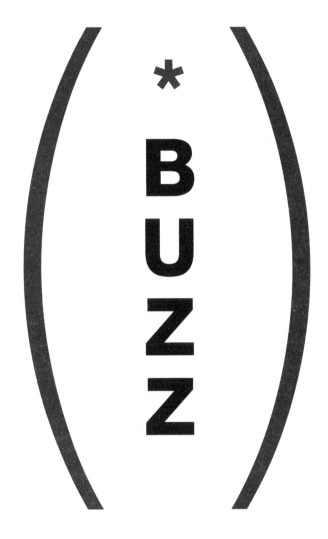

* BUZZ

A Stimulating History of the Sex Toy

HALLIE LIEBERMAN

PEGASUS BOOKS
NEW YORK LONDON

Buzz

Pegasus Books, Ltd.
148 West 37th Street, 13th Floor
New York, NY 10018

First Pegasus Books hardcover edition November 2017

Interior design by Sabrina Plomitallo-González

ISBN: 978-1-68177-543-2

10   9   8   7   6   5   4   3   2   1

Printed in the United States of America
Distributed by W. W. Norton & Company, Inc.

Contents

Preface

I was ten years old when I encountered my first sex toy. I was vacationing with my family in the Florida Keys. We had just arrived at the Sugarloaf Lodge, an old Florida hotel that had its own resident dolphin named Sugar, who lived in an enclosed lagoon on the property. I was doing what I always liked to do to acquaint myself with a new hotel room: searching for anything that might have been left behind by the room's previous occupants. I'd open every drawer and comb through every inch of the room. Usually, I was disappointed, finding little more than the Gideon Bible and a few Chinese takeout menus. But this time was different.

After finding the requisite Bible in the bedside table drawer, I began searching the bulky wooden dresser drawer by drawer. Top drawer, nothing. Second drawer, nothing. Third drawer, nothing. Then, when I got to the bottom drawer, I hit the jackpot. There was something inside! I reached my little hand in and pulled out a zippered pouch. Eagerly, I unzipped the package and discovered what was inside: an eight-inch cylindrical object.

I ran to my parents with the plastic tubelike device. "Look what I found! A pencil sharpener!" My parents' looks of horror revealed to me that I had discovered something much more interesting.

"That's not a pencil sharpener!" my mom said frantically, running toward me and taking it away. "Wash your hands."

"What is it?" I asked innocently.

"You don't need to know," my mom said.

I went and washed my hands as instructed, and we never talked about it again.

I don't remember exactly how I found out that what I had held in my hands was a vibrator. Perhaps my older and wiser twelve-year-old brother told me. Perhaps I figured it out later through the giggled gossip of my group of friends. Either way, the encounter had taught me an important lesson: the seemingly innocuous object that I had discovered had the power to make people deeply uncomfortable. I never forgot about that vibrator and the reaction it got from my parents.

Nine years later, I purchased my first vibrator, and it was love at first buzz. It was a Doc Johnson Pocket Rocket, a hard-plastic clitoral vibrator that bore a faint resemblance to a mini flashlight. And I did what anybody does when they fall in love: continuously talk about the object of my infatuation. My friends, however, didn't share my enthusiasm for the orgasm-producing powers of my new Pocket Rocket. They were happy for me, sure, but they were also concerned that I wasn't dating anyone. They wondered whether I would get addicted to my new machine; they worried I'd be unable to enjoy sex.

I took a break from my orgasms to wonder: Was I addicted? Had I, at nineteen years old, permanently broken my clitoris? Did being able to successfully give myself pleasure mean that I was ruining myself for relationships?

It turned out, of course, that the answer to all those questions was a solid no. But I wouldn't know that for a few years, until a job selling sex toys would lead me into their strange history and our complicated and surprising centuries-long relationship with them.

Selling Sex Toys

I t's 2004, and Christy is rattling off her order: a jelly vibrator, a cock ring, a bottle of Eros lubricant. Then, mid-order, she hesitates and turns to me. "I'm thinking of surprising my fiancé with a butt plug on our honeymoon," she says. "But do you think he'll think it's gay?"

"He won't think it's gay," I assure her quickly. "Lots of people bring butt plugs on their honeymoons."

I am lying. I have no idea what people bring on their honeymoons because I am unmarried, as are all my friends. My knowledge of honeymoons encompasses only my parents' honeymoon, which didn't involve a butt plug, as far as I know. But it is Christy's bachelorette party, and I am there to sell her and her friends as many sex toys as I can. It's my job. Plus, I think that in a perfect world everybody would bring butt plugs on their honeymoons and that all men would be open-minded enough to realize that stimulating your prostate doesn't automatically make you a homosexual.

"Okay, I'll take it," she says, to a round of applause from her bridesmaids.

As I add the butt plug to her order, I feel a twinge of guilt. Will her fiancé really like it, or will the butt-plug gift lead to a fight? Did my exuberant sex-toy salesmanship destroy a marriage before it even began? But these concerns pale in comparison to what I really should be worried about: whether the thirty-four-year-old, soon-to-be-married Christy is an undercover cop.

(*)

I was living in Austin, Texas, at the time, going to graduate school and working for Forbidden Fruit, a local in-home sex-toy sales business. We held events that were like Tupperware parties, except instead of selling plastic casserole containers, I sold dolphin-shaped vibrators and jelly cock rings. It was actually the second such company I had worked for, and it was one of about a half dozen that were operating in Texas at the time—a higher number of businesses than one might suspect, given that selling sex toys in Texas was illegal.

The year before, in 2003, the Supreme Court in *Lawrence v. Texas* had overturned antisodomy laws in Texas and thirteen other states because they violated the right to privacy guaranteed under the Fourteenth Amendment.[1] But the sex-toy laws weren't affected by *Lawrence* because *Lawrence* only made private homosexual sex acts between people legal.[2] Texas's sex-toy laws were about what happened in public: the promotion or sale of sex toys was their main concern.[3] Not only was the sale of sex toys illegal, but their use on a partner technically was as well, since "penetration of the genitals or the anus of another person with an object" still remained on the books as a crime in the Texas Penal Code.[4] So bringing a butt plug on your honeymoon was not only unusual but also potentially illegal. Oops.

Forbidden Fruit—which in addition to its sex-toy parties also operated a local female-friendly sex-toy store—had been raided on obscenity charges in 1989, so they were particularly concerned about not violating the law. One of the first things impressed on me by my trainer (and Forbidden Fruit's owner), Lynne, was to say that all the items we sold were for "artistic, educational, and scientific purposes." That was her way of circumventing the obscenity law, which declared that something was obscene if "taken as a whole [it] lacks serious literary, artistic, political, and scientific value." In the Texas Penal Code (Ann. §43.23, [7]), a device was illegal if it was "designed and marketed as useful primarily for stimulation of the human genital organs." And so we sold Hitachi Magic Wands as back massagers, and we sold silver bullet vibrators as point-specific massagers. As long as you lied about a sex toy's purpose, it was legal. Some of the items were harder to pass off, however. But if customers wanting, for example, a double dong with realistic balls would just sign Forbidden Fruit's form that said that they were buying it "for strictly educational, artistic, and/or scientific purposes," then they too would be in the clear.[5] I dutifully took notes as Lynne gave me her tips on how to avoid arrest.

It wasn't the first time my job had put me at risk of jail time. I had started my career in the sex-toy industry six months earlier, working for a company called Passion Parties after a friend had suggested that selling sex toys might be the perfect job for me because I was fascinated by sex toys, masturbation, and the taboos surrounding them. Part of a group of in-home sex-toy companies that emerged in the 1990s, Passion Parties had been founded in 1994 by Pat Davis, who started the company because she wanted to "create an environment of fun and trust in which a woman and her partner can discuss sex comfortably."[6] It was the typical direct-sales pyramid scheme model, in which salespeople spent just as much time recruiting women to work for the company as they did actually selling sex toys.[7]

When I first started, the company assigned me a "mentor," a sweet, young army wife at Fort Hood who peddled sex toys to women on the base. She invited me to her home, and, upon entering, one of the first things I saw was a framed biblical quote. I was surprised, to say the least. Was she socially conservative? I thought all the women who sold sex toys were bleeding-heart liberals. It wasn't the last time I'd find myself surprised by the sex-toy industry and those involved in it.

One of the first things my Passion Parties mentor relayed to me was the most important tenet about the business: that the sale of sex toys was illegal. In fact, possessing more than six sex toys was in and of itself illegal because such a quantity indicated that the owner had them "with intent to promote." The one loophole was if the owner had a "bona fide medical, psychiatric, judicial, legislative, or law enforcement purpose" for such possession.[8] Forbidden Fruit got around that by claiming that sex toys had a higher artistic, educational, or scientific purpose; Passion Parties's technique to evade obscenity laws was to use euphemisms. My mentor gave me a lexicon of such terms to keep me out of jail: The clitoris became "the man in the boat," vibrators became massagers, and cock rings were "c-rings." All the sex toys we sold were "for novelty use only." The whole scene felt surreal. There I was, standing on government property and being taught by a good Christian woman how to break the law.

"We're using this language just to be on the safe side, right?" I asked nervously. "Nobody would really be arrested for selling vibrators."

And that was when my new mentor proceeded to tell me that a Passion Parties consultant had been arrested earlier that year in Burleson, Texas, a small city on the edge of Fort Worth, about a three-hour drive north from Austin. Briefly, I pictured being locked in a cell with murderers, having to explain that I was there for peddling vibrators. I obviously didn't know how jail worked. Nevertheless, I decided to take her instructions seriously.

After I'd returned home later that night, I looked up the story my mentor had told me. I learned that the arrested woman had not been some left-wing free-speech advocate but a forty-three-year-old churchgoing Republican mother of three named Joanne Webb.[9] Local police had responded to rumors that Webb was selling sex toys by setting up a sting operation. Two officers posing as a couple went to Webb's husband's construction business where she worked the front desk and asked to buy some sex toys. The couple told Webb that they wanted a toy for anal stimulation and said that they didn't have time to host a party. (This should have been a red flag for Webb, but she wasn't exactly expecting to be the subject to a sting operation.) So she sold them a Double Hot (a vibrator that penetrates the vagina and anus simultaneously) and a Nubby G (a vaginal G-spot vibrator) and sent them on their merry way.[10] Unbeknownst to Webb, the police officers had been videotaping the encounter.

For her violation of Texas's anti-sex-toy laws, Webb faced a possible year in prison and up to $4,000 in fines, all for selling a couple of vibrators. Passion Parties started a Joanne Webb Defense Fund and raised more than $10,000 for her legal team.[11] Webb's charges were eventually dropped, but not before she spent thousands on legal fees. And, perhaps even worse, Webb was shunned in the community. The pastor of a local church in Burleson (not the one Webb attended) told *Texas Monthly* exactly why she was so upset about Webb. "The Bible teaches us that sex is a sacred act between a man and a woman, blessed by God," the pastor said. "And adding some kind of rubber toy into the sex act only diverts attention away from your partner, which is where God wants you to focus."[12]

Webb's case received international attention, which meant my mother in Venice, Florida, certainly heard about it, which resulted in teary phone calls from her, pleading with me to stop selling sex toys.[13] I told her that my chances of being arrested were very low, and besides, if I did get arrested, it would make for a great story. Not surprisingly, my arguments didn't convince her.

But Webb was far from the only person to be arrested in the late 1990s and early 2000s for peddling sex toys. In 2000, Texas resident Dawn Webber sold a vibrator to an undercover cop and was sentenced to thirty days in jail and a $4,000 fine.[14] She lost her later appeal, yet even the judge who affirmed the conviction couldn't help but comment on the law. "I do not understand why Texas law criminalizes the sale of dildos," she wrote in the judgment. "Even less do I understand why law enforcement officers and prosecutors expend limited resources to prosecute such activity. Because this is the law, I reluctantly concur."[15] In Louisiana, Christine D. Brenan was arrested three times in 1996 and 1997 for selling sex toys at her store, the Dance Box, and sentenced to "two years hard labor and a $1,500 fine." Her charges were later reduced to five years probation. After Brenan's multiple appeals, the court finally reversed her conviction in 1999. The state appealed in 2000, but the reversal stood.[16]

Adult bookstore employee Ignacio Sergio Acosta was arrested in 2003 for selling a "crystal cock vibrator" to undercover officers in El Paso, Texas, and telling the female officer it would give her an orgasm.[17]

It was such a weird position to be in: risking arrest for selling dildos. If I lived in a repressive country under a misogynistic regime, sure, this would be expected. But I lived in America, where strip clubs abound, binge drinking is celebrated, and possession of semiautomatic weapons is legal. So why the hang-up on sex toys?

It was a question that would take me more than a decade to answer.

At the time when I first started selling sex toys, Texas was one of at least five states—including Alabama, Georgia, Mississippi, and Virginia—that made the sale of sex toys illegal, with specifics varying from state to state.[18] It was a law that a number of people wanted to change and, after the *Lawrence* decision made antisodomy statutes unconstitutional, some groups saw an opening to challenge anti-sex-toy statutes. In 2004, Phil Harvey Enterprises— the corporation that ran Adam & Eve, a large sex-toy retailer with a robust website and a chain of sex-toy stores—lost their challenge against the Mississippi anti-sex-toy law. The court said that buying sex toys was not "protected by a constitutional right to privacy" because "people who are sexually dysfunctional (presumably those people who cannot achieve sexual enjoyment and fulfillment without a sexual device) should be treated by a physician or a psychologist." As a result, the court determined, since the sex toys Adam & Eve sold were "novelties," they "had no medical purpose."[19] That same year, the Alabama state court also upheld their anti-sex-toy law.[20] The ACLU appealed the decision, but their appeals failed. In 2007, the Eleventh Circuit Court of Texas again declared that the statutes could stand.[21] It took until 2008 for Texas's anti-sex-toy laws to be declared invalid, using a right-to-sexual-privacy argument as justification. It was of note that the court portrayed sex toys as devices "that an individual may choose to use during intimate conduct with a partner in the home," not as masturbatory aids.[22]

The line of distinction between masturbatory use and use in a couple wasn't the only double-standard in sex-toy law. There was also a difference in the legal standard between male and female sexuality. While vibrators and dildos were illegal in many states at the time I was selling them, Viagra was not only legal but covered by health insurance.[23] Not only was male sexual dysfunction considered a legitimate medical problem, but the pill used to cure it was advertised openly on national television—and even endorsed by former U.S. Senator Bob Dole. Meanwhile, someone could get arrested for selling a clitoral vibrator in a private home in Texas. It was ridiculous, to say the least.

But I wasn't always this cynical about sex toys. As I drove the three hours from my home in Austin to my first sex-toy party in Houston—equipped with the bag full of vibrators, lube, and massage oil I'd be peddling—I felt pretty empowered. *I'm a sex educator*, I told myself. That's the line my mentor had given me, and, in a way, it was true. I was a woman on a mission.

My confidence started to wane as I ascended the two flights of stairs and entered the cramped apartment where I was supposed to present. The host, a boisterous nurse, had invited all her coworkers over to drink a fluorescent green Hypnotiq-based cocktail called "The Hulk" and buy some vibrators. I immediately got flustered. Nearly all these women had been trained in the knowledge of the human body. Who was I to think I could teach them about the intricacies of female sexual stimulation?

I was sweating visibly as I set up my sales kit next to a table arrayed with various bottles of liquor, Boone's Farm wine, and chicken taquitos. I briefly contemplated running out the door, but I'd driven nearly two hundred miles, and turning back seemed crazy. And so I started to unpack my bag, gingerly placing down the White Chocolate Passion Pudding, Silky Sheets, Edible

Massage Lotion, Tighten Up, and various other lubes. My presentation would begin with these nonthreatening lotions and lubes; we always left the toys for later, so guests wouldn't be frightened by such intimidating devices as the nine-and-three-quarters-inch-long realistic-looking vibrating dildo deemed "Big Thriller."

As the women gathered around me in the living room, I scanned their faces, hoping they wouldn't realize that this was my first party. I began the way I had been taught to, by introducing myself and explaining the ordering process. I was nervous and unsure of what tone I should strike. I landed on a vaguely authoritarian one, which was belied by the shaking of my hands as I picked up a bottle of UniSex Enhancement Gel and began extolling its benefits of promoting arousal by strengthening penile and clitoral erection through its activation of nitrous oxide pathways. It's important to state here that I was pretty sure a lot of what I had been taught to say about this gel wasn't quite accurate. Our training materials claimed that "a group of Scientist [*sic*] were awarded the Nobel Medical Prize" for research on nitrous oxide pathways, but I wasn't sure that a gel—our gel or any gel—could actually "activate" them.[24] Yet my job was to convince these women that they ought to pay forty dollars for three ounces of this gel, so I tried to sound authoritative even though I'm sure it was obvious to anyone listening that I was just reciting statements from a training manual. But the women looked mildly interested, so I carried on.

It wasn't until I began talking about Tighten Up—our virgin-simulating gel—that things took a wrong turn. Tighten Up was made of alum, the same ingredient that was historically used to make pickles pucker up and get extra crisp. As used in our product, it was supposed to make the vagina snugger, as it would have been in its virgin state. I held up the tiny half-ounce bottle and was just starting to praise its ability to create a tighter vagina when laughter began to erupt from a corner of the room and soon evolved into raucous clapping. I had lost the crowd, if I'd even had them to begin with.

As the women all started to talk over my presentation, I finally stopped, resigned. "Why are you laughing?" I asked.

One of the women proceeded to tell me that a patient had come into their hospital after using a similar product. The patient had had an allergic reaction, and her labia had swelled up to almost three times their normal size.

I was speechless. The product I was selling—one my training manual assured me was perfectly safe—was in fact so dangerous it had sent a woman to the hospital? My mentor hadn't trained me on how to deal with this kind of development, so I decided to react the way I would have if a friend had told me the same story.

"Oh my God!" I said. "That's horrible. Nobody buy Tighten Up!"

The women seemed to accept my reaction as a sign that I had a tiny bit of integrity, but I don't think they really trusted me when I recited any of the other pseudo-medical claims. I wasn't sure how much of it I believed anymore either.

Finally it was time to bring out my first sex toy—the Jelly Osaki. This item was an eight-inch-long purple vinyl vibrator that had a rotating shaft with a woman's face on it; the shaft itself was attached to a hummingbird-shaped clitoral stimulator. Why the face? Well, Japan has anti-sex-toy laws too, and one way to get around them is to make the sex toys look like dolls.[25]

This presentation was even more challenging than the lube presentation in terms of following the law. Imagine trying to sell someone something without being able to say what it is or how it works. I couldn't say "clitoral stimulator" or describe what the Osaki actually did. Instead, I had to parrot the training manual (while cringing on the inside): "And once you put your massager on the man on the boat, you'll want to go out to sea every day." (In this confusing analogy, the "man" was supposed to be the clitoral head and the "boat" was the clitoral hood.) This atrocious euphemism for the clitoris felt like it was pulled from a poorly written children's book, and it landed like a thud in the room. To break the tension, I decided to resort to the party trick I'd been taught. I bent the shaft of the Osaki, placed it on the ground, and turned it on. The brightly colored vibrator flopped all over the place like some kind of demented robotic snake. As the women broke out into laughter, I relaxed. But I felt like a fraud. I had successfully entertained people with a sex toy, but I hadn't taught people how or why to use it. I sold a lot of Osakis and lube that night, but I had not mentioned masturbation a single time. I left feeling ambivalent: satisfied with my sales prowess but feeling as if I wasn't actually teaching people anything.

I had been so hopeful before that first party, but it wasn't long before I came to the realization that selling sex toys wasn't going to be as socially progressive as I thought it would be. Sure, there would be small moments where I would feel as if I were making some slight difference in people's lives. For example, three generations of women attended one of my parties, and as I watched them test out Pocket Rockets on their noses to feel the intensity of the vibration, the sight warmed my heart. I thought it might be possible that I was actually bringing sexual enlightenment to women of all ages. But more parties involved women gingerly calling up their husbands, asking for permission to charge sex toys on the family credit card; I couldn't help but wonder if those calls would have happened had they been spending a similar amount of money at Macy's. I'd hear them talking to their husbands as they rattled off their carefully constructed list of sex toys, explaining each with a giggle, as if they were apologizing for their sexuality. Was this really the state of modern womanhood? Even at the parties where the guests openly celebrated their sexuality, they still held up monogamous marriage as the ideal. Their hope was to bring sexual variety into marriage, squeezing the sexual revolution into a traditional framework dictated by gender norms. These women were more in line with 1950s housewives than the sexually liberated women I'd thought I'd be working with.

If I was surprised by the makeup of the clientele, the companies I worked for understood their audiences quite well. Many of the products we sold were marketed with the idea that sex was either gross or a chore to be endured. Case in point: Both home party companies I worked for sold products for oral sex that went by names like Tasty Tease, Fireworks, Happy Penis Cream, or D'Lickious Head Gel. These gels came in flavors such as cherry, piña colada, banana, mint, and more and were meant to make a man's penis taste better when performing fellatio (and for cunnilingus as well, although we weren't instructed to focus on this use). I had been taught to make jokes at this portion of my presentation like "They don't call it a job for nothing" or tell the guests that some women only give "ABC blow jobs: Anniversary, Birthday, and Christmas." There seemed to be a tacit agreement that fellatio was a chore to be endured and that the only way of improving it was to slather a man's penis with a gel that smelled and tasted like children's fluoride. God forbid any woman admit to actually enjoying the act of fellatio.

For parties geared toward women (in fact, men were barred), it was interesting how many of our wares were solely intended for male sexual pleasure. Not one of the six books we sold was about masturbation; all were about enhancing sex with your partner or pleasing a man. The first chapter of the only book we sold on sex toys, *Toy Gasms!*, was titled "How to Spring a Sex Toy on Your Lover," with a large chunk of it devoted to convincing a man that a sex toy wouldn't replace him. Passion Parties' bestselling book was *Tickle His Pickle*—a guide to sexually pleasing a male partner. Sure, women at our parties bought some sex toys for masturbation, but more of their attention seemed to be on learning to please their men and therefore keep their marriages intact.

One of our most popular items was male masturbation sleeves. Our top seller was the cheapest of these, the twenty-nine-dollar Gigi. Supposedly "modeled after a real vagina," the Gigi was bright pink, and our demonstration for it involved filling the Gigi with lubricant and sliding a penis-shaped lube bottle in and out of it to show how pleasurable it would be for a man.

Following in the blow-jobs-are-gross theme, we were advised by the training manual to tell customers, "If a woman is reluctant to perform oral sex on a man, a well-lubricated masturbation sleeve like Gigi can serve as an excellent substitute—and if you're under the covers, he may never know the difference."[26] The specter of cheating also hung over this presentation; in fact, the training manual specifically mentioned that the Gigi was a device intended to "keep him thinking about you" when "he" was traveling.

I sold a ton of Gigis.

I learned a lot of things from my time in the sex-toy-party industry, but the main takeaway was that it wasn't at all what I had been expecting. I had thought that the women hosting such parties were going to be liberal feminists whose homes were decorated with Frida Kahlo reproductions and African art. Instead, I found myself in the homes of gun-toting, religious Republicans. They were women who were buying sex toys to spice up their relationships and save their marriages. If they bought toys to use solo, it was most often because their husbands were away fighting in Afghanistan or Iraq. It was a glimpse into a world that was decidedly less progressive than the one I thought I was going in to.

The more I dove into the world of sex toys, the more I realized how sexually regressive it was. Everywhere I looked, I saw evidence that the mainstream sex-toy industry was promoting an ideology more in line with archaic gender and sexual norms than with radical sexual empowerment. Even the industry-standard term "sex toys" was infantilizing. Male sexual problems were given "erectile dysfunction" drugs, a serious-sounding term that legitimized these sexual issues as diseases. Meanwhile, women's sexuality was trite, fixed or improved by "toys." And more insulting still were the sex toys themselves. Many of them actually looked like children's toys, shaped like dolls, bunnies, monarch butterflies, or the caterpillar from *Alice in Wonderland.*

I had thought that the whole existence of the sex-toy industry was a sign of the liberation that had come out of the sexual revolution. My time in the industry itself taught me that maybe we hadn't come quite as far as I had believed. But sex toys were hard to ignore, as they were the physical embodiment of the conflicted relationship the modern world had with sexuality. Sex toys were being shown on television in shows like *Sex in the City* while, in other parts of the country, people could be arrested for selling them. And yet despite their legal status, they could be found in bedside tables across the nation—and even worldwide.

My questions were: How did we get here? How did a giant vibrating penis come to be thought of as the key to matrimonial bliss? And, why, in spite of the fact that sex toys were popular with social conservatives, did they remain illegal in many conservative states? It would require a look back at the strange history of sex toys to be able to answer these questions.

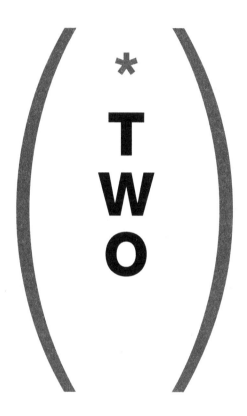

From Cavemen to Kinsey

I n 2008, I enrolled in a PhD program at University of Wisconsin–Madison. My intention was to study the history of sex toys. It wasn't an easy task. Academics had virtually ignored sex toys as a topic of study. Without a road map, I'd have to find my own way.

The first thing I learned was that sex toys were ancient. Thirty thousand years ago, our ancestors had been hunched over carving eight-inch-long penises out of siltstone.[27] Apparently, before humans invented writing or the wheel, we had invented dildos. As surgeon Joseph Richardson Parke put it in 1912, "As to the artificial penis, it is almost as old as the natural one."[28] But were these artifacts actually dildos in the modern sense?

Archaeologists are divided on this point. Made of bone, ivory, limestone, siltstone, or even teeth, these items have been traditionally classified as arrow or spear straighteners, tools to shape flint, or ritual objects.[29] On one of the oldest of these objects—one found in the Hohle Fels cave in southwestern Germany, which is about 28,000 years old—scratches are visible that indicate that it could have been used for tool-making. But given that there is no reason that our ancestors needed to use stone penises to shape flint, it is quite possible that these were used as sex toys.[30]

Archaeologist Timothy Taylor believes that phallic batons found in Eurasia—dating from the Ice Age period of 40,000 to 10,000 BCE—could have been used as sex toys because they "fall within the size range of modern dildoes." Others speculate that the dildos may have been used to perform "ritual defloration" ceremonies on young women.[31] And it wasn't just in Eurasia that ancient dildos have been found. Similar dildos were also found in Pakistan dating back to 4000 BCE, which may have been used in ceremonies worshipping the god Shiva.[32]

I knew one thing for sure: If the importance of an invention is gauged by how long it has existed, then dildos are some of the most important devices humans have created. Even if these ur-dildos were not actually used for masturbation, they still proved that phalluses have been a part of human culture since the beginning of humanity. I even found that double-headed dildos—those dildos with penis-heads on either side—were also prehistoric. Their predecessors date from about 13,000 to 19,000 years ago.[33]

Dildo-like objects show up in paintings from Ancient Egypt dated from around 3000 BCE. Women are depicted wearing giant phalluses around their waist in ceremonies honoring the god Osiris.[34] But it isn't until Ancient Greece—a civilization renowned for its embrace of sexuality—that dildos become more common. The Ancient Greeks loved phallic symbols, so it's not surprising that dildos also existed within their culture. Images of Priapus, the fertility god usually depicted with a giant erect penis, adorned gardens to "deflect the evil eye and protect humans from malign forces." The Ancient Greeks made *olisboi*, dildo-like objects, usually from leather, which was softened, before being stuffed with wool and "polished for maximum smoothness." Olive oil was used to lubricate them.[35]

Classicists are willing to admit that dildos were a part of Greek culture, even though, as scholar Max Nelson notes, the Greeks didn't have an equivalent of the word *dildo* in their language. Instead, they used at least eight different terms to refer to dildos. The most common was *olisbos*, a word meaning "leather penis" or "to glide" or "to slip," but they also used the word *toy*.[36][37] In a way, the Greeks invented the concept of sex toys.

But if *dildo* didn't come from Ancient Greek, where and when did it emerge? As I was soon discovering about all aspects of sex-toy history, there was no concrete answer. The truth was difficult to find. *The Oxford English Dictionary* defines *dildo* as "a word of obscure origin, used in the refrain of ballads."[38] Some believe that the word may have come from *diletto*, an Italian word for "a woman's delight," or *dally*, which means "to toy." Other theories point to its origins in the Old English word *dill-doll*, which comes from "the Norse word 'dilla,' meaning 'to soothe.'"[39] Another idea is that the *dildo* originated from the Latin *diliatare*, meaning "to dilate or open wide."[40] Complicating matters is the fact that in the 18th century, *dildo* was also used to describe "the round pegs that lock oars into place" on a small boat called a dory.[41] So where did *dildo* come from? It's unclear. *Dildo's* origin, like the origin of the object itself, is murky.

It's clear from existing art that the Ancient Greeks had dildos, but what's less certain is exactly what they did with them. The modern assumption would be that they masturbated with them, and, yes, it's quite possible that the Ancient Greeks did masturbate with dildos. While some scholars argue that "to the Ancient Greeks, masturbation was a normal and healthy substitute for other sexual pleasures," others claim that "female masturbation was discounted by Greek medical writing."[42] And in fact, depictions on vases do show women penetrating themselves with dildos, but that's not the only way dildos are portrayed. Vases also show women fellating dildos, holding dildos while copulating with satyrs, and sometimes just carrying around dildos in a basket for a harvest and wine festival.[43] Yet scholars don't know if the sexual depictions on dildos represent simply fantasy, routine sexual practices, or some mixture of both.[44][45]

Another clue that dildos were used for masturbation is Greek dramatist Aristophanes's play *Lysistrata* from 411 BCE. It is from *Lysistrata* that we learn that the Greek city of Miletus was a major importer of dildos. In the play, the women of the city go on a sexual strike in order to convince their husbands to end the Peloponnesian War. One woman, Calonice, worries that the sex strike won't end the war, and she will be left without a sexual outlet. Lysistrata tells Calonice that she can use a dildo if their strike doesn't work.[46] This is the first record (or second, if you count the Bible; Ezekiel 16:7— God chastises the people of Jerusalem because they "took the gold and silver" that He gave them and made "phallic images and fornicated with them"[47]—is believed to refer to dildos) that we have that hints at men being replaced by phallic devices.[48] *Olisbos* also show up in a Sappho poem, a work by Athenaeus, and two other Aristophanes plays.[49]

It wasn't just the Greeks who made and used dildos. The Romans used dildos in ritual defloration ceremonies.[50] Chinese women were buried with bronze dildos around 200 BCE.[51] Dildos are mentioned in the Indian love manual, *The Kama Sutra* (written sometime between 400 BCE to 200 CE), which advised men who were having trouble satisfying their wives to use strap-on dildos or penis extenders because they could sometimes provide more pleasure than a man's penis.[52] By the Middle Ages, the use of dildos had spread to Europe and other parts of Asia and, soon thereafter, they began appearing with frequency in literature. Italian novelist Pietro Aretino wrote in the 16th century that nuns used dildos to "quell the gnawing of the flesh."[53] Poet Thomas Nashe also addressed the items in a 16th-century poem entitled "The Choosing of Valentines, or The Merie Ballad of Nashe His Dildo."[54] In this poem, a man goes to visit his lover on Valentine's Day and, to his dismay, discovers that she now works in a brothel. He decides to visit the brothel as a client and pays to have sex with her. Yet he is so excited he ejaculates before the sex begins. So he makes another attempt, and this time he succeeds in penetrating her, but he comes too quickly for his lover. Dissatisfied, she whips out a dildo and masturbates with it. As she does so, she says that her "little dilldo" is better than a man because it "stands as stiff, as he were made of steele" and it won't cause her to become pregnant (". . . and neuer make my tender bellie swell"). The argument she makes is simple—a man is no match for a dildo—and it's the root of a male fear that has never gone away.[55]

Though at this point dildos were readily available to the wealthy, they remained controversial, sometimes being seized at customs. When the rakish John Wilmot, Earl of Rochester, imported dildos into England for his "Ballers" club (a "sexual society" that was "dedicated to such pastimes as drinking, sexual exhibitions, and dancing naked with . . . young women") in 1670, they were considered so dangerous that they were immediately confiscated and burned at customs.[56] In response, Wilmot penned the poem "Signior Dildo" three years later, which touched on the theme of dildos being more satisfying than men. The poem says that English women's lovers are so lousy that the women have to turn to a dildo (aka, the Italian Signior Dildo) to become sexually satisfied.[57] The vast majority of dildos at that point were imported from Italy, hence the object's presumptive nationality. "The fact that the dildo was . . . usually of Italian manufacture increased the upper-class English male's sexual angst since Italy was associated with effeminizing eroticism," journalist Jack Holland wrote in *A Brief History of Misogyny*. "For an Englishman, what could be more humiliating than to be superannuated by an Italian dildo?"[58] Around this time, according to turn-of-the-century physician and sex researcher Havelock Ellis, European women were even making dildos (which is incredible to think about, considering most dildos in the 20th and even the 21st century have been made by men).[59] And they were getting penalized for it too, in one of the first instances of the anti-sex-toy laws on the books. In England, laws popped up against women making dildos for themselves or others.[60]

It's clear that the history of sex toys is filled with male fear and regulation of them. Yet what's incredibly interesting is that some cultures don't fit the mold. It isn't a simple story of patriarchal cultures attempting to restrict female sexuality—it's more complicated, as the Japanese history of sex toys attests. During the 17th and 18th centuries, the Japanese were depicting dildos in their erotic books and pictures, known as *shunga*. In *shunga*, sex toys aren't shown as being as threatening to men as they are in English parodies. There was a more relaxed attitude toward sex toys in general in Edo-period Japan. The Japanese, like the Greeks, recognized the playfulness in dildos. One of the names for dildo was *warai-dōgu*, translated as "a ridiculous thing."[61]

Shunga depicts women enthusiastically buying and using dildos. In one Japanese erotic book from the 1680s, a woodblock print depicts the ideal conjugal bedroom as one filled with dildos and other sex toys, as well as sweets, for post-coital relaxation.[62] Another drawing from an erotic book from the same period shows women shopping for dildos made of water-buffalo horns from a traveling salesman. Three women crowd around the man, one woman covering her face with her hand, looking to be suppressing a laugh. Another woman is grasping a giant dildo, examining it, and saying, "This is a bit small, I want a big one."[63] Another depicts a woman masturbating with a dildo while reading *shunga*. Throughout *shunga*, women are shown as extremely sexual, even aggressively so. They show that the idea of women not only reading pornography but also being turned on and masturbating with a dildo existed in culture. Even after a code barring sex toys and *shunga* was put in place in 1722, *shunga* still thrived on the underground market.[64]

A celebration of the sex toy can also be seen in Japanese culture, where the Japanese became known for creating beautiful objects for pleasure. Perhaps the most famous sex toy the Japanese introduced is what is known in the United States as "ben wa balls." Called *rin no tama* (literally, "revolving jewels" in Japanese), these are pairs of small silver or brass balls the size of "pigeons' eggs" to be worn inside the vagina.[65] One ball was hollow while the other (referred to as "little man") was filled with mercury. Small movements would make the balls roll around inside the vagina, creating vibrations. Women wore them while walking around or swinging in hammocks. The balls would clank together and move around, creating vibrations in the vagina.[66] *Rin no tama* were supposedly very popular with geishas and prostitutes, although they were certainly "well known by name to ordinary girls." The exact age of these sex toys is unclear, though they date back at least to the 1800s in Japan, and their popularity helped them spread throughout other areas of Asia, including China and India.[67] By the late 20th century, they became controversial within some sex-toy stores (but more on that later).

(*)

Of the many regions I researched, the most difficult place to trace a culture's history with sex toys was, surprisingly enough, America. Books on the history of pornography basically ignored sex toys. I searched all the scholarly literature with little luck, aside from a few paragraphs in an article in an issue of the *Journal of Popular Culture* from the 1970s. If there was a version of *shunga* here, I wasn't able to find it.[68]

I was thrilled then when I came across Andrea Tone's book on contraceptives, *Devices & Desires*. There, on page 14, was a mention that rubber goods dealers in the late 19th century who manufactured condoms also sometimes manufactured dildos.[69] I was ecstatic. This finding spurred me to investigate further and apply to the Lemelson Center Fellowship at Smithsonian's National Museum of American History, where I knew they had an extensive collection of trade catalogs by companies, such as BF Goodrich, that made a variety of rubber goods.

When I arrived in Washington, D.C., in the summer of 2012 and entered the Smithsonian, I was in awe. It housed Dorothy's ruby slippers, a full 19th-century train car, the original Kermit the Frog—and a hidden collection of 19th-century rectal dilators and 20th-century vibrator advertisements. The archives I sought were on the first floor, in a room with a giant glass window so guests (frequently with children in tow) could peer in and watch the scholars at work. As I began digging through the archives on the first day, I felt a little uneasy as groups of people gazed at me. *If only they knew what I was studying*, I thought.

Scouring the archives led me to discover new sex toys I'd never heard of. One of the first things I found was a catalog for the Electro-Thermo Dilator, a turn-of-the-20th-century device that supposedly offered "an improved method of administering electricity to the system through the rectum, at the same time dilating the sphincter muscles." American innovation at its finest.[70]

One day a curator suggested I visit the upper floors of the museum, where all the collections that are not on display are housed. She told me that the National Museum of American History was nicknamed America's attic because the Smithsonian squirreled away their hundreds of thousands of artifacts in temperature-controlled rooms on the upper floors of the building, most never getting their moment in the museum limelight. She had seen things up there that vaguely looked like sex toys, she told me. But she wasn't sure if that's what they were. As I rode in the elevator with the curator and the elevator attendant, I tried to manage my expectations, as images of drawers full of century-old dildos raced through my mind.

We arrived on the sixth floor, and she escorted me to a thick set of double doors, waved her employee ID, and pushed through them. As I entered the room, the first thing I noticed was the freezing-cold air and a giant round metal machine, which she soon informed me was a Bakelizer, a vestige from the 1930s when the thermosetting plastic Bakelite was the height of luxury. The room looked like a well-kept thrift store, with shelf after shelf of curios: celluloid billiard balls that could explode if they got too hot; brightly colored plastic vases; an Art Deco Bakelite toaster. Beneath the shelves were drawers filled with a variety of smaller things: little plastic brooches, poker chips, figurines. Every time she opened a drawer I would feel a twinge of excitement, filled with hope that the phallic shapes within the drawer, were, in fact, dildos.

We were so primed for finding sex toys that we would excitedly examine anything that looked vaguely penis-like, only to discover, with dismay, that it was just a Bakelite flashlight. (Only later did I discover that, coincidentally enough, Bakelite was used in the manufacture of vibrators.)

After almost half an hour of searching to no avail, I was shivering, and I felt bad that the curator had to stick around for what seemed like a fruitless search. Then she opened a drawer, and I saw it: a black rectal dilator so shiny that it looked as if it had come off of Doc Johnson's assembly line that same day. I shrieked. She got excited too. The dilator, which was from the early 20th century, was beautiful. It had a curved triangular head that looked like a cross between a penis head and a Christmas lightbulb. It was a Young's Dilator, and I soon found out everything I could about it.

Patented in 1892, Young's dilators were some of the most widely advertised rectal dilators, with ads that appeared in both medical journals and popular health magazines in the early 1900s. Made of rubber, the dilators came in a kit of four different sizes, so users could increase the size as their rectum supposedly gained tone. The dilators were sold as treatments for a range of conditions, some of which seemed logical (such as constipation and enlarged prostates) and others that seemed completely off-the-wall (such as asthma). But it was Young's claim that his rectal dilators—in conjunction with his ure-thral tubes—could cure men of masturbation that was the most absurd. How exactly placing a phallic device in your rectum could, as Young said, "restore these sexual wrecks of humanity to a life of happiness" was unclear to me.[71] There was doubt in the medical community at the time as well. While a few doctors were swayed by Young's arguments, others saw through them. The editors of an 1893 edition of the *Medical Review* were especially skeptical about Young's claim that dilating the rectum could cure insanity. "Why then do these men not apply the dilators to himself or to each other?" the journal's editors wrote.[72 73]

The Young's dilator led me to fall down the rabbit hole of rubber-sex-toy history. I discovered that the Young's rectal dilator was one of several dilators produced soon after the rubber-sex-toy industry began in earnest in the mid-1800s, thanks to Charles Goodyear and Thomas Hancock. They discovered rubber vulcanization in 1844, which stabilized rubber, preventing it from melting when it came into contact with body heat.[74][75] Other devices were manufactured by respected rubber companies, including BF Goodrich. I found that most of the early rubber phallic devices were like Young's in that they were not usually sold as sex toys. Along with the rectal dilators, there were the vaginal dilators that were used to cure vaginismus ("an involuntary, spasmodic closure of the mouth of the vagina") that prevented intercourse.[76] I also discovered that not all the dilators sold at the time were made of rubber; some were made of metal or glass and contained a plunger mechanism at the bottom. They looked nearly identical to the ejaculating Asian dildos, except the American dildos were sold as rectal irrigators—almost like enemas.[77]

Although I was able to find sex toys disguised as medical devices, finding sex toys that were sold as sex toys was more difficult. I read everything I could about the sex industry in the 19th and early 20th centuries, hoping to find a lead. Most scholars wrote only about prostitution and the erotic books trade. Sex toys usually weren't mentioned; in the event they were, it was an aside, with no details provided. But one author, Donna Dennis, mentioned that there was a special type of catalog full of sex toys that was sold during this era: sporting goods catalogs. In her citation she noted that there was one housed at the American Antiquarian Society in Worcester, Massachusetts.[78] I had my next trip.

As soon as the librarian brought out the *Grand Fancy Bijou Catalogue of the Sporting Man's Emporium* from 1870, I flipped through the pages in a furious hunt for dildos, my adrenaline spiking. Then, on page 7, I found the jackpot: an ad for a "Dildoe or Artificial Penis." In front of my eyes was the first catalog from the 19th century featuring a sex toy sold without euphemisms. I was disappointed that there wasn't a drawing of the dildo, but the description gave a good approximation: "This instrument is manufactured of white rubber, and is a wonderful facsimile of the natural penis of man. For reserved females it is a happy and harmless substitute for the natural 'Champion of Women's Rights.'"[79] I envisioned a blazingly white bratwurst in my mind. The most interesting thing about the ad was that it was directed toward men. It was a sign that some American men weren't afraid of dildos at that time; they were buying them for their partners. There was some reassuring language in the description: the "dildoe" was "harmless" and the penis was a "Champion of Women's Rights" (whatever that meant).

A few more pages and I found another ad—this time for the "French Yarnal; or Ladies' Tickler." Ticklers were usually made of rubber and fit on the head of the penis, like a condom; other ticklers were like cock rings with clitoral stimulators. The description made it clear that the tickler was intended just as much for a man's sexual pleasure as it is for a woman's: The catalogue assured prospective buyers that the tickler would "cause the lady to come to Time [aka orgasm] and make her do a large share of the labor, thereby giving much more pleasure and enjoyment to the gentleman, as it would be impossible for the lady to remain still while one is being used." The description also assured men that the tickler "will cause the lady to love and stick with him who has first used it with her, as the sensation be the same as that felt the first time the act was performed in her life."[80] Although the Tickler's purpose was supposedly to give women orgasms, it was sold ultimately as a device that benefited men's enjoyment during sex. (The way we've sold sex toys seems not to have changed too much from the 19th to the 21st centuries.)

I wondered if any other 19th-century catalogs like this existed. I imagined men stashing the catalogs under their beds, hiding them from wives and moms. Who would think to save a sex-toy catalog for posterity? What had happened to the other sex-toy catalogs?

I asked my advisor, and he suggested that I look through the reports of 19th-century vice societies held at the Wisconsin Historical Society. Vice societies assisted in the arrest of citizens for selling so-called obscenity and kept detailed records of sellers of obscene goods. They must have gone after sex toys, he said. I was skeptical. Lots had been written about the society reports because they are some of the only sources on pornography, prostitution, and America's sexual culture from the 19th century. I figured that if sex toys were in these reports, someone would have written about them before. But still I went and looked.

The vice society report was housed in the Ralph Ginzburg Papers of the Wisconsin Historical Society. A publisher of *Eros* magazine, Ginzburg had been charged with violating obscenity laws in the 1960s, and he decided to investigate the history of these laws in the United States in preparation for a book that he never ended up writing.[81] He wanted to understand how the United States had come to be so obsessed with regulating sex. I immediately felt a kinship with him.

The records Ginzburg had collected were those of a vice society that started out in the early 1860s as a committee within the New York Young Men's Christian Association (YMCA), a committee looking to ferret out commercial sex products that were pouring into the streets in spite of a state anti-obscenity law. I soon learned that my advisor was right: It wasn't just pornographic books and pictures that the committee were after. They also were appalled by something not covered under the anti-obscenity laws—a group of products they called "immoral articles," an umbrella term that covered sex toys and contraceptives. "Indecent or immoral" articles were "a fruitful source of demoralization and crime," and the law needed to encompass them, the New York YMCA argued.[82] In 1868, they got their way. The law was expanded.

Around the time that the New York YMCA was helping the state crack down on obscenity, a portly dry goods salesman named Anthony Comstock was involved in a similar mission of his own. He was determined to track down an erotica dealer who had sold his friend pornography, which Comstock believed had sent his friend into a downward spiral, leading to suicide. In the process of looking for vengeance, he came across an enormous underground web of porn, contraceptives, and sex toys. Enraged, he began to scour New York City for the supposed contraband, and he reported his findings to the police, who arrested the transgressors.[83] In 1872, he joined forces with the New York YMCA and helped create their Commission for the Suppression of Vice. They believed that masturbation was dangerous and that sex for pleasure, without the goal of procreation, was a sin. Comstock's ultimate aim was to prevent masturbation, which he believed was morally and physically damaging.[84] Comstock wrote that, "If almost all of America's young men are addicted to this lethal practice, what hope remains for America?"[85]

That same year, a federal obscenity act was created, and vice organizations believed that they were beginning to win the battle against obscenity.[86] But when Comstock tried to get a porn dealer prosecuted under the law, he failed. He decided the law needed to be strengthened and expanded to incorporate rubber goods, including contraceptives and sex toys.

With the help of a lawyer, Comstock drafted a bill that was stricter and more specific, and he lobbied Congress for it. To ensure it would pass, he arrived in Washington armed with what he believed to be foolproof ammunition: an abundance of obscene rubber goods and pornography that he had collected while working as a vice reformer at the YMCA. Apparently this technique worked. Lawmakers were so upset by the mountains of sex products that they passed the bill, which made it illegal to mail any "obscene, lewd, lascivious, or filthy" material through the mail, including printed works and

B
U
Z
Z

"any cast, instrument, or other article of an immoral nature" and any contraceptives or abortifacients.[87] [88] The possible penalty was a $100 to $5,000 fine, one to ten years of hard labor—or both.

Comstock was also given the position of special agent in the United States Post Office "with power to confiscate immoral matter in the mails and arrest those sending it" and was appointed secretary to the YMCA's New York Society for the Suppression of Vice (NYSSV).[89] Within a year, he had seized "60,300 articles made of rubber for immoral purposes, and used by both sexes."[90] While many of these articles were condoms and diaphragms, some were sex toys. Comstock did not just arrest sex-toy makers; he also destroyed all their equipment and their entire stock of products.

Comstock didn't succeed in destroying the whole sex-toy industry, but he did destroy the livelihoods of many people who participated in it. He also effectively drove the sex-toy industry underground. Ads for sex toys still filled the backs of men's sporting journals, but they referred to dildos as "Old Maid's Friends" and called artificial vaginas "Bachelor's Friends."[91]

The period that Comstock worked for the federal government also gave rise to one of the most popular sex toys of the modern era: the electric vibrator. What did Comstock and the other censors think of vibrators? The answer was they didn't worry about them at all. I could find nothing in the records of the NYSSV that showed that they were concerned specifically with vibrators, although Comstock did sometimes coerce newspapers into discontinuing their "massage and electrical advertisements." Vibrators weren't specifically written into obscenity laws at this time probably because companies marketed them as medical and household appliances. Nearly every vibrator company manufactured phallic attachments, which would have been considered obscene if sold as dildos.[92] Nevertheless, Comstock let vibrator advertisements run freely.[93]

The legend of the vibrator's use in treating female hysteria has spread to popular culture, appearing in the Broadway play *In The Next Room (or The Vibrator Play)*, the film *Hysteria*, several documentaries, and many mainstream books and articles. But when I went to the source material at the Bakken Museum in Minneapolis, where the major scholar on the topic had done some of her research, I found there was something missing from them. The 19th-century gynecological textbooks and doctors' manuals on vibratory therapy said nothing about using vibrators on women's clitorises to treat hysteria.[94]

I discovered that the story of the vibrator wasn't a story of doctors masturbating female patients in their offices. Early vibrators first appeared in the late 1800s in France, England, Germany, China, Japan, and America, powered by everything from steam to water to compressed air.[95] They were used to treat all forms of disease, from sciatica to deafness. Some of the earliest medical vibrators were enormous, expensive devices. One even looked like a horse-riding saddle.

In fact, British and American doctors didn't even like vibrators that much, though the electric vibrator was invented by British physician J. Mortimer Granville in the early 1880s to treat a variety of disorders, including constipation, backache, and diabetes in both men and women.[96] He believed that the body's nerves had natural, healthy levels of vibration and that when these levels got out of balance, disease resulted. So he created a device to restore "the normal harmony of rhythm" of the body's nerves.[97] Granville's writings reveal that he knew vibrators might have sexual uses, since he instructed doctors to use vibrators to increase sexual power in their male patients by vibrating their perineums.

Although companies marketed vibrators to doctors, many doctors regarded them with suspicion.[98] In an 1898 letter to the editor of *Medical News*, a physician wrote: "After many years of vibratory therapy I am now convinced that its value is greatly exaggerated, and depends more on the creation of suggestion than anything else."[99] In 1915, the American Medical Association (AMA) said that the "vibrator business is a delusion and a snare. If it has any effect, it is psychology."[100]

After the mainstream medical community's lukewarm reception of the vibrator in the late 19th century, the vibrator was rebranded as a consumer appliance. Hand-cranked vibrators were produced in America, Germany, and Asia. Soon electric vibrators were too. The earliest ad for a consumer electric vibrator in America appeared in 1899 in *McClure's Magazine*. This ad positioned the Vibratile vibrator as both a beauty and health device, suitable for "removing wrinkles" and "curing nervous headache."[101] By 1909, Vibratile was joined by at least twenty other companies hawking similar vibrators.[102]

Vibrator ads were everywhere in the early 20th century; *Popular Mechanics*, *McCall's*, and even Christian publications featured ads for vibrators, as did regional newspapers in Racine, Wisconsin, and national papers like the *New York Times*. Vibrators were available for mail-order in Sears Roebuck catalogs, while department stores like Macy's always kept them in stock. Vibrators were even a part of popular culture. A mainstream movie from the 1919 featured a plot about a vibrator salesman. Celebrities endorsed vibrators—and not trashy celebrities either. One of the stars of Alfred Hitchcock's *Lifeboat*, Mary Anderson, appeared in Star Vibrator ads, claiming that the vibrator gave her a "beautiful complexion."[103]

These vibrators didn't look like the vibrators we are familiar with today. They weren't brightly colored, shaped like geishas, or made of plastic. They were heavy devices with a wooden handle on one end and a small electric motor on the other. Most of them plugged into the wall and ran on electricity. Nearly all vibrators featured an optional rubber phallic attachment that could be screwed onto the end. It was called either a rectal or a vaginal applicator and it was ostensibly used to treat impotence or hemorrhoids, among other diseases. They were marketed as Christmas gifts for grandfathers and grandmothers, soothing machines for babies, beauty appliances for women, and health devices for everyone. Although we now know vibrators are widely used for masturbation, there is very little evidence from consumers in this era about their use of vibrators or their masturbatory practices in general.[104] Vibrators were probably used for masturbation in the first two decades of the 20th century, but there's no way to prove they were.

So just when did we realize vibrators were sexual? It's nearly impossible to pin this exactly down. But it's likely that they were thought to be sexual from the beginning, as ads from the early 1900s were filled with busty women in low-cut dresses and ad copy that talked about the quivering and pulsating feelings of joy running through your veins after using them.

Vibrating belts were advertised as "Sexual Vibrators" as early as 1903.[105] In fact, doctors were initially more concerned with men masturbating with vibrators than they were with women using the devices. A doctor first wrote about male masturbation with vibrators in 1912.[106] By the 1930s, famed gynecologist Robert Latou Dickinson noted the autoerotic use of an electric vibrator by one of his patients, and this was not even unusual enough to provoke comment.[107]

I found that as vibrators buzzed through American culture, dildos continued marching through as well. But there was one main difference between the two of them: Dildos scared men, and vibrators didn't. To be clear, not all men were afraid of dildos, and just because there's a lack of evidence that men were afraid of vibrators doesn't mean that they weren't intimidated by them. Some depictions of women using dildos were clearly made to arouse men, such as the pictures of women masturbating with dildos that appeared in the United States in the 1930s and the images that showed women wearing strap-on dildos made of fabric, complete with pubic hair.[108] But the anxiety surrounding dildos continued. In eight-page-long pornographic comic books from the 1930s and 1940s known as "Tijuana Bibles" and "eight-pagers," many scenes featured popular comic strip characters or even Disney characters using dildos. One comic, "Snow White Makes Bashful Grow Bold and He Loves It!," showed Snow White penetrating the dwarf Bashful with a dildo, while she's saying, "Oh! So you want to be buggered!"[109] Although this comic shows Snow White using her dildo to dominate Bashful, the moral of many of the other dildo-themed eight-pagers was that sex with men is superior to masturbation with dildos.

Many eight-pagers featured the popular newspaper comic-strip character Tillie the Toiler, a secretary and model. "Tillie the Toiler" comic strips ran in newspapers from the 1920s to the 1950s. In the eight-pager *Tillie VI*, Tillie orders a dildo from Paris. When it arrives, she opens the package to see a dildo as long and thick as her forearm, and she says to herself, "Isn't it a beauty? Looks and feels just like the real mccoy—now—damn'em. I'll show all Peter-Pinching Papas that I don't need 'em. I can be as independent as hell." As she masturbates, she continues to extol the benefits of dildos over men. But after she has an orgasm while fantasizing about movie stars, she feels there's something lacking: "No kiss when I come—no hug—no dozing off all cuddled up and I know damn well it won't take me out to eat—so—to hell with it!" She calls her friend Bubbles, who is having a party, and she asks Bubbles if any of the men at the party will come have sex with her. One agrees, and when they have sex, she says, "There's no substitute for nature," implying that the dildo just can't compete with a real live penis.[110]

In the 1930s and 1940s, as men continued to be anxious about dildos, vibrators skated through culture without causing much consternation. In part, this is because vibrators were actually becoming less sexual. Vaginal and rectal attachments disappeared, and vibrator brochures no longer suggested vibrating the genitals. Rechristened as back and scalp massagers, vibrators were used by barbers to massage men. Worn on the back of the hand and attached with two sets of straps, these motors vibrated the vibrator-wearers' fingers, which they then used to transmit the vibrations to the person being vibrated.[111] As they did in the early 1900s, companies took out ads promoting vibrators as essential household devices. Vibrators were considered such innocuous devices that in 1953, *Good Housekeeping* bestowed their seal of approval upon some models.[112] Sears manufactured a Kenmore vibrator in 1956, which they advertised in their catalogs as producing "that great-to-be-alive feeling."[113]

Selling the vibrator as an innocent household appliance using traditional gendered imagery made sense in America in the 1950s. This was a period of contradictions. On the one hand, the culture was conservative, pro-natalist, and all about enforcing traditional gender norms. It was the baby boom era, where women were supposed to stick to their roles as mother and wife, and sex was supposed to be confined to marriage. As women's identities were tied to the home, masculinity was in peril. Men returning from war were now confined to office jobs. Yet the stirrings of the sexual revolution could be seen in American culture. Popular culture was becoming more sexualized. In 1953, Hugh Hefner's first edition of *Playboy* hit the newsstands with Marilyn Monroe on the cover, joining multiple men's magazines that began to be circulated widely, including *Esquire, Modern Man,* and *Look.* This was an era that saw a surge in sexual research. Alfred Kinsey published his extensive research on male sexual behavior in 1948 and female in 1953, finding that extramarital and premarital sex were common, as were homosexuality and masturbation. Around 90 percent of males and 62 percent of females masturbated, according to Kinsey.[114] Kinsey's work demonstrated that the difference between public and private sexuality was vast. Yet even as men's sexuality was openly discussed, women's sexuality was not, which is what allowed the vibrator to be sold as a household appliance.[115]

There was one contingent of society upset about the vibrator, however: the Food and Drug Administration (FDA), which began cracking down on them not because they were masturbation devices but because they were sold as weight-loss devices and cure-alls. In 1958, the FDA seized vibrators that they claimed were falsely labeled. Most companies simply removed the false claims and continued selling vibrators, with more muted assertions. But the days of selling the vibrator as a panacea were over. The FDA did not think that vibrators should be outlawed but instead thought they should be properly labeled because "the benefits of vibration are limited to temporary relief of minor physical conditions."[116]

In contrast to vibrators, dildos weren't discussed as much in America in the 1940s and 1950s because they were marginally legal. Comstock's law remained in force, and it was illegal to send them through the mail.[117] Dildos weren't really mass-produced, and there were few adult bookstores in which to purchase them.

That was about to change.

* THREE

The Ventriloquist and His Rival

Wearing thick black-rim glasses and a suit and tie, Ted Marche held his precious Georgie close to the face of a little girl as she stared back, mouth agape. Georgie looked a lot like Marche. He too had dark hair and wore glasses, suit, and tie. The one main difference between the two of them was that Marche was a famous ventriloquist and Georgie was a doll.

The image of Marche and his puppet, Georgie—decked out in a "Youth for Kennedy" button—is from the first day of the 1960 Democratic National Convention in the Los Angeles Sports Arena and Coliseum. Marche's purpose that day was to sell the young, fairly inexperienced Catholic senator from Massachusetts as a serious presidential candidate to the kids, who would then promote Kennedy to their parents.[118] Marche's efforts weren't enough to give Kennedy the victory in California. He lost the state to Nixon, but Kennedy, of course, won enough states to emerge victorious.[119]

Ventriloquism wasn't a side job for Marche; it was how he made his living. Marche wasn't his real last name, and still no one is quite sure what the original last name was. He appears to be a mystery even to some of his extended family, which is appropriate given his profession, which required him to disappear beneath other identities. One thing his son did reveal to me in an interview was that Marche was Jewish, which would explain the name change, a common tactic for performers.[120]

Other things I found out: He was born on October 25, 1923, in Brooklyn and completed two tours of service before he moved to Los Angeles to follow his passion of becoming a ventriloquist.[121] He was one of the most skilled ventriloquists of the late 1950s and early 1960s, hobnobbing with celebrity A-listers and touring the country with the Hollywood Stars Baseball Team, whose members included Mickey Rooney.[122] He entertained Dean Martin at the Friars Club and regaled Buddy Hackett at the Press Club. Famed gossip columnist Walter Winchell claimed that Marche was "the only ventriloquist I've ever seen—whose lips never move."[123] With Georgie, a hairstylist named Francois, and a talking pig in tow, Marche performed across the country, bringing his act to grocery stores, trade shows, and even a store dedicated to selling Vibra Massage Chairs.[124]

Marche was not just a professional performer; he was also an engineer. He would spend hours designing and building his dummies, creating molds and filling them with flesh-colored plastic. He was devoted. But by 1965, he was ready for a new profession. Marche wanted to solve a problem he and many men had. That problem? Eyeglasses that would slide down the nose—a particularly annoying issue for a ventriloquist whose hands were otherwise occupied with his dummy. He came up with a hinge-strengthening device made of prongs and rubber bands.[125] That invention didn't become a hit, but, later that year, he developed something that a lot more men, and women, wanted.

This product idea didn't come from Marche himself but from one of his friends, a man named John Francis. Francis was in his late sixties and was obsessed with boats, although he had recently developed a new business on the side: making prosthetic penises. He wondered if Marche could help him.

This was 1965, pre–sexual revolution, when sex toys were considered obscene and therefore illegal unless they were used as medical devices to assist in penetration during heterosexual sex.[126] In America in the 1960s, a person couldn't legally send contraceptives or dildos through the mail, and only married women could legally purchase the new hormonal birth control nicknamed

"The Pill," which became available in the first year of the decade.[127] [128] Nineteen sixty-five was the year that Ralph Ginzburg was tried for obscenity for mailing his artsy erotic publication *Eros* through the mail. Sex had been slowly becoming a topic of open, public discussion in the late 1950s as U.S. obscenity laws had begun to change. The 1957 *Roth v. United States* case saw the Supreme Court loosen the definition of obscenity for the first time in nearly a decade. Instead of judging a book or movie as obscene based on its dirtiest sex scenes, *Roth* decreed it would be judged as a whole.[129] Only if an "average person, applying contemporary community standards" would think that "the dominant theme of the material taken as a whole applies to prurient interest" and was "utterly without redeeming social significance" would a piece of art be considered obscene.[130] More sex-themed books and movies were legalized, but *Roth* wasn't all good. The ruling established that obscenity was not protected by the First Amendment.

Roth had loosened the obscenity laws, but the U.S. Postal Inspection Service continued to arrest people for mailing obscene materials. In fact, arrests for mailed obscenity had more than doubled from the period between 1959 and 1963.[131] By 1966, the Supreme Court convicted Ginzburg of "pandering" in *Ginzburg v. United States*. Ginzburg's crime? Sending *Eros* from cities with sexual names such as Intercourse, Pennsylvania, which was considered obscene.[132] "Pandering" became a new punishable offense for advertisers—and just like obscenity, pandering lacked a clear definition.

The sex-toy industry was a dicey one to be involved in. Most people, when asked if they could be of service for a dildo business, would have run the other way. But Marche was not most people. He was funny, and charming, and he loved helping people and making them happy. So he was receptive when he heard about Francis's side business: making prosthetic penis attachments, or PPAs, which were sold as devices for impotent men to strap on during sex with their wives decades before Viagra. Marche agreed to assist Francis, who had been making his hollow, strap-on polyvinyl chloride dildos one at a time in the oven in his kitchen. It was a slow process—and an imprecise one. Marche thought he could help Francis speed up the process and make the dildos more uniform.[133]

A family man, Marche decided to enlist his whole clan in his new dildo-manufacturing business. As his wife and teenage children ate dinner, Marche carved his first dildo out of balsawood. One of his children looked on with particular interest: his fifteen-year-old stepson, Marche's wife's son from her first marriage.[134]

As a sex-toy business sprang up around a kitchen table in Los Angeles, the country was awash in political changes. President Kennedy had been assassinated two years earlier, in 1963. His successor, Lyndon B. Johnson, had escalated the war in Vietnam, and 100,000 soldiers were sent there in the summer of 1965. Meanwhile, the civil rights struggle on the homefront was coming to a head. In 1964, the Civil Rights Act was passed, barring discrimination based on race, sex, religion, or national origin.[135]

Although Marche was no longer as active with the Democratic Party as he had been, making dildos in the 1960s was a decidedly political act. It was socially and politically dicey, and, depending on how you framed it, it was illegal. On top of the federal obscenity law, nearly every state had a different law regarding the products. Georgia, for example, prohibited devices "designed or marketed as useful primarily for the stimulation of human genital organs."[136]

Although the dildo business was political, it was also a skilled trade—and it was time-consuming. The first step was creating metal molds from the wooden dildos. Then Marche and his son would fill the molds with a plastic polymer and put them into a newly purchased convection oven, which perfectly tempered the dildos. The final step was placing the elastic straps on the dildos. Marche's wife had experience riveting planes at Douglas Aircraft, which came in handy for her job of assembling the snaps for the strap-on component. Francis was pleased with the output, but Marche wasn't satisfied with merely supplying Francis with toys. He wanted to start his own company.

Marche quickly realized that though he had the process down, he wasn't as sure about style: what sizes and shapes he should make them in, what styles customers would want. So Marche told his son to go investigate. His son began to visit Los Angeles–area libraries and archives on a mission to track down all examples of sex toys throughout the centuries. He went day after day, finding examples of Japanese dildos from the 1800s, ancient Chinese sex toys, and more recent Russian ones. Based on this research, they came up with four different sizes: small, medium, large, and extra-large, ranging from five to nine inches long. They decided to create solid dildos in addition to the hollow strap-ons. But there was one question they remained unsure about: What color would a 20th-century American woman want her husband's dildo to be?[137] It was a question that may never have been asked before. Or if it had, it had been answered by a man.

In America, at the time the Marches were making sex toys, dildos were hard to find. They were available only through mail order in catalogs targeted to men or in seedy XXX stores. These stores were on the outskirts of town, usually in fairly dangerous areas, as zoning laws relegated adult bookstores far away from schools, churches, or playgrounds. If a woman wanted to see a dildo before she bought it, she had to go to an adult bookstore, and the average woman just didn't go in those kinds of stores.[138]

Marche's decision to aim his dildos at a female market was a bold move. Even more daring was convening a focus group of twenty-five women to ask them which colors they preferred. Marche passed around samples of colors, including what was then called "flesh-colored"—a light pink meant to mimic Caucasian skin color—and a version in bright red. He learned that they didn't want the dildos to be too realistic in color, as that made them seem kind of creepy, steering dildos into the uncanny valley between the clearly artificial and the realistic replica. But they didn't want them to be too vibrantly colored either. A pearlescent orange won out. For the strap-on, they liked a color that was a little more realistic-looking. It was a shade of Caucasian skin color that was nearly identical to that of Georgie's face. The early dildo colors were designed after a ventriloquist's doll. Marche even mixed the color himself.

Marche wasn't just concerned about having the right color; he also wanted to make the best quality dildos on the market. For that, he had to have the best materials. He was using plastisol, a liquid form of polyvinyl chloride, for the dildos. It wouldn't be considered top-of-the-line now, but it was the finest of its time, as it was nontoxic and medical grade.[139] This too was a revolutionary approach. Most dildo companies weren't concerned about quality. Since dildos were marginally legal, the number of companies producing them was small, and the people who entered the business were usually sketchy. Consumers bought what was available because they had no choice. And when the devices broke, they didn't complain to the manufacturers. They were too embarrassed.

Marche thought of his strap-on penises as medical devices, but he sold them not just to doctors but also through wholesalers who then sold them to adult stores and through catalogs. And demand was huge. Why were Marche's dildos so popular? These strap-on dildos avoided the threat of regular dildos, which were seen as penis replacements that allowed women to give themselves sexual pleasure. These devices put men back in the picture. Strap-on dildos didn't replace men; they augmented men. They made men sexual cyborgs. A man wearing a strap-on penis is still following the sexual script of the time: penetrating a woman and being the provider of her sexual pleasure. Strap-on dildos were devices that strengthened marriage. They did not shake up the sexual status quo, nor did they alter gender norms. A dildo's purpose was enshrined within the term used to describe it at the time:

a marital aid. And letters to Marche Manufacturing made it clear that the dildos were, in fact, being used to improve marriages.[140]

Improving marriages was a laudable goal, but, for many women, marriage was increasingly being viewed as an oppressive institution, as Betty Friedan argued in *The Feminine Mystique,* published in 1963. Friedan's book was based on interviews with middle-class housewives, who, Friedan discovered, were unhappy with their traditional roles as wives and mothers. Because society told women that they should be satisfied with the domestic role, many women were left wondering why they felt a sense of existential angst.[141] Friedan "accused the entire society and culture . . . of a mass conspiracy to limit the lives of women," which she called "the feminine mystique."[142] One of the women who saw herself reflected in Friedan's book was an artist named Betty Dodson, who was mired in an unhappy marriage. In 1965, the very year Marche began making dildos, Dodson read Friedan's book and "became an instant feminist" because it "shattered forever the myth that Everywoman's complete fulfillment could be found in marriage," Dodson later wrote.[143] Dodson was part of the thousands of women questioning their gender roles as second-wave feminism washed in with the publication of both *The Feminist Mystique* and Helen Gurley Brown's *Sex and the Single Girl,* which had been published in 1962. Both books represented the two poles of the feminist movement. Brown argued that sex was the key to female fulfillment, while Friedan argued that career was.

In fact, Dodson had been struggling with fitting herself into traditional gender roles long before she read Friedan. But Friedan had been able to articulate Dodson's feelings in a way no writer had ever before. Since she was a child, Dodson had felt conflicted between what was expected of her and what she actually did. Like many girls, Betty Dodson liked to masturbate.[144] That wouldn't have been a problem, except for the fact that Dodson grew up in the 1930s in conservative Wichita, Kansas, and masturbation was just not

B
U
Z
Z

*

discussed because it was not something that young girls did. Masturbation wasn't even really something that good little boys did at the time either. It was considered physically dangerous at worst and emotionally destructive at best. Dodson felt enormous guilt about her behavior, but the guilt wasn't stronger than the pleasures that masturbation brought her.

As Dodson grew older and the guilt grew stronger, she scrounged libraries to find evidence that her habit was normal. But in the 1940s, finding any information on masturbation was difficult, and what was there to be found was not reassuring. The "dreary marriage manuals and random bits of male-oriented Victorian psychiatry" that she read did the opposite of what she intended: They told her what she was doing was wrong.[145] Messages from society were similar. The overriding message was that the only proper way to have an orgasm was through intercourse with your husband.

It took Dodson twenty years to discover just how wrong that message was. By 1950, after dropping out of college, Dodson had moved to New York with $250 in her pocket and a dream of being an artist.[146] Two years later, she got married, quit her job as a commercial illustrator, and devoted herself to being a full-time painter. It was marriage that led her to discover that she rarely had orgasms during vaginal sex. She assumed that something was wrong with her. Sex was supposed to be much more enjoyable than masturbation; she found the opposite to be the case. So she continued masturbating, even though married people weren't supposed to masturbate. She kept it a secret from her husband. She was also unsatisfied in her professional life, as her artistic career was floundering. "As a painter, I was an unknown, non-collected, not exhibited alienated, suffering starving artist in my garret economically dependent on my successful husband," she wrote to a friend. Being financially dependent on her husband was bad enough, but even worse was the fact that she was "sexually dependent upon him."[147]

In 1966, Dodson's husband ran off with his secretary, and she realized that he had probably been just as unhappy as she had been.[148] That same year, William Masters and Virginia Johnson's *Human Sexual Response* was published.

Dodson's frustration at not being able to have an orgasm during sex was legitimized through data in 1966, when masturbation finally became a topic of public conversation. Although Kinsey had publicly claimed that the vaginal orgasm was a myth, it was not until Masters and Johnson came along that the idea was truly challenged. Unlike Kinsey, Masters and Johnson didn't use surveys to get their data; they actually observed people masturbating and having sex.[149] And as anyone who has ever lied about sex knows (and that includes nearly all of us), what people actually do and what they say they do are two completely different things.

Masters and Johnson brought a variety of men and women—including graduate students and prostitutes—into their St. Louis, Missouri–based lab, hooked them up to machines and watched them have sex. They found that women frequently did not have orgasms during penis-in-vagina sex. This was groundbreaking stuff. Masters and Johnson demolished the idea that there was a special, superior orgasm that happened deep within the vagina during sex. The so-called vaginal orgasm that Sigmund Freud had touted as more "mature" than the clitoral orgasm was, in fact, an orgasm that originated in the clitoris.

Masters and Johnson also took men out of the picture in their examination of women's sexual habits by studying their masturbation. To measure this, they would place a nine-inch-long motorized dildo packed with a camera and a powerful light into a woman's vagina. Publicly, they called this dildo a piece of "artificial coital equipment" to make their research seem as scientific as possible; privately, they called it "Ulysses," after the Kirk Douglas film that was popular at the time.

What they found shocked them. During masturbation, women could have *multiple* orgasms, and these orgasms were more intense than those women had during intercourse. Much to the satisfaction of feminists, Masters and

Johnson had scientifically proven that men were unnecessary for sexual pleasure. "Males hate this machine because invariably the females speed up the machine at a rate that no male can equal," William Masters admitted. What was even scarier to men? Women were found to be insatiable. They could have orgasm after orgasm in the lab, some up to fifty in a row.[150] Masters and Johnson's *Human Sexual Response*—which was intended primarily as a medical text for doctors—went on to become a bestseller with the general public, spending thirty-one weeks on the *New York Times* bestseller list and rising to number three on the list.[151]

Some people were less than thrilled about Masters and Johnson's findings. Among them? Norman Mailer, who wrote in his book *The Prisoner of Sex* that Masters and Johnson's lab had turned sex into "fifty whips of the clitoris pinging through with all the authority of a broken nerve in the tooth." He criticized "that plastic prick, that laboratory dildoe, that vibrator!"[152] He argued that the types of women who would have such sterile, mechanical orgasms were "plain housewives" with "bewildered cunt[s]."[153]

Masters and Johnson's research findings threatened conventional gender roles because it was the man who was supposed to bring a woman to orgasm, not a machine. This is a feature that distinguished Marche's sex toys from others on the market: They weren't as threatening because they were attached to a man, allowing a male partner to bring his female partner to orgasm. Marche was, in some sense, peddling a kind of "family values" sex toy. He even used sex toys to bring his own family closer together.

One day Marche sat his teenage son down next to him and told his son that he wanted to read him a letter from a customer. It turned out that a woman had written Marche and told him that her husband had been impotent, and she didn't know what to do. Her marriage had been crumbling; it was near destruction when her doctor had suggested they get one of Marche's prosthetic penises. So she ordered one from Marche, but instead of just sending her the dildo she ordered, he sent her two of them; the second was for free because Marche wanted to make sure she got the right size. The woman was overjoyed that he would care enough to send two sizes, and, more important, that the prosthetic dildo actually worked. Her husband was now able to satisfy her. And their marriage had been saved. As Marche read the letter to his son, he began to cry. Father and son sat together on the couch in tears over the fact that their product had changed two people's lives.[154]

This isn't usually how people think of dildo makers. The popular conception of a man in the sex-toy industry, if they're ever thought of at all, is as a sleazy, sex-obsessed man who objectifies women. The Marches were the opposite. This was just one of the thousands of letters the Marches received from their customers. Marche would take the time to write many of his customers back because for him, the business wasn't just about money. Making people happy was just as important, or even more important, to him than making money. On the surface, being a ventriloquist and making dildos could not seem further removed from each other. But dig deeper and they're two professions whose principal goal is bringing people joy.

Of course, not all customer letters were filled with praise. Customers also complained to Marche. Their main complaint: They didn't like the straps that secured the dildo around the waist. They were bulky, so they asked if Marche could make a strapless strap-on dildo. This was a challenging request. Just how exactly do you get a dildo to stay on a man's body without any intervening straps? Marche and his son mulled over this question for a while. Finally, they hit upon inspiration: Use a pneumatic device, like the type used on blood-pressure cuffs. They decided on a square pneumatic balloon device that attached to the base of a man's penis. Since it was inflatable, men could pump it to the exact size they needed.

To create the new strapless strap-ons, his son (who was now sixteen years old) transformed the garage into his personal workspace and hired twelve workers to assemble the "pneumos" for a dollar fifty an hour. While most high schoolers were busy worrying about their physics homework, this teenager was overseeing the production of one of the most high-tech dildos around. There was just one catch: The workers didn't know they were building pneumatic bladders for dildos. Marche and his son kept that a secret. The finished product was on display only inside the house, not in the garage. And the workers were just happy to have a job. They quickly outgrew the garage and opened a factory on Hollywood Boulevard, where they employed twenty-four people. The dildo business was continuing to grow.[155]

Marche continued to focus on quality, using medical-grade material. This also served a practical purpose, as the more medicalized the dildos, the less likely they were to be considered illegal. But medicalizing a dildo was no guarantee of evading trouble. Even when companies presented dildos as medical devices or marital aids, they still risked being charged with sending obscenity through the mail or, at the very least, reported to the American Medical Association's Department of Investigation. The AMA would then sometimes alert federal or state authorities about fraudulent claims or supposed obscenity.[156] Prosthetic penises drew "hundreds of complaints."[157] For example, in August 1967, Frank E. Wilson, the executive director of the Association of Military Surgeons, wrote to the AMA, complaining about an advertising brochure for the United Artificial Penis, a strap-on penis similar to the ones sold by Marche. Even though the device was marketed as a medical device for men "who are unable to perform marital relations by reason of organic impotence" from injury or other reasons, it still offended Wilson. Wilson said that the brochure was "pornographic and exciting to homosexuals and people of low mentality."[158]

(*)

Around the time that the Marches were making dildos in their garage, a major change occurred to obscenity law. In 1966, a two-hundred-year-old novel written by Englishman John Cleland, *Memoirs of a Woman of Pleasure* (more commonly known as *Fanny Hill*), was declared not obscene, and this decision liberalized the obscenity law again. *Memoirs v. Massachusetts* built on *Roth*, and it established that a work was obscene only if it was "utterly without redeeming social value" and "patently offensive."[159] The test, like the obscenity tests before it, was vague and difficult to enforce. But according to First Amendment scholar Donald Downs, "*Memoirs* pushed the Court along the path to concluding that only 'hard-core' pornography . . . could be designated obscene."[160] A year later, in 1967, the Supreme Court tried three cases that also loosened obscenity restrictions. In *Stanley v. Georgia*, the court established the right to possess obscene materials in your home. *Redrup v. New York* and *I. M. Amusement Corp. v. Ohio* established that distribution of many sexual magazines and movies was legal.[161] But sex toys remained marginally legal as well as controversial.

(*)

As the obscenity laws loosened, Betty Dodson, now thirty-five years old, single, and sober, began to explore erotic painting. When one couple posing for her started having sex, this experience drew her into going to orgies. Soon she was having sex with whomever she could, whether they were male or female. This was a daring thing for anybody to be doing, let alone a single woman from Wichita. Group sex opened her mind. It was "incredibly liberating," she said, because it "forced [her] to get rid of [her] jealousy." Instead of being in a monogamous relationship where "you spend all your time and energy worrying about what your lover is doing when you're not with him," during orgies "you can see what he's doing, and it's not nearly so terrifying."[162]

One man she was seeing stood out from the rest: a former English professor named Grant Taylor. Taylor did one thing that her other lovers did not—he stimulated her clitoris during intercourse.

Still, Dodson's sexual anxieties did not just evaporate. She had her deep, dark secret that she had never admitted to anybody else: She liked to masturbate. She had been doing it so much that she worried she had deformed her genitals. Dodson had held on to this secret for nearly three decades, as it gnawed at her, making her feel tremendous guilt. Then one day her anxiety disappeared thanks to five magical words uttered by her lover Taylor: "You have a beautiful cunt." He had been performing oral sex on Dodson when he stopped to admire her vulva. He told her he wanted to look at it in more detail. Dodson demurred, insisting that her inner labia were deformed and elongated and "hung down like a chicken" because of her childhood masturbation. He protested, saying that many women had genitals like hers.

To prove it, he went to his closet, emerged with a stack of porn magazines, and flipped through them to show her the "split beaver" pictures, which featured women spread-legged and displaying their vulvas for the camera. Dodson was skeptical. As a feminist, she found pornography degrading. It was how she was supposed to feel, but instead her lover was insisting that porn would do the opposite: make her feel better about herself.[163] It took a little while, but soon she began to appreciate the vulva photos. "By the time we'd gone through several magazines with him pointing out models that had genitals like mine," she said. "I realized I was 'normal,' and maybe even beautiful like he said." To learn that her labia were not only normal but also sexy enough to be featured in porn magazines was a revelation for Dodson. She felt empowered.[164] Unlike other women's activists who saw pornography as destructive to women's self image, Dodson saw it as liberating.

Soon after learning that her genitals were "normal," Dodson admitted to her lover that her masturbation habit had not stopped during childhood. She had masturbated all throughout adulthood, including during her marriage. Instead of being shocked, her lover said that he had done the same. They had hidden their masturbation habits from their spouses, so they decided that they would no longer hide their masturbation from each other.

They chose to masturbate in front of each other, but she wanted to masturbate by herself in front of a mirror first to get a sense of what she looked like. When she saw herself masturbating, she realized, "I didn't look funny or awful—I simply looked sexual and intense."[165] Watching herself masturbate was the "beginning of my freedom from the romanticized image of sex—a Sexual Independence Day," Dodson said.[166] She then felt comfortable enough to masturbate in front of Taylor, and they both masturbated together.

Even though she felt empowered, she still felt a deep anxiety. For a woman, masturbating in front of a lover is fraught with a kind of nervousness that no man would feel when engaging in the same act. Not only are women taught that masturbation is wrong, but they are also taught that a man should be bringing them sexual pleasure. So even though Dodson saw her masturbation as a celebration of her sexual independence, she still feared that her lover would leave her if he realized that she "wasn't dependent on him for orgasm."[167] She was also worried that if he felt threatened by her masturbation, she would end up "scurrying back to the missionary position."[168] Dodson's lover did not leave her. And their sex got better. Much better. Something about sharing this sexual act that they had both been socialized to think of as shameful had deepened their bond.

Despite her sexual openness, Dodson was still skeptical when Taylor returned from the barber one day with a vibrator he wanted to try. He'd gone for a haircut, and when the barber strapped an Oster vibrator to his hand and proceeded to massage the back of his neck, Taylor had thought it would be the perfect sex toy, so he purchased one from a barbershop supply store the same day. He brought the vibrator home to use during sex play. Dodson was wary.

"Although I was not all that crazy about getting off on a mechanical device, my motto is to always try everything at least once," Dodson later said.[169]

Her hesitation demonstrates how deeply ingrained the antitechnology ethos was in the 1960s and 1970s. Nature was fetishized, and many thought that an electric vibrator couldn't be further from nature. Ironically, animals have been documented using objects as sex toys, including orangutans, a close relation to the human, who have been seen using twigs to stimulate their genitals, as have female porcupines.[170] To corrupt the "natural" act of sex by enhancing it with a machine was widely considered anathema among many, like public intellectual Lewis Mumford, who "wanted technology to be organic rather than mechanistic."[171] But Dodson's first experience with the Oster was so intense that she overcame any philosophical justifications for not enjoying the vibrator. "I gasped when his fingers made contact with my clitoris and in moments, the orgasm I had was so powerful I was terrified!"[172] And she was aided in her change of heart by the design of the Oster itself. "I was able to rationalize that since his fingers were touching me, it was still skin on skin—so it was probably okay to use the vibrator from time to time," Dodson said.[173] Dodson began masturbating with the vibrator soon after, and Taylor was thrilled, as her sexual appetite had exhausted him. "He wanted to watch the ball game and I wanted to have more orgasms," she said.[174]

As Dodson had been exploring her sexuality through practicing with her lover, as well as many other lovers that she had during their open relationship, she had also been exploring it through her art, painting images of nudes. In November 1968, she had her first show at the Wickersham Gallery in New York City, the same year that women liberationists protested the Miss America pageant. It was her first solo exhibition, and she was panicked. "I envisioned irate citizens throwing rocks at the gallery or my getting busted for pornography," she wrote.[175] Dodson attended the art opening dressed in full-on dominatrix style, without even knowing what a dominatrix was. Clad in black leggings with a "jeweled chain belt" and "black leather-riding crop," she created quite an image in the staid art world.[176]

The show displayed Dodson's charcoal drawings of her having sex with her lover, Taylor, and another lover, Roy, with the drawings placed behind multi-colored Plexiglas.[177] The show was a resounding success. Within the two weeks of the exhibition, eight thousand people came to see drawings of Dodson having sex, the largest crowd the gallery had ever seen.[178] But what affected Dodson the most were the stories patrons were telling her about their own sex lives. Women were much more interested in discussing sex than men; they shared their "fears and hangups" with Dodson.[179] Some men talked to her too. One man took her aside and whispered that he had "the same disease as the model in one of your pictures."[180] The "disease" he was referring to was that of having a curved penis. In some ways, men were as ignorant about sex as women were. She learned something important from the show: "Nearly everyone was affected by socially imposed sex-negative attitudes." The key to fixing these attitudes was to teach women about masturbation, thought Dodson. [181]

(*)

As Dodson was becoming motivated to change societal views on sex, Marche was experiencing a new feeling as well: the feeling of having competition. In 1968, the same year of Dodson's show, a fifty-something novelty-goods salesman named Fred Malorrus decided to enter the sex-toy business. Malorrus had been selling novelties for nearly four decades before he turned his attention to sex toys.

Born in 1915, Malorrus began traveling the country as a rack jobber, a salesman who peddles goods to retail stores, at the young age of fifteen. The Malorrus family, like the Marches, was Jewish, and Malorrus's son believes his father's ethnicity may have influenced his choice of profession. "The Jewish people had trouble getting jobs if they weren't lawyers, doctors, or accountants," said Malorrus's son, Farley. So Fred went into what has historically been a classic profession of Jews: itinerant peddler. From 1930 to 1938, he drove "all over America with a trunk full of pens, costume jewelry, perfume, condoms," said Farley. "He was the guy who would pull up at a gas station or a pool hall and open up his trunk" and men would come racing out to see what he had, they'd purchase a few things, and he'd go to the next gas station down the road.[182]

Malorrus was taking a risk by selling condoms in 1930, even though this was the year when Comstock's nearly five-decades-long ban on selling condoms was loosened. But there was a catch: Condoms were legal only if they were sold to prevent disease, not for contraceptive purposes. Hence the name some still use for condoms today—prophylactics. Six years later, the condom's legality was further strengthened when a federal appeals court decided that doctors could legally prescribe condoms to prevent disease.[183]

After his successful experience as a rack jobber, Malorrus decided to form his own company, which he called United Sales. He began selling only steel wool, but by 1942, he expanded to selling watches, rings, costume jewelry, perfume, and condoms. A few years later, in the mid-1940s, he added a new sex product: a flip book of a woman flashing her breasts. A variety of sex-themed goods soon followed, including nudist magazines, erotic playing cards, a wind-up toy of two pigs having sex ("Makin' Bakin"), and his first sex toy—French ticklers.

According to Farley, it wasn't until his father met a Mattel employee that he decided to sell dildos.[184] This employee had honed his skills working with plastic through making children's toys, and he was now making rubber dildos on the side and selling them to a store on Sunset Boulevard. Fred thought he could expand the employee's customer base, and he convinced him that he could sell the dildos all across the country.

Fred's first step was packaging each dildo in a box with the words "Ladies Home Companion" stamped on the outside. That way the dildo could possibly be considered a novelty or practical joke item and Fred could skirt the law. Another way they tried to preempt prosecution was by placing a sticker on every box that read "sold as a novelty only." (Sound familiar?) Even the size of the dildos themselves was influenced by legal concerns. "The dildos were so huge, I mean, we're talking ten inches long," said Farley. "I'm looking at my dad, saying, 'Dad, how's a woman supposed to . . .' and my dad says, 'We can't make it real, Farley, or we'll go to jail.'"

Unlike Marche's dildos, the ones that United Sales was selling weren't medical grade. They were "made of the same rubber used to make tires," Farley said. "[They] had a gasoline smell." Farley was so alarmed by the low quality of their dildos that he tried to convince his father to include a condom with them, so the rubber wouldn't come into contact with users' skin. But his efforts were unsuccessful. In 1968, Fred began making his own dildos, after he moved out to California and went into business with the Mattel employee. They manufactured their dildos in a factory in Hermosa Beach on the cheap. It cost only thirty-five cents to make the dildos, which they then sold to wholesalers for a dollar. But dildos weren't cheap for consumers, who paid seven to ten dollars for them. United Sales's dildo business took off, and after graduating from college, Farley joined his father at the factory.[185]

Soon United Sales became Marche's biggest competitor. Because United Sales wasn't concerned with quality, they could undercut Marche in price. Since dildos were a largely underground business not regulated by the FDA (and they still aren't), consumers were left unprotected from the low-quality sex toys from the Malorruses and other companies. These were products consumers were putting directly into their bodies, with the potential to cause great harm, and the government wasn't concerned about safety. Because sex toys were rarely discussed or reviewed, consumers weren't able to educate themselves. All people had to go on was price. So many of them bought the Malorruses' dildos. This didn't go over well with the Marches.

"Fred Malorrus was my dad's nemesis," Marche's son said.

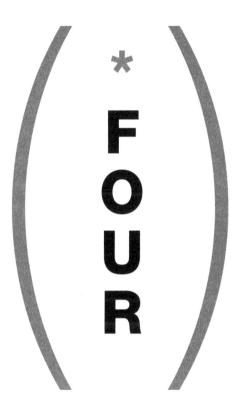

Fake Vaginas, Female Masturbation, and Porno Empires

Faced with increased competition from the Malorruses, the Marches branched out into a new product: strap-on prosthetic vaginas.[186] Like dildos, artificial vaginas also have a long pedigree, dating back to at least the 17th century with Japanese versions made of velvet.[187] But artificial vaginas, or pocket pussies as they're more commonly known, have nearly always been less discussed and feared than dildos. Women, it seems, aren't afraid their spouses will leave them for a rubber vagina. Artificial vaginas were marketed the same way prosthetic penises were: as devices that allowed married people to have sexual intercourse. The Marches sold Caucasian flesh–colored vaginas that were designed to be worn around a woman's waist almost like underwear. They had a tube that simulated a woman's vaginal canal and an attached bulb that allowed the vagina to be inflated so it could be tightened to the man's specification or to simulate orgasmic spasms.

Following soon after the Marches, the Malorruses added artificial vaginas to their sex-toy line. According to Marche's son, Fred and Farley copied everything they did. "We only had six months lead time on a product before he would duplicate it." And because they used cheaper materials, the Malorruses were able to sell them at a lower price than the Marches. As D. Keith Mano wrote in *Playboy*, United Sales "doesn't excel in sex innovation, but it's superb in cut-rate marketing." Farley claims that the copying went both ways, and the Marches copied them too. But the Malorruses weren't the only ones the Marches had to worry about. "One of our competitors copied [our artificial vagina], sent it to Hong Kong, and ordered 10,000 in flesh color," Marche's son told *Playboy*. "They came back yellow. And when they looked at the sleeves—instead of three inches in diameter so you have plenty of room to move around in—they came back the size of a quarter."[188]

While the Marches sold their vaginas the same way they had sold their penises, as prosthetic devices, the Malorruses initially went the novelty route. They called their strap-on vaginas a "Silly Millimeter Longer" to ensure that the vaginas were seen as gag gifts. But soon they took a cue from the Marches and began selling prosthetic vaginas and penises under the guise of medical marital aids. Like strap-on dildos, strap-on vaginas were another product designed and marketed to improve marital sex. For legal reasons, a typical brochure claimed that the purpose of a prosthetic vagina was "to provide a substitute means of physical gratification to the husband when the wife is unable to perform sexually for physiological or psychological reasons."[189] Of course, this was not how they were always used. "Men would strap them on to an inflatable doll or pillow or whatever, and masturbate with them," Farley said.[190]

Selling fake vaginas as marital aids was no guarantee that legal action wouldn't be taken. In 1967, one seller of rubber vaginas was reported by the AMA to the post office for possible indictment under laws prohibiting sending fraudulent products through the mail, one of the laws used to indict sex-toy sellers.[191] The Malorruses and Marches seem to have escaped indictments, but it was impossible to not be affected by the climate of censorship. Even during the manufacturing process, things had to be done in secret. When there's no regulation and a business is conducted on the margins of society, there are bound to be complications. By going after sex-toy makers, the government helped push the industry underground.

Since strap-on vaginas required different manufacturing materials than strap-on penises, the Marches had to outsource the work to another maker, a man in Santa Fe Springs, California, who created a high quality, thin, plastic vagina with foam. Because what he was making was potentially illegal, he hid it from the rest of the workers, running the production line only after 10 p.m. Marche would then arrive early in the morning to retrieve the vaginas before the factory opened. The vaginas were popular, although not as popular as the dildos. Still, Marche began receiving a flood of letters of thanks. Many of the letters were written by men who wrote how relieved they were that they were finally able to have sex with their wives, who had had medical conditions like vaginismus that didn't allow them to have sex. There were significantly fewer letters from the men masturbating into vaginas for fun.[192]

The success of their strap-on penises and vagina spurred the Marches to expand into vibrators. Even though Masters and Johnson's research had shown that masturbation was more pleasurable for women than sexual intercourse, the Marches didn't market their vibrators for masturbation. As they did with their dildos, the Marches sold their hard, plastic, whitish phallic vibrators as marital aids.[193] Vibrators like these were usually used for masturbation, so why sell them as marital aids? It wasn't just due to the law. From a marketing point of view, selling vibrators as couples toys made sense.

Masturbation was still widely taboo, even among health professionals. Psychologist and sexologist Albert Ellis wrote in 1966 that when he spoke at a symposium a few years earlier, "several prominent psychologists and psychiatrists objected strenuously to my statement that masturbation is quite harmless." Few women would have been comfortable admitting to masturbation, let alone purchasing a special tool for it, during a time when even many sex manuals said that "masturbation while not completely harmful, is still not 'good' or 'desirable'"—statements that according to Ellis, had "no scientific foundation and constitute a modern carryover of old antisexual moralizings."[194] And especially because many female-centric sex toys were bought by men, the appeal to marriage and partnership worked because it was less threatening.

Around the same time as the Marches began selling vibrators, the Malorruses entered the vibrator business. Instead of creating their own, they bought the rights to a Japanese vibrator called the Stim Vib, thus beginning what would become a big business of importing sex toys from Japan. It looked similar to the standard white vibrator sold by Marche, except that theirs was curved at top and it was marketed in a nonsexual way, as a scalp and facial massager.[195] In the 1970s, Japanese products didn't have the cache that they have now. They were considered low quality. But the Stim Vibe was a powerful vibrator made of soft and flexible plastic, and it was rated as one of the best vibrators in *Playboy*'s "Sex Aids Road Test." Vibrators remained controversial, though, even to the *Playboy* testers. The testers noted that vibrators still possessed a "bad image."[196]

(*)

Although the Malorruses aped many of the Marches' medical-style sex toys, they never aspired to be taken especially seriously in the business. They just wanted to make money. And if it was money you were after, it didn't matter too much what you were selling as long as it was cheap to make and somebody was willing to buy it. After all, Fred Malorrus had entered the business as a novelty salesman, selling Makin' Bakin'. So Fred and Farley Malorrus began producing more sexual novelties, including penis-shaped lighters and "Time to Fuck" watches. They cost pennies to make, and they were absolutely ridiculous, but thousands of people bought them.

Soon after, the Marches joined in the novelty game with a penis pencil topper. They decided that if they were going to make a penis pencil eraser, it would be the best-made adult novelty the world had seen. Constructed out of high-quality medical-grade plastics, the penis pencil topper was a gag gift that was small enough to not be too upsetting to those with a more conservative streak. Ever the entertainer, Ted Marche used penis erasers as props for his gags. He'd ask a person for a cigarette, they'd hand him their pack, he'd place a penis eraser on one of the cigarettes and hand it back to them. Marche would watch in amusement as the person looked in horror to discover that his cigarette was now bearing a penis emerging from its filter. The penis erasers were a hit. *Penthouse* bought one hundred thousand of them. The Marches expanded their line of novelties. And the war between the Marches and Malorruses was on.[197]

A penis gear shift. A penis key ring made of leather. A light switch cover that made the switch look like a fat man's penis. Marche and his son dreamed up a phallic wonderland. They saw the world through penis-shaped glasses, which were another product they made. There's a reason why bachelorette parties are full of penis trinkets and not vagina ones: It was men who created the mass market in genitalia jokes. While feminists made vagina art to be hung in museums, it was the men who monetized their genitalia as commodities.

The Malorruses and Marches continued to churn out novelties and sex toys, with the Malorruses not caring too much about quality, as was illustrated by their new line of aphrodisiacs. Aphrodisiacs are ancient and have always held a certain appeal throughout the centuries, and some have actually shown to be effective, such as ones containing ambergris, a lump found in sperm whales' stomachs.[198] Until the 1990s, some doctors did prescribe aphrodisiacs such as Yohimbine before drugs like Viagra were available.[199] Medical literature has shown Yohimbine to be effective.[200] But aphrodisiacs have also been the province of hucksters. Pills and potions that purportedly increase lust are nearly irresistible to humans because they make the amorphous and complicated process of sexual desire seem concrete and within a person's control. But, as with illegal drugs, with over-the-counter aphrodisiacs it's difficult to know just what you are getting because they aren't regulated. Of all the aphrodisiacs in the world, perhaps the most famous is Spanish fly, which the Malorruses sold. Although Spanish fly, or *cantharidin*, has been used as an aphrodisiac for thousands of years, it is one of the most dangerous of its kind. Spanish fly is not, in fact, made from flies but from another insect: the blister beetle. The same properties that supposedly make it an effective aphrodisiac—the fact that it causes irritation in the body—also make it potentially toxic. It can cause the stomach to bleed so severely that it results in death.[201]

But what the Malorruses sold as Spanish fly was related to the real thing in name only. What they were selling was a mixture of cayenne pepper and whey in the pill version, and sugar water in the liquid version, known as Spanish fly drops. The drops came in eight different flavors, including chocolate and coconut. And as Farley points out, the pills did actually heighten people's sexual desire, if only via the placebo effect. Another possible reason the Spanish fly "drops" were so effective? They instructed customers to rub the drops "on her love place, massage them in, and lick it off." What they were really asking their male customers to do was perform oral sex on their female partners. Of course the drops worked.[202]

It was selling bogus products like sugar water as Spanish fly that gave sex-toy producers a bad name in the 1960s and 1970s and continues to give some of them a bad name today. If one of a company's products is fraudulent, how is a consumer supposed to trust the rest of them? Then again, if the Malorruses had sold the real Spanish fly, they could have killed their consumers, and if they'd said it was sugar water they were selling, it wouldn't have had the placebo effect. The Malorruses probably helped many people's sex lives with their fake Spanish fly. Most certainly they raked in a lot of cash. The sugar water cost ten cents for them to produce, and they sold it for a dollar to the wholesaler. Consumers shelled out ten dollars for it. But this time the Marches didn't follow them into this new line of products. They just didn't have it in them.

The fake aphrodisiacs and penis gearshifts undermined the credibility of the sex-toy industry by literally making sex seem like a joke. But you can't just blame the Marches and Malorruses. America's laws and social mores were more to blame. Novelties were less likely to be considered legally obscene. They also didn't threaten gender or sexual norms. While decorating motor-cycle handles with penis sheaths may have been in bad taste, it was considered boys just being boys. Some people even argued that these sex novelties were a response to women's liberation, a pushing back against newfound female power in the bedroom. A penis golf-club topper was a way to assert sexual dominance.[203]

It is these laws and cultural norms that have caused the sex-toy industry in America to swing between these two disparate poles of purely medical device to novelty, from a medical prosthesis to a wind-up jolly jumping pussy. Sex toys sold for masturbation fell in the middle: They were the most dangerous. A dildo or artificial vagina sold for masturbation was undermining traditional values and promoting singledom a retreat from social norms, a furtive antiso-cial masturbation practice.

The legal gray area that sex toys lingered in required manufacturers to hedge their bets by producing products that were least likely to be prosecuted: those that upheld heterosexual family values and those that were gag gifts. To make a profit, usually the same companies would produce both types.

But a big difference existed between the Malorruses and Marches. Malorrus saw little distinction between the novelties and the prosthetics. They were all products that turned a profit. For Marche, all his products—even the penis erasers—were made to exacting specifications and the same medical-grade plastic as the dildos. But from an outsider's perspective, both companies looked similar. And it was hard to take seriously a company that designed prosthetic genitals for Johns Hopkins (which Marche Manufacturing did later) if, in the same factory, they also churned out a penis ring-toss game.

Although the Marches and the Malorruses were vicious competitors, there was one thing they agreed on: They needed better distribution for their products. And they knew just who to turn to—a charismatic wholesaler based in Cleveland, Ohio, named Reuben Sturman. He controlled the distribution of pornography and sex toys for nearly every adult bookstore in the country and owned many of the stores too. To have Sturman distribute your dildos was like winning a contract with Walmart today. The only problem was that Sturman took a big cut. How was Sturman able to have such a big monopoly? Because distributing sex toys and porn was a quick way to get arrested, few people wanted to do it. Most of the other people willing to take such a risk were members of the mob.

Sturman hadn't always aspired to be the largest porn and dildo distributor in the United States, but he had always wanted to be rich. Sturman was a first-generation immigrant, born in 1924 in a Jewish immigrant community in southeast Cleveland to communist Jewish parents who had recently immigrated from Russia. He spent three years in the U.S. Air Force and then enrolled in Case Institute of Technology, graduating in 1948 with a business degree. After graduation, Sturman's neighbor suggested that he join his cigars and candy distribution business.

In 1951, Sturman persuaded his neighbor to add comic books to the line. It was the height of the comic book craze, and their comics were so successful that Sturman broke off from his neighbor's company to start his own wholesale business, Premium Sales Company. Because Sturman was incredibly charming and skilled at schmoozing with retailers, his business was immediately successful. For the next five years, Sturman peddled the comics from the trunk of his old Dodge.[204]

Around this time, Sturman married a woman he'd met a year earlier during a trip to Los Angeles. Esther was a strong New York–born woman with a six-year-old daughter, Peggy, who Reuben adopted. Soon they had two more children, Lee and David, and Esther joined Sturman in the business.[205] They weren't rich, but they were comfortable. Then one day at work, one of

Sturman's employees, a man named Wally, came in clutching a sex-themed paperback. Wally wanted to start adding sex books to their line. "'Wally, we're busy," Sturman told him. "If you think it'll sell, take it but I don't want to pay any attention to it." Wally's instinct was right. The book sold and sold and sold. Suddenly sex books seemed appealing to Sturman. And once publishers found out that Sturman was distributing sex novels, they began seeking him out because Sturman had what they needed: an extensive distribution system he'd created when distributing comic books. Sex books were just another product to him.[206]

Even though he claims to have felt no real affinity for sex books, once he started selling them, he never really looked back. Soon he moved onto other sexually themed materials, including cheap black-and-white sex magazines that distributors began creating to compete with a new men's magazine called *Playboy*. Then "he realized that you could make a ton more money from pornography," said his son David.[207] Sturman's wholesale business was so successful that he was distributing girlie magazines all across the country to wholesalers. He changed the name of his company to Sovereign News to make it seem regal, and in his three-story brick warehouse in Cleveland, he began creating a porn empire.

By the early 1960s, with his wife Esther's blessing, Sturman had graduated to distribution of hard-core porn, and he had added another product category to the line, a type of good few others would touch: sex toys. As he had with pornography, Sturman very quickly became the go-to distributor of sex toys in the Uunite States. And he wasn't just distributing his product outside of Cleveland; he was also setting up distribution centers across the county with grandiose-sounding names, including Crown News and Majestic News.[208]

Sturman had it all: a happy family, a successful business, and a large Tudor home. He was well-loved by many in the community thanks to his generous gifts to charities. But building a big sex empire in the early 1960s was risky. The country was still stuck in quaint notions of sexuality and gender. A woman's place was in the home, abortion was illegal, and birth control was impossible to obtain without a marriage license. Pornography didn't sit well with a large portion of the populace. Even books like James Joyce's *Ulysses* were deemed obscene.

It was only a matter of time before Sturman got in trouble with the law. One day in 1963, the Detroit police raided his Royal News warehouse, seizing his stock of nudist camp magazines, which they believed were obscene. It turned out that the magazines weren't obscene, at least not by any legal definition. A few months later, the police showed up again and destroyed twenty thousand magazines. Sturman responded by suing the police for $200,000, claiming that not only had he lost money in his business but that the cops were harassing him.[209] His lawsuit didn't end the raids, however. It had the opposite effect: It began a war, and not just with the Detroit police, but also with the FBI.[210]

In the 1960s, Sturman's businesses were raided all over the country.[211] He was dragged into court on obscenity charges in California, Michigan, and Ohio. He always beat the charges; he even sued J. Edgar Hoover at one point.[212] But being hounded by the federal government took its toll on Sturman. He began breaking up his company into smaller corporations, incorporating them in the United States and internationally.[213 214]

Sturman wasn't deterred, however. Instead, he expanded his business. He was always on the lookout for new products to distribute. One day, a friend of his showed him a few wind-up machines that displayed films. They were usually placed in bars, where customers could put a quarter in and flip through them. Sturman had an idea: He would put the machines in his stores, but he'd place them in private wooden booths with a lock on the door. That way, male customers could masturbate while watching the films.[215] Soon Sturman was not only distributing the films but also distributing the machines and building the booths through his company Automated Vending. He set up these peep shows in the back of adult bookstores and stocked them with eight-millimeter sex films. Men would put a quarter in the machine to watch a minute of a short film.[216] Peep shows became wildly popular and profitable because most people had no way of watching pornography at home since VCRs hadn't yet been invented. One other great thing about the peep-show business? Most of the profits were in cash. On a per-week basis, a store could earn up to $10,000. Sturman's associates would travel from store to store, draining the machines of their quarters, giving the owners a percentage, and placing the rest of the heavy loot in bags.[217]

As his businesses succeeded, his marriage to Esther was crumbling. Sturman began sleeping with women he met in a calisthenics class he was teaching.[218] Reuben and Esther separated, and Esther moved out of the house. Esther wanted to continue in the business, but Reuben disagreed. He barred her from the office and forged documents so her name was removed from the board of directors of his companies. When they finalized their divorce, she had one request: Don't let the kids join the business.[219]

Post-separation, in the late 1960s, Sturman was the king of the peep show and the largest pornography distributor in the United States. He also owned a huge number of adult bookstores. Although he'd been indicted several times on obscenity and his businesses were controversial, he had always beaten the charges. He was a man on the rise, with an empire built on the phenomenon of male masturbation.

As Sturman was profiting from male masturbation, Betty Dodson was making art out of it. She'd already had the first one-woman erotic art show at the Wickersham Gallery in New York City in November 1968.[220] Because it went over so well, she was asked back. For her next show, she created a series of "Sex-Role Cartoons." Each painting featured a dichotomy of traditional women's roles like "Madonna/Whore," which showed a woman nursing her child on the top half of the image, with the bottom half showing her reddened genitals getting penetrated by a penis. To contrast the cartoons, she decided to create a complementary series of women masturbating. One of these was a six-foot-tall portrait of Dodson's girlfriend masturbating with a vibrator, which was the most contentious of them all.

Even knowing that her work would be controversial, Dodson was still surprised at the responses. Some female visitors to the gallery confessed they were afraid of using vibrators because they thought they would get addicted to them. Others mentioned that they thought the drawing subjects had to be single, as women in a relationship would never need outside tools. These reactions led Dodson to a revelation that changed the course of her life. "The two weeks I spent in the gallery made it very clear that repression relates directly to masturbation," she says now. "It follows then that masturbation can be important in reversing the process and achieving liberation."[221] For Dodson, masturbation was the key to women's liberation because masturbation was the first stepping-stone to sexual freedom. This was a radical idea then, even among radical feminists. How could touching yourself in private, such an insular and seemingly selfish activity, actually be a form of liberation? According to Dodson's philosophy, masturbation was liberating because it allowed women to learn about their bodies' own sexual responses. Until women knew how to bring themselves pleasure, they would not be able to take control of their own sexuality. A woman could not have a successful sexual relationship without knowing how to give herself orgasms because they would not be able to transmit that knowledge to their partners, she said.

"If I couldn't touch my own body for pleasure, I was a victim hoping to get the kind of sex from a partner who would provide adequate stimulation of my clitoris that lasted long enough for me to have an orgasm," Dodson says. "Even if that happened, I would still be dependent on each lover for all my orgasms. This kind of sexual dependency led to resentments, which fueled the war between the sexes."[222]

One major point in Dodson's argument was her insistence that orgasms were clitoral. Dodson was furious that women were taught to believe in the Freudian view that they should graduate away from the "immature" clitoral orgasm and into the "mature" vaginal orgasm as they became adults. She promoted Masters and Johnson's research proving that all orgasms are clitoral, and other feminists used those findings as a rallying cry to demolish existing gender and sexual roles.

Feminist Anne Koedt's seminal 1973 essay "The Myth of the Vaginal Orgasm" argued that both men and women perpetuated the idea that a superior vaginal orgasm existed. Each gender had a different reason for hanging on to this myth, wrote Koedt. Since men enjoyed penetrative sex, they wanted to perpetuate the myth because it ensured that intercourse would be seen as superior to other forms of sex, like cunnilingus. Koedt also said that men wanted to control women's sexuality. They thought of women as subordinate, and they were afraid that clitoral orgasms would make men expendable. Women perpetuated that myth because they had a desire to please men and were ignorant about the functions of their own genitals, argued Koedt. Although her essay was convincing, Koedt lacked a practical solution to getting the two sexes to agree to retire the myth of the vaginal orgasm.[223] Other feminists proffered practical changes. For example, Alix Kates Shulman argued that Americans should transform sex education so that the clitoris, not the vagina, was described as women's primary sexual organ.[224] But aside from Dodson, few other feminists saw Masters and Johnson's findings as a call for masturbation.

Dodson's focus on sexual pleasure was controversial within the women's movement, where many feminists believed that a focus on orgasms and sexual pleasure divorced from emotional connection was a "male-identified" and antifeminist form of sexuality. The Boston Women's Health Collective (BWHC) espoused this view while advocating for masturbation in their seminal 1970 booklet "Women and Their Bodies: A Course," which went on to be published as *Our Bodies, Ourselves* in 1971. Although they promoted clitoral stimulation and masturbation and argued that that all orgasms are clitoral, the collective declared, "Orgasms are not that important in life. What are important are loving, giving, free relationships between people." The BWHC's focus was more on relationships than sexual pleasure, which made the book less sexually progressive than it could have been.[225]

Dodson then published an article called "Masculine Mystique" in *Screw* magazine, provocateur Al Goldstein's weekly publication primarily directed toward heterosexual men. In the article, she explained that missionary sex rarely provided women with orgasms, and she also criticized porn for not focusing on clitoral pleasure. But few feminists read *Screw*, so her article did not have much of an impact.[226]

An article in Barney Rossett's avant-garde *Evergreen Review* followed in 1971, in which she spoke out against feminists' antipornography stance and argued that feminists should create their own porn. It was this article that made the feminist establishment take notice. *Ms.* magazine called her to ask her to write an article on masturbation a few months later. In the article, Dodson fully articulated her masturbation philosophy and advocated for the use of vibrators. But after commissioning the article, *Ms.* rejected it. They were afraid that a pro-masturbation article would offend their readers. It was the beginning of the feminist masturbation fight.[227]

NOW, Sex, and Women's Liberation

O n a warm day in New York City on August 26, 1970, Betty Dodson joined fifty thousand women marching through the streets in the Women's Strike for Equality. Organized by National Organization for Women (NOW) founder and *Feminine Mystique* author Betty Friedan, the Women's Strike for Equality had three main goals on its agenda: to legalize abortion, to make childcare more affordable, and to give women equal opportunities in education and employment. It was supposed to be a work strike for women, with women forgoing cooking and cleaning for a day, to show men what life was like without women's unpaid labor. Friedan believed that the only way to change women's place in society was from the top down, by changing the law. Dodson, who had recently shorn her hair bald, "was marching for women's freedom to choose how [women] wanted to have sex," which wasn't exactly the official goal of the march.[228]

As Dodson marched, another woman stared longingly out the window of the Hodes Advertising at the mass of protesters on Fifth Avenue. Dell Williams didn't know that Dodson was about to change her life. Williams went to the water cooler to get a drink, and as she did, the agency's copywriter sidled up to her. "Oh, look the women are marching outside, the women libbers," he said.

"Maybe I'll join them," she replied.

"Guess they don't have anything better to do," he scoffed.

Williams was taken aback. "Was I just the house broad then? The career gal making good in a man's world and not making a fuss about who really ran the place?" she remembers thinking.[229] She liked this copywriter, and she had thought of him as a sweet man. How could he be so dismissive of the women's movement? "Now I know I'm going to march," she told him.

She stormed out of the office, made her way to the line on Fifth Avenue, and began marching. She was handed a poster that read "Women Unite," which she proudly carried. As she marched and met other women who told her about the feminist movement, she "had a metamorphosis and thought, 'That's why they are always pinching my ass.'"[230] Suddenly it all came together: that she'd been treated differently than men, that her husband had expected her to support his career, that so many men had wanted sex in exchange for a job. That day she wrote that she "had been called by some power greater than my own to some higher purpose."[231]

(*)

Born in 1922 in Manhattan as Dell Zetlin, Williams barely made it through childhood. At age three, after suffering with an illness for days, doctors declared her dead. Then suddenly her mother heard Williams squirming and making noise. She was alive. "I like to think of it as the first time I defied established authority," she later wrote.[232]

Williams was raised by two activist parents and was purportedly named after the socialist journalist Floyd Dell, who was a champion of Margaret Sanger. Williams's parents were both Russian Jews who were subjected to pogroms and fled first to Paris and then to America at the turn of the century to escape.[233] Her father, Isaac Zetlin, was a successful women's clothing designer who sold his creations to Bergdorf Goodman's. Williams's mother, born Sarah Bronstein, was a dressmaker. Life wasn't easy for them. During the Depression, Isaac Zetlin lost his job, and the family was evicted from three different homes. After the third eviction, he disappeared for five years, an abandonment that devastated Williams and ended up shaping her life.

Williams's mother was politically progressive, and Williams learned from her that making the world a better place was possible. A serious tennis player, her mother sought change on the court. Her tennis league was sex-segregated, but she got the league to incorporate mixed doubles by challenging a male player to a match, which she won. She also successfully integrated the league in the 1920s by convincing the league to allow black players in it.[234]

From an early age, Williams was bisexual, though she wouldn't have called herself that at the time. She knew how she felt, yet she was entirely ignorant about sex itself, lacking even basic information. During the 1930s, when she was a teenager, most schools didn't teach sex education. Although a school board member tried to implement a sex education program in New York City high schools in the late 1930s, it was too controversial and it failed.[235] And Williams's parents were no help either. She made it all the way through high school thinking that babies emerged from the anus. It wasn't until she turned eighteen, and her boyfriend taught her about her clitoris, that she started masturbating.

While in high school, Williams had dreamed of becoming an actress and singer, and she performed at her synagogue. Then at age twenty, during World War II, she unexpectedly got pregnant with her boyfriend Peter's baby. Because she wanted to continue following her dreams of stardom and she knew she simply wasn't ready to have a baby, she decided to have an abortion. Not only were abortions illegal, but they were also exorbitantly expensive. Peter's parents paid $500 for the abortion, which is the equivalent to about $6,000 today.[236] Even though a doctor performed her abortion, it was still extremely painful for her. The doctor refused to use anesthesia because anesthesia was more likely to cause complications; complications meant that Williams would have to be admitted to a hospital, and the doctor's illegal

BUZZ
*

abortion could be found out, which could have potentially caused him to be stripped of his license.

Shortly after her abortion, Williams joined up with the Bronx Variety Players, a group that specialized in political satire. Its leader, Madeline Lee, was a communist, and she encouraged Williams to join the party. Three years later, in 1945, Williams became a member of the Women's Army Corps, where she did clerical jobs in addition to being an "entertainment specialist," a gig in which she traveled to Army bases in the United States performing a show penned by a female lieutenant, entitled *Call Me Mrs.*

Within a few years, Williams decided to follow her dream to become a Hollywood star. She was accepted at the prestigious Actors' Laboratory Theater, which Marilyn Monroe attended. Williams landed some theater roles, but what she really wanted to do was work in film. Yet every time that somebody offered her an opportunity, there was always a quid pro quo—the old story of the casting couch. Williams refused to trade sex for film roles.

Meanwhile, Williams kept busy as an artists' model and secretary during the day and having affairs with married men at night. One of her paramours was the famed avant-garde composer George Anthiel, who was married and nearly triple her age; he was happy to have the dalliance but declared that he would never leave his wife, so Williams moved on. The next affair was with her singing instructor, who was separated and kept telling her he would get a divorce. He even bought an apartment where they lived together for a while. When he went to Las Vegas to get a divorce, he came back two weeks early and empty handed; he wasn't getting a divorce, he told her. He was getting back together with his wife.

It wasn't until 1949, when she was twenty-seven years old, that Williams began to think about sex more deeply. Williams was walking by a bookstore when she saw a book with "orgasm" in the title. The very fact that such a book existed was incredible to her. She bought Wilhelm Reich's *Function of the Orgasm* immediately and took to Reich's philosophy that orgasm was the epitome of life and was intimately tied into natural processes like ocean waves.[237]

In 1951, with her Hollywood dreams dashed, Williams returned to New York City and landed a job at the United Nations as a secretary, which was the best position a woman could get at the UN at the time. To get the job, she had to sign a "Loyalty Oath" saying that she had never been a communist. So she lied. She hadn't given up on acting, however. She enrolled in another famous acting academy, Paul Mann Actors Workshop. There she met and partied on the weekends with people like Buddy Hackett, Ted Marche's friend who'd been particularly fond of Marche's penis pencil toppers. She even went on a date with the actor and producer Mel Brooks, who she thought was crazy.[238]

A few months later, Williams received a notice to appear before the House Un-American Activities Committee. This was at the height of Cold War communist paranoia. The government had discovered that Williams had spent time at the Jefferson School of Social Science, a socialist camp, and that she had volunteered with a committee to help the Hollywood Ten. When she told one of her coworkers of the investigation, the woman shared her own experience of being the subject of such a probe. "Dell, it was a harrowing experience, don't go through it," the woman told her. So Williams resigned instead of being subjected to it.[239]

Even after graduating from Paul Mann Actors Workshop, Williams didn't seriously pursue acting. She was deeply insecure and afraid that she wasn't talented enough. So instead of acting, she ended up working at an ad agency that specialized in real estate advertising. Then, in the early 1960s, when she was in her late thirties, she decided to try her hand at something significantly more traditional than she'd ever done before: She got married.

Her marriage wasn't conventional, however. The man she married was a photographer named Ted Willms, and he was fifteen years younger than her.

Like a good wife was supposed to, Williams quit her job and devoted herself to helping his career while they tried to start a family. The road was rocky, however, as Ted's career went downhill and Williams found herself unable to get pregnant.

One night in 1962 while a group of her husband's friends were visiting, Williams discovered that they were producing a short movie called *The Cliff Dwellers*, about a young Texas man living in New York City who is unable to find a woman willing to date him. Williams asked if she could be in the movie. They said there was a part for a middle-aged waitress who the man tries to woo; the waitress is shocked when she learns that this younger man is interested in her. It was a small part, but Williams leapt at the chance.[240] The movie went on to be nominated for an Academy Award in 1963 for Short Subject (Live Action). A small part of her dream had finally come true.[241]

Williams's relationship, however, didn't work. She separated and had the marriage annulled. She did leave with one consolation prize: a new last name. When she returned to her job at the ad agency, they suggested that she keep because it was "more common . . . and more memorable" than Zetlin. She wasn't happy with keeping her former husband's name of Willms, so she changed it to Williams, a name that was hers alone.

Williams soon realized that she didn't really want her old job back. She wanted a better job. She wanted to be an advertising executive. It was 1962, and the advertising industry was one of the few professions that placed women in higher-ranked positions. Still, even in ad agencies, the prospects for women were fairly dismal. The agency with the best record for women was McCann-Erickson, which had six female vice presidents out of one hundred total.[242] To find a job, Williams had to scan the male jobs section of the classified ads and apply for jobs hoping that they would be willing to hire a woman. This was a ballsy move that few women would have done, but it paid off. She got a job.

In 1970, the year she joined the Women's March, she was forty-eight years old and working as a vice president for Hodes Advertising.[243] The feminist movement was just really beginning to get national publicity, but she hadn't gotten involved in a major way quite yet. Williams had "heard about Women's Liberation," she says. "But I didn't take it too seriously because I figured I'm liberated and I'm doing what I want to do because I owned a house at Fire Island."[244] Once she went to the march, she had a change of heart, as did Dodson.

(*)

Although Dodson had already become inspired to become a feminist from reading Betty Friedan years earlier, she didn't attend her first NOW meeting until after the march. But the minute she entered the room where the New York City chapter meeting was held, Dodson felt alienated from the conservatively dressed, upper-class women who were more interested in discussing sexual discrimination than sexual pleasure. Their lack of interest in sex came as a surprise to Dodson, as she felt that it was all part of the same puzzle.

Feminists were divided about the importance of sex to women's liberation. NOW feminists were cultural feminists, who were usually more traditional, in that they celebrated gender differences between men and women and believed in gaining women's rights through political channels. Sex wasn't high on their agenda. As historian Carolyn Bronstein pointed out, "NOW tried to advance equal rights for women without challenging the basic structures of American society." Dodson was too avant-garde to fully commit herself to such a group. She abandoned NOW soon after attending her first meeting, but she didn't want to abandon the women's movement. She just needed to find a different side of it.[245]

Fortunately for Dodson, New York was the epicenter of radical feminism at the time. Dodson attended a meeting for the New York Radical Women (NYRW), a group formed in 1967. Less conservative than the NOW feminists, radical feminists were interested in fundamentally changing gender norms within society and demolishing the patriarchy. Radical feminists "argued that all forms of social domination, including the oppression of women, originated from male supremacy." To radical feminists, male domination of women was woven into the fabric of women's lives so tightly that they might not even recognize it. "Men exploited and victimized women, primarily exerting their power through sexuality, through the heterosexual institutions of romantic love, marriage, the family, sexual violence, and through the sexual objectification of women in mass media," Bronstein wrote.[246] The only way to stop such exploitation and change the situation was not through official political channels but at the home, on an individual level, hence Carol Hanisch's 1969 catchphrase: "The personal is political."[247]

Radical feminists believed that the best way to take down the patriarchy was to share stories of exploitation with other women in a safe, female-only space via consciousness-raising (CR) groups. These groups involved women gathering in one another's homes to discuss women's health and social status, including taboo topics like abortion, reproduction, incest, or genital anatomy. Women in CR groups believed that sharing their experiences with other women and normalizing them was the starting ground for women to cope with a misogynistic world.[248]

Dodson was very much on board with this idea, so when she visited a New York women's center, she was disappointed to find that they weren't currently putting on any consciousness-raising groups at the time. The center's organizers suggested that Dodson form her own. "But I have no experience," she said. The organizer told Dodson that her experience of being a woman more than qualified her. "Just get the women together, and let it happen," she said.[249] Dodson took the advice and called two of her friends to help her put together a group. In time, they had gathered about a dozen people at weekly meetings. They talked about their personal experiences but pretty much avoided discussions of sex.

That group didn't last long, disbanding after a short stint, but then Dodson joined a new CR group, mainly populated by single women. One day she decided to share some of her personal sexual experiences with the group. She told the group of women what she had witnessed at sex parties she'd attended: that while the men were having orgasms, the women were faking them because it's what they thought their partners wanted. How could a woman "love herself if her sex life was based on pretending?" Dodson wanted to know. She then opened up about the fact that she was having sex with both men and women and that she called herself a heterosexual bisexual lesbian. After sharing her heartfelt confessions, she was met with silence. "I was shocked to discover that the personal wasn't political, at least when it came to sex," she wrote.[250]

Although that was Dodson's experience, it wasn't necessarily true across the board. In fact, Betty Friedan—Dodson's inspiration—believed radical feminists were too focused on "orgasm politics." Change should happen in "City Hall not the bedroom," Friedan argued.[251] Some CR groups did discuss sexual pleasure and the importance of the clitoris, but few were devoted solely to the subject. Radical feminist groups such as the Redstockings believed that women's sexuality should be used to transform traditional marriage. As founding member Shulamith Firestone memorably said, "A revolutionary in every bedroom cannot fail to shake up the status quo."[252] But not everybody in the Redstockings agreed with this view. Some members left in protest to found a rival group that believed that "heterosexual desire was nothing more than a male fabrication designed to keep women enslaved to men." Other radical feminist groups, such as Cell 16, thought that sexual liberation should mean a "liberation from sexuality" entirely by becoming celibate. One of its leaders, Dana Densmore, argued that most women didn't find sex enjoyable because they "don't have orgasms."[253] Because orgasm was considered masculine by many radical feminists, groups asserted that women's sexuality was based not on sex but on "belonging and social bonding."[254]

In the 1960s, abortion and other reproductive rights issues were more prominent topics of discussion than orgasm in most feminist circles, since abortion was still illegal in most of the country. Yet Dodson had assumed that because most of the women in her group were high-powered, single, creative women that they would be more "sexually open-minded." To her dismay, she discovered the opposite: that "job insecurities and financial problems still made finding the right man the emotional bedrock of security."[255]

The radical feminists who did think female orgasm was important had very particular ideas about how those orgasms should be obtained. Anne Koedt, a founding member of New York Radical Feminists and demolisher of the "myth of the vaginal orgasm," helped to empower some women to have sexual pleasure. Other feminists argued that re-centering the "location . . . of the female orgasm" to the clitoris was problematic, because it denied women "the ability to define and control sexual experiences for themselves," according to scholars Ann Snitow, Christine Stansell, and Sharon Thompson.[256] While Koedt advocated clitoral orgasms through both heterosexual sex and masturbation, the other group she founded, the Feminists, which was separate from the New York Radical Feminists, argued that women should avoid sex with men altogether in favor of masturbation.[257] This was the male fear of female masturbation made concrete: that women would stop having sex with men once they could satisfy themselves.

Even though she had her differences, Dodson didn't abandon her CR group. Instead after learning that "many of the women knew very little about sexual pleasure, and several admitted they'd never had an orgasm," she decided to become a sexual mentor. She taught women how to be more assertive with men, suggesting that they touch their clitorises during sex or that they ask men out. Masturbation was an activity they should all be doing, Dodson told them. After she discussed her own masturbation, many of the women opened up about their experiences. It turned out that many of them had had similar experiences to Dodson's: orgasms during masturbation but not during sex with their male partners.[258]

Dodson then shared information about a new device she had discovered: the vibrator. She brought in a box of electric vibrators. These weren't the hard plastic, battery-powered types of vibrators that Marche or Malorrus sold. These were high-powered vibrators built by respected American and Japanese companies like General Electric and Panasonic. They weren't marketed as sex toys. They were sold as back massagers. As Dodson passed the vibrators out, she persuaded the women that "a sexually turned-on woman was a joy for a man, not a threat."[259]

Not all men would agree with her.

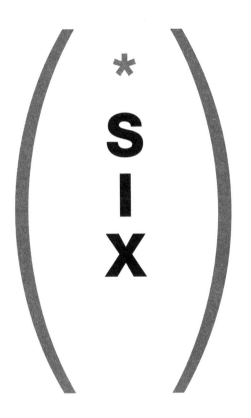

Duncan's Dildos

A few years before Dodson introduced vibrators to her consciousness-raising group, Gosnell Duncan was miles away in Chicago, working at the International Harvester Company. One fall day in 1965, during the early-morning hours of the overnight shift, he was welding the bed of a truck, and the car fell on top of him. Within seconds, the thirty-seven-year-old recent émigré from Grenada was paralyzed from the waist down.[260] A skilled Calypso dancer and handsome ladies' man, Duncan was never able to have an erection again.[261]

Growing up on the island of Grenada, Duncan had been raised as a Seventh-day Adventist, but as he grew older, he had abandoned the church. He became a father while he was in his early twenties, and he ended up having four children, all with different women. In 1963, Duncan decided to enroll in a medical engineering program at a college in New Brunswick, Canada; en route to Canada, he stopped off in Brooklyn to visit a friend, Angela, from Trinidad. Angela introduced Duncan to another friend, at whose house Duncan could stay, and, with his eye on Angela, Duncan decided to abandon the Canadian degree program and stay in Brooklyn. Angela and Duncan started dating, and Duncan began looking for a job in New York, to no avail. He was able to land a job in Chicago at International Harvester, and despite the distance, they continued dating, with Angela making frequent trips to visit him. It was in Chicago that Duncan had his accident in which his spine was severed. Angela stayed by his side, and they were married in his hospital room. Soon thereafter, they moved back to Brooklyn.[262]

Although Duncan's medical expenses were covered by International Harvester, his income was limited, so Angela got a job as a lab technician. Things weren't easy for either of them as they confronted Duncan's new life as a paraplegic. Duncan tried starting a number of businesses, but none of them really caught on. Meanwhile, he remained frustrated with his inability to get an erection; his spine injury had made him completely impotent. He read up on all the current literature on penile substitutes he could find, but his options were limited in 1965, and he didn't know about Marche's dildos yet. As Duncan became involved in the disability movement in the late 1960s, he learned that he wasn't alone. Many other disabled people wanted to have good sex, but they didn't know where to turn for help. While many saw themselves as sexual beings, their doctors—not to mention the sexual revolution—did not. Even in the disability movement at large, many chose to focus on other more "serious" issues.

"As I was learning to live my life from scratch, no one even mentioned the word 'sexuality,'" Duncan said. "The women in particular had problems. They couldn't get out of the house to find themselves a lover, or if they had one, there would be nowhere they could take him."[263] In fact, many disabled people were "more concerned with sexual functioning than walking again."[264] Duncan began brainstorming on his own how he could make sex aids for the disabled.

(*)

Life for Duncan wasn't easy. In the 1960s and 1970s, many public spaces were not wheelchair accessible, and most colleges didn't admit disabled students. Duncan connected with any disabled people he could to try to share information. One person he reached out to was former Brooklyn Dodgers catcher Roy Campanella, who had been paralyzed in a car accident in 1958. Campanella was one of the first black players in Major League Baseball. He started playing in 1948, a year after Jackie Robinson made his debut.[265]

When Duncan became a paraplegic, the disability movement was still in its infancy, but it was the start of large-scale change in the status of disabled people, and Duncan was at the forefront of the movement. An offshoot of the larger counterculture movement, the disability movement got its start in the early 1960s in Berkeley, California, when—at his mother's urging—community-college student and quadriplegic Edward Roberts chose a four-year college based not on whether it was handicapped accessible but on its academic merits, which was a radical idea at the time. Roberts chose the University of California–Berkeley, but when he began talking to the administration about attending school there, they told him, "We tried cripples and they don't work." So he sued. Roberts won and paved the way for other disabled students to go to Berkeley and went on to cofound the Center for Independent Living, a national organization.[266]

Roberts's victory didn't change the world for the disabled overnight. It did, however, spur others to get involved in the disability rights movement. When Duncan began taking part in the movement, the time was right for a new approach to handicapped sexuality, as the incidence of paraplegics and quadriplegics had increased dramatically due to injuries sustained during World War II. The U.S. Public Health Service estimated that there were nearly one hundred thousand paraplegics in the country in 1953.[267]

The issues facing disabled people were manifold, and it was wonderful that they were finally being addressed. Still, Duncan was troubled by his sexual limitations, and so he was thrilled to see a session on sex and disability at an Indianapolis disability conference in 1971. During the session, he patiently listened to speakers discuss their challenges with sex but didn't hear many solutions. He saw his chance and took it: Surrounded by his target market, he asked if they would purchase a dildo. The answer was a resounding yes.[268]

Duncan returned to Brooklyn armed with confidence and began investigating the dildos that were already on the market, like the Marches' and Malorruses'. "In the 1970s . . . most dildos were made of heat-treated rubber and would melt with heat," Duncan said. "I wanted to have a product that was different. . . . . Something that . . . you couldn't [melt] by washing and cleaning it." Besides the melt factor, he found many dildos were also made of irritating materials and had strong chemical odors that people were often sensitive to.[269] [270]

Dissatisfied with the current offerings, Duncan decided to start his own dildo business. Unlike most of the men who had come before him (and they were usually always men), he didn't just want to make dildos for money. "He was the most generous person I've ever met to the point where he'd give away everything he had," his niece Lurline Martineau said. He saw himself as a healer, and he simply wanted to help.[271]

He began by investigating newer, safer materials for dildos. At the time, most sex toys were made of polyvinyl chloride, which had major drawbacks, including porousness, a "plastic" smell, and the inability to retain heat.[272] While working as an auto mechanic, Duncan had been impressed by the pliable silicone rubber that didn't melt even when exposed to the intense heat of an engine. This heat resistance meant that silicone could be sterilized in boiling water. Plus, silicone lacked the strong chemical odors found in other materials. The only problem was that the silicone used in automobile parts was not exactly safe for the body.[273]

If he could develop a silicone safe enough for the body, he thought, he could create a dildo different than anything on the market. A silicone rubber dildo would be nonporous, making it appealingly smooth and capable of being sanitized between partners. He couldn't create a new form of silicone on his own, though. He needed help.[274] Following the conference in Indianapolis, he reached out to General Electric. "I sent them a letter explaining that I needed a rubber-based product that is nonirritating to the human body," he said later. They put him in touch with one of their chemists.[275]

GE was the leader in silicone development at the time, selling the material for use as adhesives and footwear, among other products. Duncan and the chemist corresponded for nine months, tweaking various formulas to get the perfect silicone: Smooth, flesh-like, and safe for insertion into the human body. They finally hit on a formula, and Duncan set up a test lab in his basement.

Since sex toys were still a marginally legal business, there was no road map on how to proceed, no trade associations to consult with. Duncan just had some vats of silicone and his ideas. "The designs were all my mental creations," he said. "I remember writing to the Kinsey Center, and I corresponded with them. From what I read, and using myself as the normal, I was able to come up with sizes." These sizes ranged from six to nine and a half inches long and one to two inches wide in girth. He began by making a model out of clay, then a mold after that. He would pour the silicone into the molds and then mix in a catalyst to help the silicone solidify. Then he added scents to the mixture, such as licorice smell.[276] The silicone dildos were produced under the brand name Paramount Therapeutic Products.[277] There was nothing sexy about the marketing for his dildos. In fact, he didn't even call them dildos. As Marche had done before him, Duncan sold his dildos as prosthetic strap-on devices.

Even with such clinical marketing, selling sex toys to the disabled community was no easy feat. Not only were sex toys taboo among the general populace, they were doubly taboo within the handicapped community. For starters, disabled people weren't thought to be sexual. The majority of doctors didn't address sexuality with their disabled patients. "Most people regard the sexuality of the disabled as nonexistent," wrote a woman to *The Squeaky Wheel*, a magazine produced by the National Paraplegia Foundation. "What ignorant write-offs of such moments of joy."[278]

To be fair, not all physicians were ignoring disabled sexuality. Some doctors even suggested that disabled men use vibrators on their penises to stimulate erections. These doctors recognized that, as numerous handicapped men had reported, an inability to have an erection or orgasm was nearly as devastating as not being able to walk. One 1972 study even looked specifically at the use of vibrators on disabled men, finding that vibrators more than doubled the percentage of paraplegic men who were capable of ejaculation (from 10 percent to 27 percent).[279]

Although using sex toys to improve partnered sex among disabled people was starting to become seen as a positive thing, masturbation among the disabled—especially female masturbation—was still somewhat stigmatized. A 1977 Planned Parenthood brochure called "Toward Intimacy: Family Planning and Sexuality Concerns of Physically Disabled Women" was hesitant to unequivocally encourage handicapped women to masturbate. Although the brochure quoted a quadriplegic woman saying that masturbation was one of the few "pleasant" feelings she had and that it "helped get rid of the pain," it later cautioned that masturbation "may conflict with your religious or ethical values."[280]

Despite this work to improve sexuality for the disabled, popular culture still didn't portray handicapped people in a sexual light. Disabled people were almost never eroticized in film or TV but instead were either depicted as objects of pity or examples of courageous people who had overcome obstacles. Although sometimes disabled people were portrayed as objects of desire or even romantic interests, this was rare. One example is the 1978 movie *Coming Home*, starring Jane Fonda as a woman who falls in love with a paraplegic. The only place where disabled sex was usually depicted was in porn, as fetishistic eroticism.

Duncan's dildos were filling a void left by the many doctors and sex educators who were ignoring the needs of the disabled. His connections with the disabled community allowed him to spread the word of his dildos to doctors, physical therapists, and leaders in the community.[281] He began sending his catalogs throughout the country to medical centers that worked with handicapped patients. Duncan's line expanded to include not just strap-on dildos but also sex toys for quadriplegics that were held by the mouth.[282]

In the 1970s, Duncan began working with a pioneering center for the disabled, Goldwater Memorial Hospital in New York. Goldwater had made major advances for disabled people, but, in the late 1950s, disabled people who were placed in Goldwater were expected to live their whole lives at the hospital, completely separate from the rest of society. They were not expected to live normal lives, go to college, or get married. That changed when, in 1958, a young quadriplegic woman at Goldwater named Anne Emerman decided not to settle for this cordoned-off life. Despite the objections of the social worker assigned to her (who said her aspiration for higher education was "a fantasy, and fantasy can lead to mental illness"), Emerman applied and got into college and went on to get a master's in social work from Columbia University. Emerman also married and had children. Her courageous efforts led her to be the first "test case" for independent living, and her success led Goldwater to become a center that was at the forefront of disability care. By the 1970s, they were true innovators, and they invited Duncan to work with them and give lectures on the "Sexual Functioning of the Spinal Cord Injured Person" and the larger issues surrounding sexuality and disability.[283]

It was an incredible opportunity for Duncan's work to be on a national stage, but working with healthcare professionals at Goldwater and other hospitals also brought with it complications. Although the more open-minded centers were receptive to Duncan's sex toys, they also wanted a say in how they were marketed. When Duncan tried to make his brochures more consumer-friendly—with a lighthearted and sexy touch—he got backlash. "While I am all for fun in sex, I am somewhat leery of whimsey [sic] in or out of bed," wrote Mary Romano, who worked in the Social Service Department of the Presbyterian Hospital at the Columbia-Presbyterian Medical Center. "I wonder if you might consider modifying those of your brochures geared to a handicapped population so that they look and read a bit more clinically." One of her suggestions was that he change the name of his newly named dildo from "Joy Boy" to "artificial penis #1, #2, or #3."[284] This wasn't the kind of business Duncan had envisioned.

Duncan's dildos were revolutionary not just because he was designing them for the handicapped or because he was using silicone but also because they appeared in different colors. At the time, the standard dildo was in an off-white pinkish color referred to as "flesh-colored," which alienated all those whose flesh wasn't the color of the dildo. It was only when Duncan, a dark-skinned Caribbean paraplegic, started making dildos that the colors and styles changed radically. Duncan wanted to make his dildos in a variety of shades of black, so he contacted A. S. Crouse, a technician at General Electric, for help. Crouse informed him that there were no off-the-shelf shades that would work, so he suggested Duncan create his own and gave him advice on which silicone pigments to use. Duncan experimented in his basement lab to create just the right skin colors, blending brown and black organic pigments with silicone oil.[285] Duncan sold his dildos in four different colors: three different shades of black (Mulatto, Negroid, and Black), and Caucasian.

There were further innovations in the design of the devices. Unlike Marche's prosthetic penis attachments, Duncan's strap-on dildos were solid, not hollow. They were "designed to be strapped directly over the pubic bone . . . leaving the penis and testicles free." This was for a good reason. Many of the people in the target audience had catheters attached to their penises and bags strapped to their legs. Duncan's selling point was that his creations were sex aids "developed and manufactured by a paraplegic for use by paraplegics and quadriplegics and their mates." In the late 1960s, before Duncan came along, some paraplegics and quadriplegics had already been using strap-on dildos, but there was no company solely devoted to selling dildos to them.[286] So this availability meant a whole new market.

Handcrafted dildos came at a steep price, however. They came in a kit with a harness and lubricant and ranged in price from $19.95 to $39.95 (approximately $100 to $200 today), which was prohibitively expensive for many.[287] Most sex toys at the time ranged in price from $10 to $25, with most closer to the $10 mark.[288] One customer wrote a letter to Duncan saying that "'pricing' a product out of the reach of the buying public . . . is my first concern." He suggested reducing the price by 30 percent or renting them to customers. The latter was an idea that thankfully Duncan never took up.[289]

Price was a minor concern in light of the larger concern Duncan was facing: that he could be charged with pandering. The Anti-Pandering Act was enacted in April 1968 supposedly to crack down on sex-related advertising sent through the mail. While obscenity was nearly impossible to define, pandering was an even looser term. The definition of pandering rested upon the person receiving the mail. Anybody who received what they considered to be an "erotically arousing or sexually provocative" ad could report that to the post office. The post office would then send a "Prohibitory Order" letter to the person who mailed the ad and demand that the sender stop sending the mail to the address under threat of law. Even if the ad itself was not legally obscene under the law, if it seemed too sexual for the person receiving it, it would be considered a pandering ad. (If this seems like it violates the First Amendment, well, many people argue that it does.)[290]

In 1970, Duncan made the mistake of sending his catalog to a family in Streator, Illinois, with four young children. Now, it may not have actually been a mistake. It's possible that wife ordered it and then the husband found it or vice versa. Whatever the case, they alerted their post office, and Duncan received his first notice that he was violating the law by sending a "pandering advertisement offering for sale erotically arousing or sexually provocative matter."[291] Now he had yet another thing to worry about: the federal government. No matter that what he was making actually was designed to help disabled citizens pursue happiness, or that many of these people were disabled due to fighting wars for the government. He was swept up in an epidemic of chasteness. By 1970, Americans had requested 450,000 prohibitory orders for various companies' publications; more than 80 percent of these were deemed credible enough by the government for them to issue official stop orders.[292]

But that was not all that Duncan had to worry about. During the late 1960s, President Lyndon B. Johnson created the U.S. Commission on Obscenity and Pornography, which was made up of eighteen people representing a wide variety of fields, including legal experts, clergymen, sociologists, and psychologists. The commission's goal was to determine whether pornography and obscenity actually harmed society. Social scientists performed rigorous studies about the effects of pornography and surveyed the scope of the adult industry. Although the focus was mostly on pornography, they also studied adult bookstores.[293]

When President Nixon was elected, he appointed antiporn crusader and founder of the Citizens for Decent Literature Charles Keating to head up the commission. Nixon was hoping to get the result he wanted: that pornography was dangerous and we needed stricter laws. But when the results came in, they were the opposite of what he had hoped. The commission found that pornography did not cause any negative effects, and porn-watchers were not more likely to commit crimes. The commission determined that porn could actually be good for sexual relationships and recommended that all "federal, state, and local legislation prohibiting the sale, exhibition, or distribution of sexual materials to consenting adults should be repealed."[294] In other words, the commission said that all the obscenity laws should go and porn should be legal. Even more surprising, the majority of the Americans they had polled agreed that there should not be any restrictions on sales of sexual material to adults.[295]

Since this was the opposite of the result President Nixon and Commissioner Charles Keating wanted, Nixon decided that he would ignore the findings. He announced, "So long as I am in the White House, there will be no relaxation of the national effort to control and eliminate smut from American life."[296] Nixon believed that getting rid of the laws would be the equivalent of "condoning anarchy in every other field"—and Congress agreed, nearly unanimously rejecting the commission's findings.[297] Obscenity continued to be a target.

(*)

That didn't stop Duncan from making dildos in his Brooklyn basement. Since he was handcrafting them, he had the advantage of being able to make dildos to his customers' specifications. Just as men would order tailored suits, his customers would order tailored dildos. How he did this was simple. He'd ask male customers to record the length of their penises and then measure the diameter of their penis with a piece of string; they'd then send that measurement and string back to him and he'd make a dildo to those specifications.[298] Even in the era of Etsy, such personalization is rare.

Asking for this kind of intimate data automatically made Duncan seem like a confidante to many of his customers, and they shared their personal problems with him as if he were a therapist. Customers wrote lengthy letters to him that went far beyond simply requesting sex toys. They shared intimate details of their sex life and marriages and their secret sexual desires; his disabled customers shared the struggles their disabilities had brought them. The letters are at turns erotic, heartbreaking, and inspiring. One customer spent two pages describing his penis and its ability to stay hard for more than an hour, and then seemed to recognize that he was conversing with a complete stranger. "Could you tell me a little more about yourself?" he wrote. "I feel a little strange telling these things to someone I hardly know."[299]

Customers' letters to Duncan show that his dildos, and the vibrators he later sold, brought people a joy they had never experienced before. "The vibrator and dildo have been a great source of pleasure for me for the past year," one woman wrote to him. "With both I am able to reach orgasm, which I was unable to do in twenty-five years of marriage." Although sex toys had brought her first orgasms, she still thought of masturbation as a way to improve sex with a man. "I think what convinced me [to masturbate] was a statement my Doctor made when I complained of my problem. She said, 'When you masturbate and learn how to bring yourself pleasure, you can be in a better position to have successful sex relations with a mate.' I thought about what she said and decided that I would purchase a vibrator." Even though a mate had never been able to give her an orgasm, she still could only be convinced to purchase a vibrator when it was presented as a way to improve partnered sex.[300]

Other customers were content to stay single and masturbate, but they always evaluated sex toys in terms of how they compared to men. "I've had a few men in my life and except for one of them I have never enjoyed sex as much as I do now," one woman wrote to Duncan.[301] Another woman wrote to say, "Pleasantly I'm on two weeks vacation and everyday as a rule I leave myself properly satisfied as many as four times! After which I don't really need a man."[302]

Sex toys could coexist with relationships with men, some customers asserted. They insisted that they weren't using sex toys because they weren't able to land a man. For example, a woman named Louise wrote to Duncan in 1980, saying, "The vibrator is not really a substitute for a mate, but in addition to a mate. At the present time I am seeing two men, trying to keep them."[303]

Not all of Duncan's customers were heterosexual. A woman wrote to him on May 27, 1975, saying, "I am a lesbian and would like to know anything in that line, I allsa [*sic*] am married, 'But' my husband does not know I am Lesbian." Although she remained closeted, Duncan's mail-order store allowed her to at least explore her lesbian desires surreptitiously.[304]

The letters and calls poured in, but it was the disabled customers who seemed to reach out the most. Duncan viewed these customers as friends, calling them and writing them extensively. Duncan and his customers would not just share information on sexual matters but also share resources on living with disabilities. In this pre-Internet time, basic information about navigating the world in a wheelchair was hard to come by. One letter writer wrote to Duncan that she couldn't attend college after she graduated high school in 1961 because colleges weren't equipped for the handicapped. Disabled customers whose partners were also disabled presented unique problems. "I have Athetoid Cerebral Palsy and my partner is a spastic CP [Cerebral Palsy] man," wrote one woman. "Therefore, you see we do possibly have multi-problems? He cannot spread his legs whereas I CAN." She asked if a vibrator would be useful for her partner, but she added this caveat: "Sorry to ask questions, but I FEEL I MUST TRUST YOU IF YOU WANT TO HELP ME. I also hope in turn, that you'll trust in me?"[305]

Some customers wrote him in part because they thought sharing their experiences could benefit the disabled community. One disabled customer wrote in detail about how he had sex with his able-bodied wife. Instead of having sex on a bed, which was too uncomfortable, she would lay on the kitchen table with her knees bent while he sat in front of her. "Please keep this infor[mation] private between you and I when communicating," he wrote.

"Altho [*sic*] you can use our situation as an example when talking to other disabled people who you think would benefit from our case. . . . I hope I've helped out some."[306] Duncan believed that all of it—the devices, the open dialogue—was indeed helping very much.

(*)

Although sex toys were one solution to the problem of expressing sexuality while handicapped, this solution was not completely satisfying to some people. They wanted human connection. Since it was difficult to connect with people who shared similar disabilities in the pre-Internet era, Duncan created a one-to-one advisory service from his home. For a small fee, he would give handicapped people around the country information not just on sex but on life.

After receiving an inquiry by mail, Duncan would usually send back a questionnaire tailored to the writer with questions that ranged from details on their spinal-cord injuries to their ability to have erections to what religion they practiced. One Kentucky man wrote to Duncan out of frustration. He was a virgin who wanted badly to have sex, but his doctors and nurses didn't give him any advice on how to accomplish that. Instead, they told him statistically how likely he was to have an erection, to ejaculate, or to be fertile. They emphasized that any individual questions couldn't be fully answered until he actually had sex with a woman. Not only did they keep mum on the topic of masturbation, but they also were asking him to jump into the sexual wilderness armed with no specific information. Since this man was a virgin who lacked a frame of reference, he turned to Duncan. Duncan suggested that he start masturbating, get in touch with his female friends, and buy a dildo and a vibrator.[307] Practical and basic advice, certainly—but something not being offered to this man anywhere else.

While giving advice and selling sex toys to the disabled was emotionally satisfying, it wasn't bringing Duncan the money he had hoped it would. He needed a new market. Duncan had also tried selling some of his dildos to transsexuals in Canada, but that market also wasn't big enough.[308] He needed to find another group of people to target or his business wasn't going to survive.

Inflatables

At the same time that Duncan's business was being tested, another former Seventh-day Adventist living in New York City was opening up a waterbed store with his friend. Tall and lanky with a wide smile, Duane Colglazier was just twenty-four years old. With his clean-shaven face and parted straight brown hair, he could have passed for a Bible salesman if it weren't for the leather pants and stylish shoes that he was fond of wearing.[309] It was 1971, and Colglazier and his thirty-year-old friend Bill Rifkin started small, literally. They sold only two products: waterbeds and mood lights. The Pleasure Chest on Tenth Street and Seventh Avenue was tiny—just forty-seven inches wide, sandwiched between two buildings. The space was basically a narrow alleyway that someone had put a roof over. If you wanted to sell waterbeds in New York City, you couldn't have picked a worse location to do it. The store was so small that they couldn't even fit a fully assembled waterbed within its walls. No matter. They were going to make this work. Even though the store was minuscule, there were two things about the location that made it a wise choice: The rent was cheap—only seventy-five dollars a month—and it was in the West Village, near the gay area of the city.

Still, Colglazier and Rifkin had a tough proposition: selling their customers on a product that they couldn't see in store. It was difficult to entice customers to a store whose signature products were only available in a catalog. After a few months selling waterbeds, they decided to expand their stock to something that could actually fit within the store.

But what to sell alongside mattresses? Most mattress stores didn't sell much else, maybe some pillows or sheets. Mattress stores were focused on the piece of furniture itself, not what went on between the people using it. As everyone knows, beds are for two things: sleeping and sex. Perhaps they could sell something sex-related?

The legend goes that it was Rifkin who had the idea to sell sex toys and suggested it to Colglazier. According to Rifkin, Colglazier had reservations about the new product line, but he eventually gave in, and soon there were sex toys hanging from pegboards on the wall.[310]

By placing sex toys in their waterbed store, Colglazier and Rifkin were upending the idea of where an adult store in New York could be located. Until this time, most of the sex-toy stores were sequestered near Forty-second Street, which was home to most of the commercial sex industry in New York City, including strip clubs, live sex shows, adult bookstores, and prostitution.[311] Yet the Pleasure Chest was adjacent not to a strip club but to the upscale Italian restaurant Julius Lombardi, which Craig Claiborne had favorably reviewed in the *New York Times*.[312]

If Rifkin's version of the story is true, Colglazier was initially embarrassed to talk up sex toys with customers.[313] Colglazier had been brought up as a Seventh-day Adventist and stayed with the religion through much of college, much longer than Duncan had. He'd inherited the group's fairly close-minded views toward sex, and he found them hard to shake. The group's founding prophet, Ellen G. White, believed that masturbation was the cause of most of the ills in the world. White shared her antimasturbation beliefs in a book published in 1864 called *An Appeal to Mothers: The Great Cause of the Physical, Mental, and Moral Ruin of Many of the Children of Our Time*. In the book, she argued that masturbation—or "the solitary vice," as it was called at the time— would not only ruin life on Earth but also life in Heaven. She shared her visions of people who had become physically deformed from masturbation.

The masturbators had ailments ranging from "misshapen heads" to dwarfism. Because masturbation was so common, she argued, most young people were doomed. But there was something people could do to stop masturbation: Eat bland foods and learn self-control.[314] There is a great irony in that a person steeped in White's religion became rich selling devices to aid in the very practice that its founder thought was destroying the world.

Colglazier grew up on a ranch in Holyoke, Colorado, in the 1960s, which was an awkward place to be a young man questioning his sexuality. After graduating high school, Colglazier moved to Lincoln, Nebraska, to attend the Seventh-day Adventist Union College. After two years in Lincoln, he abandoned his studies and moved west to Los Angeles. It was 1964, and the city was teeming with possibilities. Colglazier arrived in Los Angeles ready for anything. He was twenty years old and finally able to come out as a gay man, at least to his friends. His family was still in the dark, although his mother suspected he was gay.[315]

Colglazier's first job was a brief one at the Los Angeles County Hospital. After that, he drove an ice-cream truck and sold frozen treats to kids throughout Los Angeles. It wasn't a terribly ambitious business, but it was a good job for an energetic young man. Piloting an ice-cream truck suited Colglazier's childlike, playful personality perfectly. As he drove, he'd pump music out of his truck, craning his neck to spot the kids chasing the truck. "I think that's when he really picked up the power of retail," Colglazier's nephew, Brian Robinson, the current owner of Pleasure Chest, said in a 2016 interview. "When you're driving around in those neighborhoods, and it's a hot day and you've got what people are wanting, [you come to understand] the power of retail and demand and supply." But Colglazier wasn't happy in L.A. He missed the changing seasons he'd become accustomed to in Colorado. In Los Angeles, it was summer all year long. That was good for an ice-cream truck business, but it wasn't a good fit for a Colorado boy.

After less than a year in L.A., he decided to move cross-country to New York City. Although there was still harassment and discrimination against gay people as there was everywhere at that time, New York was a fairly good place to be a gay man in the 1960s. Gay bars and saunas lined Christopher Street. Male hustlers cruised Times Square; the adult bookstores carried gay-male porn. New York was a city full of possibilities, and Colglazier was ready to work hard and make some money. He found his opportunity on Wall Street as a stockbroker, working for a firm called Dempsey-Tegeler. He quickly discovered that he was as good at selling stocks as he was at selling ice cream. He also met another financier, a gay man named Bill Rifkin, and they became lovers soon after they met. Their romantic relationship didn't last very long, but they remained friends.[316]

Meanwhile, Colglazier was tiring of grinding out long hours as a stockbroker. He'd been at it for a few years, and it no longer held as strong an appeal. Besides, what was happening outside Wall Street was decidedly more interesting. It was 1969, and the sexual revolution and gay rights movement were just beginning. On June 27 of that year, the patrons of the gay bar the Stonewall Inn were commemorating the death of Judy Garland, which had occurred five days earlier, when suddenly police raided it. Raids were actually fairly common; usually the owners would be tipped off in advance, but this time the raid was coming from the Federal Bureau of Alcohol, Tobacco, and Firearms and not the local police, so there was no warning. The feds were raiding the bar because it was mafia-run (which was common for marginally legal businesses), and they thought there was an illegal bootlegging scam. When they raided the establishment, instead of being greeted with "limp wrists" as *The Village Voice* wrote, they were greeted with beer bottles and bricks being thrown at their heads. It was the smashed beer bottle heard 'round the world: Finally gay men and women had stood up to the police harassment that they were constantly subjected to in bars and other public areas.[317] The Stonewall riots spurred the development of both the Gay Activist Alliance and the Gay Liberation Front (GLF), which had as its statement of purpose: "We are a revolutionary homosexual group . . . formed with the realization that complete sexual liberation for all people cannot come about unless existing social institutions are abolished."[318]

Colglazier didn't join the movement. Instead, he decided to go back to school. This time he didn't attend a religious college; he chose a secular one: New York University. But Colglazier didn't just want to study business; he wanted to start his own. While he was still in school in 1971, Colglazier and Rifkin started the Pleasure Chest.

(*)

In their stumble into selling sex toys, Rifkin and Colglazier actually did something revolutionary. They brought sex toys out of the dark, dingy pornography stores and sold them in a well-lit boutique environment. It was a far cry from the porn and sex stores in Times Square. "We treat our customers as if they are coming into Gimbels to buy a table and chairs," said Rifkin in an interview, noting that they were the first adult store to "not black out the windows and hide merchandise."[319] Pleasure Chest's location legitimized the products within the store because customers didn't have to feel ashamed to walk in. While other stores were ashamed to sell erotica, Rifkin and Colglazier (once he came around to it, which he finally did) were proud of selling sex toys because, to them, it was a political statement.

Colglazier and Rifkin distinguished themselves from the other adult bookstores at the time not just because they made the store more upscale but also because they educated themselves about the products they sold. This was an important step because, as the Malorruses' Spanish fly drops and low-quality dildos attest, not all sex-toy producers were as assiduous as Marche. Colglazier and Rifkin educated their employees too. It seems now like a no-brainer, but no other sex-toy retailers were doing this at the time.

Even after they expanded their store's stock to include sex toys, Colglazier and Rifkin continued to sell waterbeds, at least for several months, but the beds were by then positioned as sex accessories. The company was growing not just through their store but in catalogs, which allowed the sale of sex toys and waterbeds nationwide. They were definitely catering to a gay male audience. The Pleasure Chest's first catalog, which was drawn and hand-lettered, was a work of art, full of drawings of naked, buff, mustachioed men using all manner of sex toys—classic gay iconography, à la Tom of Finland. Every item was accompanied by a drawing of a different man with a different story. The catalog featured "Alex" laying naked on a waterbed, his buttocks perfectly sculpted, a big smile on his face. The accompanying text informed readers that Alex "discovered that waterbeds are good for exercising as well as sleeping."[320] There was "Tony," the "well-constructed Italian construction worker," shown with an erection encased in a cock sheath, which the catalog said "come[s] in any desired length ($1.25/inch)." There was also "Al," the locksmith, who "spends most of his day working with keyholes" and "is an ace with a dildo and really knows how to use that big black one ($12.00) he's holding." Rounding out the crew was Brad the telephone repairman, Ivan the Russian Cossack, and Gary the bad boy, among others. It's worth noting that some of these men were presented in stereotypical ways, and that black male sexuality was fetishized in the form of the big black dildo, which was commonplace at the time.

Why didn't Colglazier and Rifkin just put a picture or a drawing of the sex toys in the catalog and call it a day? Why sell sex toys using such complicated backstories? For starters, their catalog sent a message that masturbation was sexy and that using tools to masturbate was fairly normal. The characters in the catalogs humanized sex toys. The story format made sex toys seem like everyday objects used by men from all walks of life. Employing a narrative style allowed them to explain in great detail how the sex toys were used, which was helpful at a time when sex toys—especially those for gay men—weren't commonplace. Not everybody would have known how to use the "B.D. Special Cock and Ball Ring" or what "Joy Jell" was. The catalog put everything in context.

Where the catalog was elaborate, the store was more subdued, although it was adorned with erotic art on the first floor. On their "toy chest floor"— which was only about four feet long—they housed their sex toys and sadomasochism, or S&M gear. As customers entered this space, they were greeted with a hand-written sign—probably inspired by Colglazier's burgeoning attention to the law—assuring them that "All items sold on this floor sold as novelties only. They have not been approved by Good Housekeeping, Department of Agriculture or Board of Health."[321] Nipple clamps hung from the wall, next to realistic metal handcuffs, whips, and strap-on harnesses, all labeled with prices. One wall was strung with realistic-looking dildos: veiny and Caucasian flesh-colored. If the dildos hadn't been so large, the display could have been mistaken for one in a medical museum, as the dildos looked like disembodied penises, unless you looked closely and saw the straps visible on some of them. Arrayed on shelves were leather cock rings adorned with studs on the outside or internal pinprick-like stimulators on the inside. Joining them were various types of erotic jewelry, including penis key chains, which made sense, given where Colglazier and Rifkin were getting their stock: Marche Manufacturing and United Sales (the Malorruses' company), by way of Reuben Sturman's distribution companies.[322]

(*)

In the late 1960s, a few years before his company began supplying sex toys for the Pleasure Chest, Reuben Sturman had been looking to expand his porn and sex-toy empire in Cleveland. One day, the peep-show king entered his local Baskin Robbins for a generous scoop of one of their thirty-one flavors of ice creams. In the store was a teenager, Ron Braverman, who was looking for a way out of Cleveland.[323] Sturman was a big shot in Cleveland. If there was anyone who a young Jewish aspiring businessman would have looked up to in Cleveland as a model for success, it was Sturman. A multimillionaire, Sturman dressed fashionably, smoked expensive cigars, and was always driving a Cadillac or Mercedes Benz. Braverman asked if Sturman could give him any work. Sturman said yes.

Braverman was twenty-four years younger than Sturman, and his only sales experience was in appliances (and not the sexual kind either), but his extended family—grandparents and uncles—were experienced salesmen. The fact that Braverman was Jewish didn't hurt. Sturman hired Braverman, and Braverman's life was about to drastically change. He just didn't know it yet.

Sturman offered Braverman a job selling magazines in the New England area, and Braverman was relieved to get out of Cleveland. He happily moved to Boston, where he drove around his six-state territory with a stack of Sturman's porn magazines in his trunk. "There were days I got pulled over," Braverman told *Los Angeles Magazine* in 2012. "Sometimes the cops just wanted a few magazines. Sometimes I ended up using the attorney's card."[324]

In 1972, Sturman sent Braverman to Europe to grow the company's burgeoning adult bookstore business in Amsterdam.[325] What Braverman saw in Europe changed his idea of how a sex toy could be sold. "There was a completely different attitude to sex toys," Ron Braverman says now. "They were in blister packs on the wall. They had descriptions on them about how to use them."[326] The biggest difference of all: The adult stores weren't just full of men. Women and couples visited the stores and picked sex toys together. Braverman's eyes were opened to new possibilities for selling sex toys—and the thought of bringing female consumers into adult stores.

(*)

While Braverman was looking to get more women into adult bookstores, Farley Malorrus had the opposite idea. He thought there were enough profits from the dildo business; it was time for men to get their chance. By the 1970s, both United Sales and Marche Manufacturing were swimming in money, with around $5 million in revenue from their novelties and prosthetic devices.[327] This should have been a good thing for the heir to the Malorrus fortune, but he wanted out. So in 1972, Farley broke off from his father and started his own company: Bosko's Oso, which sold blow-up dolls "for all the lonely guys that weren't getting laid" during the sexual revolution.[328] In the era of waterbeds and inflatable furniture, no sex novelty was more emblematic of the 1970s than the blow-up doll.

Sex dolls date back much further than the 1970s. The idea can be traced as far back as the Pygmalion myth in which a king falls in love with an ivory statue of a woman that he has carved. He prays to the gods for it to come alive, and Aphrodite answers his prayer. The statue turns into an actual woman, and he has children with her. The idea of having sex with an inanimate woman is ancient, and sex dolls go back at least to the 17th century, the time when the Japanese began making variations on artificial vaginas: tortoise shells with velvet linings known as *azumagata* ("woman substitute").[329] By the 19th century, cloth sex dolls, known as *dames de voyage*, were carried aboard European ships so the sailors could have sex with them.[330] In the 1960s, it was the Japanese again who were innovating with sex dolls, this time with the company Orient Industries's blow-up dolls, nicknamed Antarctica 1 and Antarctica 2 because scientists took them to the Showa Station on the icy continent.[331] These dolls were flawed, however. They had the unfortunate tendency to pop.

Farley Malorrus didn't make his own blow-up dolls. The Judy Inflatable Doll he sold was imported from Japan.[332] Constructed of vinyl, Judy was five feet two inches with the alluring figure measurements of 37"-23"-36". At least two different companies imported her to the United States before Farley began selling her. She was sold as a "loving companion" who could accompany men on rides in their convertible or recline on the couch, sipping martinis. Farley saw one major mistake: The doll didn't have any orifices. So Farley strapped an artificial vagina on her (with a pubic hair option), which allowed him to double the asking price for the doll.[333]

Judy was somewhat of a TV star. Before Malorrus imported her, she had appeared on the Emmy-nominated comedy show *Love, American Style* in 1969, in an episode in which a man tries to make his neighbor jealous by pretending he has another date.[334] But that was just the beginning of blow-up dolls in popular culture. They soon appeared in other TV shows, cartoons, and song lyrics.[335] Their appearances in pop culture may be related to Americans' uneasiness with the changing gender roles and sexual behavior that occurred during the sexual revolution. Blow-up dolls returned the new sexually autonomous woman to male control. A blow-up doll is always ready for sex, never talks about her rights, and always looks perky. They were the ultimate sex objects.

A few years after Farley started his company, the Police sang jokingly about the advantages of blow-up dolls in their 1978 song "Be My Girl–Sally," which tells a story of a lonely man who "needed inspiration" but "didn't want a wife." His solution? A blow-up doll named Sally. Unlike a human wife, Sally is "loving, warm, inflatable, and a guarantee of joy." She's completely within a man's control, like his little pet. "I sit her in the corner," he sings. "And I sometimes stroke her hair." That same year, Joan Rivers also referenced blow-up dolls in her directorial debut, *Rabbit Test* (1978). In the opening scene, Billy Crystal, in his film debut, is depicted from behind, sitting on a couch, seducing what appears to be a real woman, plying her with red wine, as he kisses her on the check. Midkiss, she pops, flies around the room, and lands in his lap. "You really know how to turn a guy off, Jackie," he says. "A simple 'no' would have been sufficient." Unlike in the Police song, this blow-up doll is not within a man's control, and in fact is used to mock the man who is using her. It's easy to tell which blow-up doll story was written by a woman.

Malorrus periodically tested out Judy to make sure the doll was sturdy enough. The best way to do that: research and development. Farley didn't want to spend much money on R&D, so he enlisted a friend to test out Judy. "Every night he would come home drunk without a girl . . . and he would bang the doll," Farley said. Then one night, when the man was having sex with Judy in his apartment on the twentieth floor of a St. Louis high-rise, he was interrupted by a loud pop followed by a hissing sound. Judy began slowly deflating underneath him. Drunk and angry, his friend began punching her. He threw her out the window into traffic on the major thoroughfare—to the horror of the drivers below who skidded to avoid what they believed was a real person.[336]

Farley continued to experiment with blow-up dolls. In 1974, he added a new doll to his line: the Barby, which had a built-in vagina—an improvement on Judy.[337] He advertised Judy and Barby in alternative and underground newspapers in California: the *Berkeley Barb* and *Los Angeles Free Press*.[338] Soon he added "a boy doll with a penis in it and an ass and an open mouth" to his line. Farley and other companies imported male dolls primarily for the gay markets but also for women, with vibrating penises and open mouths and anuses. Farley needed a place to sell these new dolls, and one of the places he turned to was a boutique called the Pleasure Chest.[339]

(*)

Although by 1972 Colglazier and Rifkin of the Pleasure Chest had replaced their waterbeds entirely with toys like Malorruses' blow-up dolls, they didn't formally remarket their store as a sex-toy shop.[340] They wanted to keep its boutique vibe. Preserving the upscale feeling was important not only strategically as a sales tactic but also because of the law. The same year that the Pleasure Chest opened in 1971, New York City Criminal Court judges found Al Goldstein's sex magazine *Screw* obscene due in part to its dildo ads, which it said violated the penal code. Goldstein was forced to strip *Screw* of sex-toy ads, even though these were arguably the least offensive part of *Screw*, a magazine that delighted in detailing Linda Lovelace's bestiality porn.[341] "The only thing I can think of to account for this, myself," wrote Dean Latimer in *The East Village Other*, "is Betty Dodson's illuminating suggestion that the more enlightened authorities don't mind male-directed pornography, but still despise female directed pornography. Seeing an ad for a dildo . . . it perhaps occurs to the magistrate that *this* horrible thing might turn on *women*. Instinctively his mind rebels against this. Women aren't supposed to get turned on."[342]

The Pleasure Chest managed to avoid a run-in with the law, and their sex toys sold so well through both their store and their mail-order catalog that in 1972, they moved to a larger store on Seventh Avenue South in Greenwich Village. Their new store was right in the heart of New York City's gay mecca, yet it still attracted female customers. Colglazier's reticence about sex toys had completely evaporated by this point. Times were changing. As Colglazier told the *New York Times*, "There were a lot of indications that sex had caught on in a respected and dignified manner. First there was nudity in the theater, and then abortion was legalized [in New York], and then just a few weeks ago New York had its first Erotic Film Festival."[343] Colglazier was aligning his store with high culture, putting the Pleasure Chest in the same category as Broadway shows and film. This was a smart move considering that the Pleasure Chest was trying to distinguish itself from the seedy porn stores.

But Colglazier and Rifkin faced a major challenge: They were selling gay-centric sex toys at a time when homosexuality was considered both a sickness and a crime. The American Psychological Association regarded homosexuality as a mental illness, and sodomy was illegal in most states. These laws were enforced too. In New York alone, more than one hundred men were arrested for sodomy during the 1960s.[344] Even though this was post–sexual revolution and the gay rights movement had already begun, creating a sex-toy store targeted to gay men was incredibly risky. In fact, the sexual revolution was, in many ways, a revolution for heterosexuals. In the early 1960s, the revolution "celebrated the erotic, but tried to keep it within a heterosexual framework of long-term, monogamous relationships," according to historians of sexuality John D'Emilio and Estelle B. Freedman.[345]

Even within the sex-toy industry itself, heterosexuality dominated. Gay-centric sex-toy companies didn't really exist at the time. The burgeoning sex-toy industry may have seemed to reflect sexual progress, but in fact it promoted the same ideals of heterosexual marriage and monogamy that many in the gay rights movement were trying to overturn. Even the most common euphemism for sex toys at the time—"marital aids"—seemed to indicate that gay men and women were excluded from the dildo revolution.[346] Colglazier and Rifkin soon discovered this fact when they recognized that Marche's dildos didn't satisfy their gay customers.

"Fist fucking became popular in the gay community," Colglazier said. "And the dildos that were made at the time were very small . . . they didn't compare with a fist. We had a lot of requests for much larger dildos." So Colglazier worked with a sculptor and Marche to design larger dildos, as well as dildos shaped like fists and hands.[347] But given the antigay sentiment of the time, Marche Manufacturing didn't indicate on their packaging that the dildos were for gay men.[348] Yet the very fact that heterosexual men were collaborating with gay men to create gay sex toys in the 1970s was remarkable—and the collaboration worked out for both sides. By the late 1970s, the Pleasure Chest had purchased a half million dollars' worth of dildos from Marche, and the sex-toy industry in general was growing at a rapid clip, about 28 percent per year, with sales around $100 million.[349] [350]

The Marches weren't the only ones creating products targeted to the gay community: Farley and Fred Malorrus also began crafting products that appealed to gays and selling these products to the Pleasure Chest. Similar to the Marches' toys, the Malorruses' products promoted a heterosexual ideal on the package. They sold a lidocaine-based numbing gel called Anal Eaze for anal sex, but they sold it with a picture of female pornstar Seka's posterior on the package, despite the fact that the predominant market for Anal Eaze was gay men.[351] Although Farley Malorrus said that "the gay people in this world . . . made the industry," he had mixed views on the gay sex toys they sold. "My dad sure invented thousands of products that had to do with the rear end," Farley Malorrus said. "I sold 'em, but I wasn't a big advocate of it. . . . I don't believe in sodomy. I'm a Christian."[352]

Colglazier and Rifkin knew that selling products associated with sex, especially products associated with gay sex, was making a bold political statement. But the two entrepreneurs weren't content to let their butt plugs and gay iconography speak for themselves. Starting with their second catalog, they boldly set out their philosophy in the front of their catalog. "The Pleasure Chest is a new concept," they wrote, "reflecting the changing attitudes of our society towards sex." Their catalogs mixed high and low culture. Interspersed among the dildos and vibrators were everything from quotes taken from *The Oxford English Dictionary* (a definition of love) to a concise history of sex toys, dating the devices back to cave drawings that "indicated that primeval man employed crude prosthetic devices."[353] Illustrations in the margins mimicked classical art, showing intertwined bodies engaged in cunnilingus, fellatio, and various other sexual acts.

It was not just gay sex that they were interested in legitimizing. They also advocated for women's sexuality. "The most important fact to know is that orgasms will not occur in the vagina or urethra unless the clitoris is participating," the catalog proclaimed. "The clitoris is the key that unlocks female sexuality."[354] This was heady stuff, reflective of Masters and Johnson's work and the feminist movement's advocacy of the clitoris most famously elucidated in Koedt's "The Myth of the Vaginal Orgasm." Colglazier and Rifkin did not couch their discussion of women's sexuality in overtly feminist terms, but the underlying philosophy was undoubtedly feminist. In a way, the first feminist sex-toy store was, in fact, not started by women; it was founded by gay men.

Lesbians and gays made up a big portion of the Pleasure Chest's customers, but Colglazier and Rifkin estimated that more than half of their customers were straight. It wasn't just its location or the fact that the store was more inviting than the Forty-second Street adult bookstores that attracted women to it, even though many of the products were directed toward gay men. It was also the fact that they didn't sell pornography. The Pleasure Chest was one of the first adult stores to not sell porn alongside sex toys, which attracted women to the store. Women likely felt more comfortable shopping in a store run by gay men and full of gay male shoppers than they did at an adult bookstore full of straight men, many of whom who had come to masturbate in the peep-show booths. And these weren't just young women shopping at the Pleasure Chest. Colglazier and Rifkin said they were surprised to have a sixty-something "grey-haired woman" enter the store, buy $145 worth of sex paraphernalia, and then "carr[y] it off [in a] 'little knit shopping bag.'"[355]

Lesbian customers too were drawn to the Pleasure Chest. The store advertised in lesbian magazines, including *Echo of Sappho*, where they referred to the Pleasure Chest not as a sex emporium, but as a "Love boutique" that featured "Every thing for sex."[356] Among the lesbians who the Pleasure Chest attracted was a specific subculture: lesbian feminists who liked S&M.

This subculture was highly controversial within the feminist movement. Most feminists came down on the side of seeing S&M as a form of ritualized violence against women, even if it was only women who were participating. Stores that sold S&M gear were targeted by protesters demanding that the establishments stop carrying such goods.[357] As a result, some women were hesitant to shop at the Pleasure Chest. For example, an actress who played a promiscuous carnival worker in Steve Martin's movie *The Jerk* told the *Los Angeles Times* that even when she was auditioning for the part, which involved being "a motorcycle daredevil—a very S/M type," she "was too afraid to go into the Pleasure Chest for leather and chains," so she "shopped at a pet store instead."[358] The feminists who came out in favor of S&M were lambasted, called all manner of names, and accused of working for the CIA.

Gayle Rubin, who founded the lesbian S&M group Samois, spoke out against the feminist anti-S&M rhetoric. Samois argued that lesbian S&M practitioners were an "oppressed sexual minority" who "believe that S&M can and should be consistent with the principles of feminism." Rubin argued that antiporn feminists unfairly used S&M porn for their cause. "The use of S&M imagery in antiporn discourse is inflammatory," she wrote. "It implies that the way to make the world safe for women is to get rid of sadomasochism."[359] It wasn't just antiporn feminists who were critical of S&M. For the most part, S&M was too controversial a practice to appeal to even left-wing radicals, even though sadism and masochism is as old as the Marquis de Sade. But it's been misunderstood since that time too. Consensual violent-seeming or actual violent play seems just like violence to outsiders, but those within the community have developed a series of intricate codes, rules, and restrictions that actually make S&M as safe or safer (both physically and emotionally) than other sexual practices.

The Pleasure Chest was somewhat of an outlier in the range of sex stores because of its focus on S&M. "Most of us probably don't consider instruments of torture sources of sexual pleasure," intoned the narrator in a nasal voice in the 1972 documentary *Pornography in New York* as he stood outside the original Pleasure Chest location dressed in a suit and tie. "And you probably didn't believe that sadomasochism existed or if does, certainly not outside medical journals. We questioned this and opened a veritable Pandora's box called the Pleasure Chest." In the documentary, Rifkin escorted the narrator around the store, showing him handcuffs, leather cock rings with pinprick-like interiors for stimulation, and penis key chains. While he was showcasing slave collars and all manner of handcuffs, Rifkin tried to distance himself from the S&M scene. "I don't have to be a sadist or a masochist to sell restraints," he said. "They don't care if I am or not. If they want restraints, this is where they can get them. My sexual preferences don't really influence theirs at all."[360]

By the mid-1970s, the Pleasure Chest had added a second store on East Fiftieth Street and another on West Seventy-fourth Street. In spite of the government's stance that obscenity was dangerous, the Pleasure Chest—with its stock of dildos and leather ball harnesses—was gaining more success and more visibility.[361]

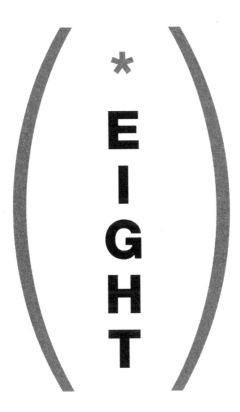

Female Masturbation

As the Pleasure Chest expanded in New York City, Betty Dodson entered a yoga retreat not knowing what to expect. She made her way to her room, and there she found her roommate: a forty-something spunky woman with short curly brown hair named Dell Williams. Her first impression of Williams was that she was a smart, pushy New Yorker, but she liked her immediately. They soon bonded over their love of Austrian psychologist Wilhelm Reich. "I'd never met a woman before who read Reich," Dodson said.[362] Dodson learned that although Williams spent her time developing advertisements as vice president of the Hodes Advertising, her true passion was making the world a better place for women. One of the first things Dodson did was show Williams her nude drawings, which Williams thought were amazing because they featured "strong, beautiful bodies engaged in ecstatic sex."[363] Dodson told her about the new sexual-consciousness-raising groups she was starting, where she taught women how to masturbate. Williams was fascinated.

Although Williams felt an instant connection to Dodson and pledged to stay in touch with her, she didn't contact Dodson after the retreat was over because she was too afraid. She knew that she wanted Dodson to teach her how to masturbate, but she wasn't sure she was ready to learn. "I didn't think masturbation was a good thing to do," Williams said. In part, this attitude had come from her mother, who had caught her brother Lorenz masturbating when he was a kid and was so appalled that she told him, "If you touch that again, I'll cut it off." Williams couldn't shake the feeling that "if somebody caught me jerking off, they'd think I'm a terrible woman."[364] It wasn't until three months later that she finally picked up the telephone.

(*)

It was the spring of 1973, and fifty-one-year-old Dell Williams was terrified. Her feet were unsteady as she entered the elevator en route to Betty Dodson's twelfth-floor New York City apartment, wondering whether she would have the nerve to participate in Dodson's bodysex workshops.[365] Dodson had only two requirements for participants: that they pay the fee and that they attend the workshops completely nude. It was the latter that Williams struggled with. "I was not prepared to be nude among complete strangers, all women or no," she said. To cope with her nervousness, she reminded herself of why she had come in the first place. It wasn't just to become more comfortable with masturbation, but it was also because of Betty Dodson's magnetic personality. "To be with her was to share her sense of joy and aliveness, her total command of her self, her body."[366] The elevator stopped, the door opened, and Williams worked up the courage to walk down to Dodson's apartment and ring the doorbell. As she did so, she told herself that the workshop would actually be fun; after all, it was about masturbation.

When Dodson answered the door, she was completely naked with a huge smile on her face. Williams was shocked. "I was the type who was still wearing fashionable hats on a daily basis," she said. Soon her shock subsided and her "whole consciousness changed" when she realized that Dodson "wasn't worried that the neighbors would see."[367] Williams realized that Dodson's nudity was "a source of power." She wanted what Dodson had.

When Dodson asked her to take off her clothes immediately and hang them on one of the fifteen hooks she had strategically installed at the front of her entranceway, Williams didn't flinch. Dodson did not want to give women a chance to think about whether removing their clothes was a good idea because, if they thought too long about it, they might not want to do it. Williams dutifully followed Dodson into her living room, which was full of nude women milling about between the blue pillows strewn across the floor.[368]

Dodson sat down on a pillow and crossed her legs. She asked her flock to join her, and the naked women followed her lead, sitting on cushions as Dodson presided over them like a Buddhist guru. "The personal is political, including sex," Dodson declared.[369] Williams looked around the room. It was full of women whose bodies ran the gamut from skinny to obese, young to old, flat-chested to big-bosomed.

Dodson opened with a discussion of her own body insecurities. Then she asked Williams and the others to share their own. Nearly everybody had negative things to say. Even the most conventionally beautiful women in the room were down on themselves.[370] "I hate my body," said one woman, as Dodson assured her and the other participants that she used to feel the same way. As Williams realized her feelings of insecurity were shared, she felt stronger, which was the point of this consciousness-raising technique: It was empowerment through the sharing of "commonalities."

Then Dodson asked them to say something positive about their bodies. As they shared things they liked, the whole room changed. They all became "better and more confident," Williams said.[371]

To truly overcome their insecurities, Dodson told them, they had to face their fears by gazing at their bodies in their mirror. Dodson placed a small mirror in front of each woman and asked them to spread their legs and gaze at their vulvas as well as their neighbors' vulvas. Next, she told them to spread their outer labia so they could get a better look. Williams did as she was told. Dodson provided a short anatomy lesson, naming each part of the genitals.

Williams looked in the mirror as Dodson moved around the room, showing women how to fully appreciate their genitals, arranging "with care and an artist's eye the butterfly wings" of one woman's labia.[372] Williams was transformed. She had never thought of her vulva as attractive before. In fact, she had never even really looked closely at it. Now she thought of it as incredibly beautiful. And she saw that each woman's vulva was different. "This was revolutionary information," she said. She went home feeling better about her body than perhaps she ever had.[373]

During the next session, Williams had an even greater transformation. At this session, Dodson first led them in some yoga and breathing exercises, and then she got to the pièce de résistance. Dodson took out an oblong device with a soft vinyl head about the size of a tennis ball. It was a Hitachi Magic Wand. Then she explained how she had transformed her "feelings of guilt about masturbation to feelings of celebration so that masturbation became an act of self-love."[374] Dodson and her assistant, Sheila Shea, both plugged their devices into the electrical outlet, cranked up their dials, and placed them on their clitorises. A wave of pleasure washed over their faces. For twenty minutes, Williams and the other participants sat silently and watched as the naked Dodson and Shea vibrated themselves to powerful orgasms. After Dodson and Shea climaxed, the room erupted into applause.[375] Williams's views on masturbation were never the same. She found "a new sense of power . . . independence, and control" over her sexuality.[376]

After witnessing her mentor's powerful orgasm, Williams and the other participants were each given a Magic Wand. Following Dodson's lead, they began to masturbate. Orgasms came quickly for some, not so for others. Many women stifled their moans, embarrassed. Dodson urged them not to. After the women had orgasms, she told them to continue, to have more.[377] Dodson then gave them a homework assignment: Masturbate at home. They could use a vibrator if they wanted to, but they didn't have to. Dodson offered to lend out her vibrators, or for those who wanted their own, she directed them to go to purchase a vibrator.

Williams wanted her own vibrator, but only sex-toy store that was inviting to women existed in the early 1970s: the Pleasure Chest. Adult bookstores were clearly men's spaces, full of pornographic magazines, which displayed gynecological close-ups of vulvas, as well as peep-show booths, which were full of sticky seats and masturbating men. They were temples to male sexual fantasy, masturbation palaces where men went to either jack off or buy a magazine to masturbate with later. Women entered at their own peril, which meant that they rarely entered at all.

If a woman was brave enough to push past the patrons who were flipping through porn magazines, she would find—in a small back section of the store, hidden among an array of dildos, artificial vaginas, whips, and female blow-up dolls—just one or two plastic, battery-operated phallic vibrators of about six inches in length. These were low-quality devices unsuitable for clitoral stimulation, so it was no wonder only 1 to 3 percent of adult bookstore patrons were women.[378] So Williams went instead to Macy's—a store that had been stocking vibrators under the guise of medical devices since 1910.[379]

Upon arrival at the department store, Williams asked the male sales clerk—two decades her junior—if he could direct her to where the "body massagers" were. In Williams's recounting, he crowed, "'What do you want it for?' loudly enough that people turned to look." She "mumbled something about having a bad back." She ended up buying the vibrator, but not without "a sense of guilt and shame." *Buying vibrators shouldn't be fraught with shame*, she thought. But she filed this thought away, took her vibrator home, and did something else that she'd been told she should feel guilty about. She masturbated.[380]

Williams showed up to the next bodysex session having completed her masturbation homework. At this meeting, Dodson directed her and the other women in a discussion of their masturbation experiences. About half of the women had experienced success, if you define success by having an orgasm. The remaining women either didn't have orgasms or were not sure if what they felt was an orgasm. After listening to everyone's experiences, Dodson explained what an orgasm feels like. She then focused on the next step in her sexual awakening plan: how to use vibrators during partnered sex. This was not as simple as it seems, given that the vibrators they were using were more than a foot long and plugged into the wall. The best position was woman on top, Dodson said, and then she demonstrated it by using her female assistant as a surrogate sex partner.[381]

(*)

In the meantime, Williams had been active in the New York City branch of NOW, and she had increasingly come to believe that sexual liberation was key to women's liberation. In early 1973, the president of NOW, Judy Wenning, asked Williams to co-organize the first NOW sex conference. The first person Williams thought of to join her was Betty Dodson. She called up Dodson and asked her to become a member of the planning committee for the conference, and Dodson agreed.

From the minute she joined, however, Dodson caused trouble. At an early meeting, Williams asked Dodson what she planned to do at the conference.

"I'd like to do a slide show of split beaver for feminists," Dodson responded.

Silence filled the room as women's faces showed no sign of recognition. Dodson explained to the group that "'split beaver' was porno slang for a photo of a woman holding her vaginal lips open." The idea of having a split beaver session didn't go over well for some in the group, who were offended by the phrase, believing it to be a "derogatory male term." The group was resistant to Dodson's idea until Dodson shared her story of insecurity about the look of her genitals and explained that many women had been transformed by her workshops. The other women tentatively agreed to the slide show under one condition: that she didn't use the term "split beaver." One woman suggested that Dodson use the term "open otter" instead because it was more feminine. Dodson declined.

To get the NOW members on her side, Dodson decided to host a free bodysex workshop for them. Once they saw what Dodson's workshops were like, she surmised, they were sure to be won over. But during the workshop that Dodson held with Sheila Shea, none of the NOW women wanted to open up. "Lesbians didn't want to discuss their private sex lives, and the political lesbians weren't having any sex," Dodson said.

Things only got worse from there. When Dodson showed her vulva to the group and referred to it as a "cunt," a woman yelled, "I object to that word!" The group then spent thirty minutes having a "long, boring discussion about what to call our 'things,'" Dodson later wrote. "We finally agreed on 'genitals,' but Ruth's angry outburst had effectively ended the Genital Show and Tell process." Her co-coordinator Shea developed a headache and excused herself.[382]

Sexuality was such a charged subject for NOW members that they couldn't even agree on what the conference flyer should look like. It didn't help that Dodson was drawing it. Dodson was a natural choice to make the flyer because she was a classically trained artist, and the image she came up with was influenced by her training: an homage to Leonardo da Vinci's Vitruvian Man, only the figure was reimagined as a Vitruvian woman. Although Dodson intended the drawing to be a triumphant demonstration of women's sexuality, the nude, muscled woman splayed on top of a vulva caused an enormous amount of controversy among the NYC NOW chapter. Much of the controversy centered on the woman's clitoris, which many women mistook for a penis because they thought it was too large. Dodson reduced the size of the clitoris, even as she argued that she was trying to create a new image of women in culture, one that was not the "classical image of woman" with curves. (Dodson's poster was controversial enough that Judy Wenning, as president, felt the need to defend it in her opening keynote speech: "I have heard a lot of complaints about the drawing, done by Betty Dodson. . . . The body on this conference poster is a strong, functional body. I think it's a body that this woman would be enjoying," Wenning said.)[383]

After much argument and compromise, the conference was a go. On June 9, 1973, more than one thousand women and one hundred men gathered in Intermediate School 29 on Park Avenue and Ninety-fourth Street for the NOW Women's Sexuality Conference to talk about sex in all its permutations, from lesbianism to masturbation to sadomasochism. There were thirty-eight workshops for women to choose from, with such titles as "Alternatives to Monogamy," "Women Loving Women," and "Reaching Your Sexual Potential." Although men were excluded from the women's workshops, they had nine of their own, including workshops on "Masturbation and Orgasm" and "Sexual Roles, the Macho Mystique, and Male Intimacy." This didn't sit well with some of the lesbians in attendance, who protested and even booed at a man who attended a women's session.[384] Women of all ages came; some even brought their kids, whom they dropped off at the day care set up on site.[385] Although there were numerous speakers and break-out groups, it was really Dodson and Williams's vision that shaped the conference.

To prove that sexuality was sufficiently political, Williams began the conference proceedings by describing how women's sexuality has been suppressed since biblical times, beginning with the story of Adam and Eve, which was "created by the patriarchal mind to entrap women," Williams later wrote. "What better way to subjugate women than to deny her sexual freedom?" Although Williams's logic was sound, the split among feminists who believed that sexual enlightenment was the key to political gains or was a distraction ran deep. Many members thought that focusing on sex was not the best way to gain rights for women. "Some of my sisters dismissed the significance of the conference because of 'our many political struggles,'" Williams wrote. "If freeing ourselves from sexual imprisonment is not political, I don't know what is."[386]

Dodson took the podium after Wenning's keynote speech. She was the first woman scheduled in the "speak out," where women shared stories about their sexual histories with the group. Williams decided to have Dodson go first because she thought, "If I opened the conference with Betty talking about jerking off, everybody would drop their shyness about sex."[387]

With her shaved head, the forty-four-year-old Dodson nervously took the stage because she "knew this was [her] big change to get masturbation out of the closet and up in the headlines as a feminist issue."[388] After Wenning had focused on how controversial Dodson's drawing was, Dodson was already in a defensive crouch, so she opened her speech with a justification of the poster. "I stuck my neck out and a lot of people didn't like [the drawing]," Dodson declared as she stood at the podium. "I'm sorry, but I do think we ought to try to experiment with new images [of women]." This was a prelude to the many defensive postures she would take throughout her career, as she battled frequent criticism by other feminists. After she finished the apology, she declared herself a "sex freak," saying that sex had made her "feel better than I have ever felt." To say that this was not an attitude that many feminists had at the time is an understatement. Enjoying sex was one thing, but abandoning marriage and being proudly promiscuous was quite another.

Dodson's promotion of masturbation was probably even more controversial. She wasn't just extolling the benefits of jacking off; she was also suggesting that women use a machine to do so. "I'm probably hooked on my vibrator. I'm probably going steady with it, but I'll worry about that later. I don't know," Dodson said.[389] "I've got four with me at the conference . . . and I mean it's like a groove. I change them over. Actually, the reason I do that is that they get hot and you have to change over to the next one. Wait till we

B
U
Z
Z

*

start designing vibrators. It'll be a trip."[390] After describing her unhappy marriage, laying out her philosophy of the liberating power of masturbation, and urging women to get over their genital shame, Dodson finished her speech by telling women to come to her "Liberating Masturbation and Orgasm" workshop later in the day.

That afternoon the workshop was packed, with women milling around in the hallways of the repurposed high school auditorium, craning their necks to catch a glimpse of an enthusiastic Dodson. After a short discussion, Dodson removed three vibrators from her briefcase, plugged them in, and, as a reporter for the *Los Angeles Times* reported, "began to discourse on the fine points of each vibrator—when used not for muscle relaxing but for sexual pleasure."[391]

She started with the Panabrator made by Panasonic, the Japanese company known more for their TV sets than their sex toys. The Panabrator was a foot-long plug-in vibrator with a dial to modulate the speed. It wasn't considered a sex toy by Panasonic—far from it. They advertised their vibrator in the *New York Times* as "The Healthy Way to Ease Mother's Tension and Backaches."[392] What could be less sexual than that? Panasonic also didn't sell their Panabrator in sex stores; they distributed it in department and clothing stores and marketed it to men as well. "Plug in the massager and pulsate away the tension, aches, and pains," read one 1972 *New York Times* advertisement, which featured a man massaging his back.[393]

When Dodson stood in front of the captivated women discoursing on the finer points of masturbating with the Panabrator, she gave it a new meaning. A radical one. It was no longer a device for Mom. Instead, it was a toy that allowed women to "dial a come," as Dodson put it.[394] As she plugged it in and turned it on, a buzzing sound filled the audience and instead of making apologies for the loudness of the vibrator, Dodson eroticized the noise. "I'm at the point where just the sound of a vibrator turns me on," she said. The women in the audience were rapt as Dodson discoursed about the three different types of vibrators: large plug-in, battery operated, and a smaller new plug-in clitoral model. The phallic battery-operated vibrators were "a man's idea of what a woman wants in a vibrator," Dodson said dismissively, claiming that they didn't reliably give women orgasms. One woman in the audience agreed, and she complained that "the battery runs out at the wrong time."[395]

The age-old fear rose up: What would men think of vibrators? Would they be threatened? "The vibrator doesn't have to replace the penis," Dodson assured everyone. She was echoing the advice given by British physician Alex Comfort in his bestselling sex manual published a year before the conference, *The Joy of Sex* (1972). Although Comfort was enthusiastic about vibrators, writing that they "can produce some sexual feeling in almost any woman," he too assured his audience that "vibrators are no substitute for a penis."[396] Dodson argued that men would welcome vibrators because they would "relieve the pressure" on men to provide women with orgasms. "Any guy that I've ever talked to that's really sexual and digs women has no objection to a woman using a vibrator to have an orgasm with," Dodson said. "You bring out your vibrator and it will separate the chauvinists from the lovers."[397]

Dodson ended the workshop by setting up a small vibrator shop, placing two vibrators on a table and plugging them in, allowing women to feel the vibrations. Within a half hour, her inventory was gone.[398] Both Dodson and Williams were excited that the vibrator inventory sold out. It was proof that there was a market for vibrators among feminists.

(*)

Dodson's vibrator workshop had been an unabashed success, as had her speech, but she was only just getting started. At 11 a.m. on the second day of the conference, a large group of women filed into the high school auditorium to see her other presentation, the split beaver for feminists slide show that she had renamed with the innocuous academic title of "Creating a Female Genital Aesthetic."

Dodson began by projecting large images of anatomical vulva drawings from textbooks, which she critiqued. The audience laughed along with her as she pointed out mislabeled clitorises. So far, so good. "We need new images of women's genitals," Dodson told them as she began projecting one of the many photographs that she had commissioned of her friends' vulvas. This was daring stuff. Although vulva imagery is now so tied in with the feminist movement that vagina puppets are a running joke in *Portlandia*'s feminist bookstore sketch and feminist Instagram accounts are dedicated to vulva imagery, at the time, such images were highly controversial. Pornography was reviled among a lot of feminists, even as the pro-sex feminist movement was just beginning, with the publication of Germaine Greer's *Female Eunuch* in 1970, in which Greer urged women to abandon monogamy and get in touch with their vast sexuality.[399] [400]

As photographs of her friends' genitals were projected on the screen, Dodson described their unique beauty. She wanted women to recognize the wide variation of vulvas and clitorises and be inspired to realize that their genitals were "normal." Although her overall message was greeted warmly, the words she used to make it were not. "I call this a Baroque Cunt," Dodson said proudly as she beamed at the photograph of her friend's vulva on screen. Suddenly a woman burst up from her chair, hands on her hips, and said (echoing what the NOW members had said earlier), "We object to you using that word! We've heard enough of that kind of talk from men." Most women would have been rattled by such a public dressing down, but not Dodson. She was undeterred.

"I'm sorry the word offends you," she said. "But saying it happens to turn me on, so I intend to keep using it."[401] And she stayed true to her word, introducing all manner of cunts as the presentation wore on. The audience warmed to her.

Williams loved it. "When she finished showing all the different types, because we're all different, our lips are all different, there was such of an out-pouring of acknowledgment," said Williams of Dodson's show. "The place was in an uproar. I never heard such acceptance as if all the oppression that women had felt about it being bad and not good exploded and we were all good."[402] Dodson received a standing ovation. But the lone dissenter presaged the trouble that was to come, as Dodson refused to kowtow to the feminist orthodoxy.

(*)

At the NOW conference, Dodson introduced the feminist movement to masturbation as a political act, and vibrators as political objects. So it was only natural that about a year after the conference, in August 1974, *Ms.*, the magazine founded by NOW co-founder Gloria Steinem, published Dodson's article on masturbation. According to Dodson, the editors of *Ms.* were initially wary of featuring an article on masturbation, worried that the subject would destroy the credibility that second-wave feminism had built up. They required Dodson to make a number of changes, toning down the article title from "Liberating Masturbation" to "Getting to Know Me" and refusing to allow Dodson to include the opinions of other participants in the workshops, requiring Dodson to be "designated the lone masturbator." [403] [404] To be fair, *Ms.* wasn't exactly prudish, as they let Dodson include a nude photo of her arching her back in a yoga pose.

In her article, Dodson encouraged women to masturbate for political reasons: to overcome the sexual double-standard that women were held to. Society was guilty of "depriving [women] of direct sexual self-knowledge—especially masturbation," Dodson argued. The only way to regain this knowledge was to "become very aware of our genitals" through masturbation. She shared the most effective masturbation technique: using vibrators. "I have found that the vibrator gives me the strongest and most consistent form of stimulation and is especially good for women who have never experienced orgasm," Dodson wrote.[405]

Ms. editor Harriet Lyons had suggested Dodson include a pitch promoting her masturbation pamphlet, "Liberating Masturbation." Dodson listened to her advice, expecting only a few orders to come in.[406] After the article was published, thousands of orders rolled in, along with handwritten notes from women who were relieved to discover that their own masturbation was not abnormal, nor a sign of mental illness. Dodson decided that these women—who seemed as if they'd been waiting for decades for someone to admit that masturbation was not only fun but also political—deserved more than an eighteen-page pamphlet. She tripled its size and included fifteen pages of her vulva drawings.

Dodson's ambition meant that the more than two thousand readers who ordered a copy of *Liberating Masturbation* would have to wait for three months to get it, so *Ms.* sent out postcards to women alerting them to the delay. But they made one mistake: they wrote the title of the book on the postcard. This did not sit well with many of the *Ms.* readers. "Instantly angry women wrote back, shocked that the word 'masturbation' had appeared on a postcard that could be seen by postal clerks, mailmen, and members of their family," said Dodson.[407] Ordering a book on masturbation was one thing; letting everyone know about it was entirely another matter.

Although abortion had been legalized with *Roe v. Wade* in 1973 and porn had gone mainstream with *Deep Throat* and *Behind the Green Door,* masturbation was still stigmatized in the 1970s. In a 1974 survey, a quarter of women said they felt guilty, perverted, or feared going insane from masturbation, while 21 percent of men said the same.[408] Dodson realized she had much more work ahead of her.

Liberating Masturbation was one of the first books about masturbation ever to be written by a woman.[409] Merely writing this book was a political act, but the message inside it was also explicitly political. Women should masturbate, Dodson argued, because "sexuality and economics" are inextricably intertwined. "Ultimately [sexuality and economics] are not separable—not as long as the female genitals have economic value instead of sexual value for women. Saving sex for my lover/husband was my gift to him in exchange for economic security—called 'meaningful relationship' or 'marriage,'" she said.[410] Women lost in this exchange because married sex was usually unsatisfying as it was routinely missionary style, and women rarely had orgasms. Many women were faking orgasms, she wrote, so as not to bruise their partners' egos. Women were giving up their own orgasms for financial stability. Basically, Dodson was reframing an older feminist argument that marriage was a form of prostitution. Although the kernel of the argument wasn't new, the solution to the problem was: masturbation.

Liberating Masturbation was basically a print version of Dodson's bodysex workshops and NOW slide show. It spread her message nationwide. The book featured Dodson's drawings of women masturbating while gazing into mirrors, etches of penises, and diagrams of nude women doing yoga poses. The drawings served to educate women about the different styles of vulvas, to reduce their shame. But it was the illustrations of women using vibrators that were revolutionary. She showed women both masturbating with vibrators and using them during sex with men.

In *Liberating Masturbation,* Dodson pushed masturbation into the spotlight and made it a part of the sexual revolution. Up until this point, the sexual revolution primarily benefitted men. Although women were now able to have sex before marriage without worrying about the fear of pregnancy, for the most part, women weren't able to have multiple partners without being branded a loose woman. The double standard was still in place, even within much of the feminist movement, which castigated promiscuous women as male-identified. Dodson didn't transform the sexual revolution overnight, but she made a place for masturbation and female sexuality at the table.

Although masturbation "is our first natural sexual activity," Dodson said, society doesn't see it that way. Instead, society had repressed women's natural sexual instinct and had actually normalized repression. Women were not supposed to know anything about their bodies or their sexuality until they got married and men taught them. But the only way a woman could enjoy sex was if she learned how to pleasure herself, Dodson wrote. Yet Dodson did not think that masturbation was simply a stepping-stone to sex. She thought masturbation should be celebrated for its own sake. Women could not truly be liberated until they were sexually liberated, she argued, and they wouldn't be sexually liberated unless they learned how to masturbate, because only then would the "paralyzing sex roles" be destroyed. If you depended on your spouse for an orgasm, she said, then you could never be truly free.[411]

Dodson's masturbation theory should have easily fit into the radical feminist movement, since they were hailing the clitoris as a feminist body part.[412] Yet Dodson was a leader, not a follower, and she was allergic to orthodoxy. While some feminists were on board with Dodson's argument that masturbation would help women become more self-reliant, others were critical.[413] Because she believed that women could have sex without love and that orgasms were important, Dodson was not universally accepted by radical feminists because she was too "male-identified."[414] Even feminists who liked *Liberating Masturbation* worried that conflating pleasure with liberation was misguided.[415] Lesbian feminists were the most critical of Dodson, accusing her of being a closeted lesbian because even though she had sex with women, she described herself as heterosexual.[416]

Dodson's biggest challenge in *Liberating Masturbation* was making vibrators seem appealing. The prospect of an orgasm was not a convincing enough argument for many women in a society where women were still socialized to think that their sexual pleasure was subordinate to that of a man's. Women worried that using a vibrator would scare off men.[417] [418] This was not an idle fear. One way to get men to like vibrators was to use vibrators on them, Dodson argued.[419] It wasn't just men's fear of vibrators that women were worried about; they also were afraid they'd become addicted to vibrators. Dodson didn't deny that vibrators were addictive; she just claimed that they were a harmless addiction. "It's not fattening, illegal, or immoral," Dodson wrote.[420]

(*)

The *Ms.* article and the sexuality conference couldn't change attitudes toward female sexuality overnight. But Dodson's article and her rousing vibrator workshop helped transform vibrators into symbols of women's liberation for some feminists. Before the NOW conference and *Ms.* article, vibrators were barely a blip on the radar of the feminist movement. Now they were tools that could transform gender roles by empowering women to stop depending on their partners for sexual pleasure.

Yet the effect of Dodson's work was limited. No matter how much Dodson advocated for vibrators, the fact remained that it was not so easy for a woman to acquire a vibrator in the 1970s. Aside from the Pleasure Chest, which was an anomaly, woman had two choices: Buy one at Macy's and possibly be shamed by the store clerk, or trek to a porno store in a bad area of town. There had to be another option. According to Williams, she asked her friends to carry vibrators in their feminist stores, and they all said they weren't interested.[421]

So Williams thought that perhaps she should start a store herself. She asked Dodson to join her. Dodson would provide the educational side of the operation, and Williams would use her advertising expertise to sell sex toys. According to Dodson, when Williams asked her to be business partners,

Dodson seriously considered it. But the more she thought about it, the more hesitant she became. "I knew that in a month I would kill her," Dodson said. "She would have become a total bottom: indecisive, always regretting her decisions."[422]

Dodson turned Williams down. "Why don't you just do it yourself?" she asked.[423]

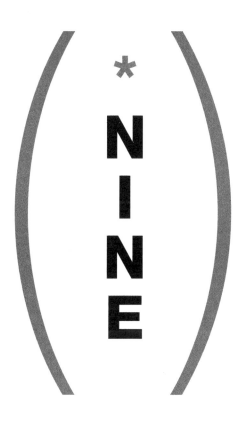

A Garden of Sex Toys, Condoms for All, and Sturman's War

Williams wasn't sure if she wanted to head into a business by herself. She had a lucrative, high-status career as an advertising executive, and becoming an entrepreneur in her off hours would eat up the little free time she had.[424] Besides, she wasn't sure that a vibrator store was really the best way to spread feminism throughout the United States.

She thought back to Dodson's workshop, where Dodson had argued that masturbation meant no longer having "to rely on a lover for orgasms."[425] Then Williams recalled Wilhelm Reich, who had argued that society "repressed sexuality in people in order to deprive them of their own personal power." It suddenly came to her.

"I had a vision that orgasmic women could transform the world, not only to achieve equality for women, but peace on the planet," she later told *Ms.* magazine.[426] A sex-toy store could be the tool for political revolution.[427]

As Dodson had before her, Williams decided to become a masturbation evangelist, except instead of selling a workshop to teach women how to get off, she was selling the tools to do it with.[428] Williams racked her mind for a store name that was inspiring and sexy but not salacious. As she went through possibilities, she took out the NOW conference program. Right there on the cover, Williams saw Dodson's reimagining of Leonardo DaVinci's Vitruvian Man as a nude, splayed woman. It reminded her of "Eve . . . emerging with awe and fearlessness into her wonderful, unknown world, before she was shamed into that fig-leaf getup."[429] Inspired, Williams came up with idea of naming her store Eve's Garden, but she hesitated because she wasn't sure that she wanted to name her store after a Christian symbol of the source of original sin. Even though Williams wanted to reclaim the image of Eve from that of "a fallen, shamed woman to a strong, powerful woman proud of her strength, sensitivity, and sexuality" and transform Eve into a feminist symbol, she was doubtful if this was the right move. Was it really a good idea to associate her store with a patriarchal religion that had kept women from autonomy by shaming them and demonizing their sexuality? Was naming her store after the original temptress who led to the fall of man a good move for a Jewish woman whose idea of spirituality was informed by Reich?[430]

It was risky, but it felt right. "Eve," Williams thought. "I'm going to help you reclaim your garden."[431]

In September 1974, Williams opened Eve's Garden in her apartment in New York City. Because she had no room to hold inventory and would only sell things that she personally vouched for, she developed a catalog with just three items in it: A Hitachi Magic Wand, Dodson's *Liberating Masturbation*, and the Prelude 3 vibrator. Notably, Williams didn't have any pornography in her catalog.[432] Her choice to eschew porn magazines was a huge change in sex-toy retailing. Up until this point, most venues that sold sex toys (aside from the Pleasure Chest) sold porn alongside them. Porn and peep shows had kept feminists away from adult bookstores. A true feminist did not watch pornography, according to Andrea Dworkin and the leaders of the women's movement; if she needed a sexual outlet, she read or watched erotica. The distinction between the two was fuzzy, of course, as neither the Supreme Court nor Women Against Pornography (WAP) were able to agree on a satisfying definition of pornography. Thanks to Williams, feminists could now buy sex toys without abandoning their ideals.

All Williams needed was somewhere to advertise. She contacted popular women's magazines like *Redbook*, which seemed like natural places for her to advertise, but they all rejected her ads, even though mainstream media outlets like the *Los Angeles Times* and the *San Francisco Chronicle* had no qualms running ads for 1972's porn juggernaut *Deep Throat*.[433] With its plot line of a woman discovering a clitoris in her throat, *Deep Throat* was immensely popular. Celebrities flocked to the movie both out of curiosity and because being photographed leaving a showing was a sign that you were hip and progressive. And it wasn't only male celebrities like Jack Nicholson who were spotted taking in the Linda Lovelace flick. Even Jacqueline Kennedy Onassis saw it. Why was *Deep Throat* more socially acceptable than sex toys? Because it reinforced current gender norms—women were reliant upon men for their orgasms.[434]

Williams next turned to feminist publications.[435] She went with the most well-known and popular one first: *Ms.* Even though Williams had experience as a copywriter, she labored over how to distill the essence of her company into a short sentence that would generate interest among an audience of feminists, many of whom were wary of sex toys. She finally decided upon: "Liberating vibrators and other pleasurable things for women from a feminist-owned business. Send 25 cents for our catalog. Eve's Garden, 119 W. 57th St., NYC."[436] It wasn't the most memorable piece of ad copy; it didn't possess poetic charm or a clever tagline. But it was the best Williams could do in the short time period. She submitted the ad, it ran in *Ms.*, and Williams waited nervously, wondering if she would get even a handful of requests for her catalog.

She shouldn't have worried. Her ad was a resounding success. Requests for catalogs poured in. Orders for vibrators and books soon followed, which she piled onto her kitchen counter, many accompanied by handwritten letters of women expressing their gratitude. One customer wrote, "As a woman and an active feminist, I greatly appreciate efforts by other women to liberate the minds and bodies of our sisters . . . to provide us with information and quality merchandise, to help us understand and release the full beauty of our sexuality."[437]

Williams had tapped into the hidden desires of hundreds of women who wanted to discover how to have an orgasm, have more orgasms, or at the very least be reassured that masturbation was normal. She didn't just tell them that masturbation was acceptable; she made it something to celebrate. "Light candles," she told these women. "Take your time. Have some fun."[438]

(*)

Within a year, Eve's Garden began to make enough money that Williams quit her job at the ad agency and devoted herself to the business full time. The first thing she did was look for a space for an office and a showroom. The only problem was that nobody wanted to rent to a sex store, which is surprising in the 1970s in a city that was packed with strip clubs featuring fully nude women grinding on their male patrons' laps.[439] But the sexual revolution was fairly patriarchal and full of double standards. Men were supposed to be highly sexual, so commercial establishments catering to their needs were not considered out of the ordinary.[440] Women, on the other hand, weren't supposed to be as sexual as men, so setting up a sex shop just for women was unheard of. She finally found a place on 119 West Fifty-seventh Street on the twelfth floor.

As Williams got more attention for the store and began advertising more widely, feminists began to question her intentions. Although most of Williams's feminist friends had been supportive of Eve's Garden from the beginning, not all of them were. A few of them "kind of snickered," Williams said. "That's because they didn't get the political meaning."[441] Williams decided to spread the word to Betty Friedan, sending one of her brochures to her. A little while later, Williams and Jacqui Ceballos (then-president of the NYC NOW chapter) were picking up Friedan from the Washington, D.C., airport to drive to a funeral of a mutual friend. While in the cab, Williams turned to Friedan and said, "Betty, did you receive my brochure on Eve's Garden?"

"What?" Friedan asked. " But that was just about flowers or plants." She hadn't even read it.[442]

As the company grew, customers began to challenge Williams. One prospective customer wrote to Eve's Garden: "Dear People: I'm not quite sure what feminists are doing in the vibrator business (it seems rather anti-social or anti-people to me) but please send me your catalog anyway. Thank you."[443]

Williams didn't back down; she responded to the criticism in a positive way. "What a feminist is doing in the vibrator business," Williams wrote back, "is creating space for women to touch base with their potential power which lies in the release of the orgasm . . . the ability to sense more pleasure and change the world from the standpoint of pleasure-based power rather than hostile/anger-based power." She also took aim at the writer's assertion that vibrators were an antisocial technology. "P.S. Vibrators are not meant to replace people . . . they're fun things too."[444]

That wasn't the only customer who challenged Williams. Another began her letter with this declaration: "As a feminist and an activist against pornography and other forms of violence against women, I am somewhat skeptical in writing to you! . . . If you are another sleazy sex-company parading as a feminist erotica store, that is not what I'm looking for."[445]

Vibrators continued to hold a contentious place within the feminist movement. At a second NOW feminist sexuality conference held a few months after Eve's Garden opened, the organizers extolled the benefits of vibrators, yet many participants weren't happy about the vibrator focus. Vibrators "were presented as the messiah—everywoman's dream come true (only $19.95)," complained three members of Washington, D.C.'s NOW chapter who attended the conference.[446]

In fact, criticism of Eve's Garden and its later imitators was so common that in the magazine *New Women's Times*, noted feminist Pat Califia—co-founder of the lesbian S&M group Samois—satirized the views of the radical feminists opposed to stores like Eve's Garden. "Has anybody thought of launching an investigation of so-called 'feminist' businesses which sell vibrators, lubricants, dildoes, and sexually explicit material to women? Obviously these shops must be on the cutting edge of an attempt to undermine feminist sexuality. Perhaps they are all secretly funded by Hustler or even the CIA!"[447]

Why were some feminists so upset about vibrators? Samois's other co-founder, Gayle Rubin, had a theory of the sexual value system that provides a bit of an explanation. Rubin argued that certain types of sex are prized over others for being "'good,' 'normal,' and 'natural.'" Good sexuality is "heterosexual, marital, monogamous, reproductive, and non-commercial." Bad sex is its antithesis. According to this theory, sex toys and masturbating, she argued, were bad sex.

The commercial aspects of sex toys were upsetting to many feminists because many radical feminists were wary of any enterprise even marginally connected with capitalism.[448] As historian Alice Echols argues, most radical feminist groups believed that all female "oppression derived from capitalism," so the idea that any commodity, even vibrators, could be liberatory was unfathomable to them.[449] Yet it wasn't just radical feminists who were critical of capitalism. The mainstream feminist movement was also wary of consumer culture. In 1969, mainstream "political" feminists organized protests against bridal fairs that promoted expensive wedding dresses.[450]

Criticisms of Williams's commodification of feminism were justifiable. Most attempts to commodify the women's movement—aside from women's bookstores and women's coffeehouses—were made by slick corporations incorporating feminist themes into their campaigns to sell more stuff. The 1960s Virginia Slims campaign with the tagline "You've Come a Long Way, Baby" typified feminism as branding, according to Thomas Frank in *The Conquest of Cool*. Frank argued that the campaign mixed "militant feminist rhetoric . . . with some less radical aspects of American femininity (like makeup and fashionable clothes)." It's no wonder that feminists were wary of Eve's Garden, given that feminist themes were being used by corporations like Philip Morris to sell dangerous, addictive products to young women.[451]

Although both Williams and Philip Morris used feminist rhetoric in advertising, there was one major difference between the two of them: She was sincere. Education was the primary goal of Eve's Garden. Williams said her goal was to "turn shy inhibited women into powerful women capable of changing the world."[452] But prospective customers had to be convinced that Williams was a true feminist activist. So Williams tried to communicate her feminist credentials any way that she could. Instead of treating her customers as people to make money off of, she treated them as like-minded compatriots to the feminist cause. She addressed her customers as "sisters" she was helping explore sexuality. Many customers responded in kind with personal letters that they attached along with their orders. For example, one woman wrote, "I know we've never physically 'met' but I miss hearing from you. I felt I'd found a friend—someone who understands so much more about being a woman than most other people ever could."[453]

Williams attempted to make shopping into a political act. She turned women's traditional role as consumers on its head. No longer was shopping the idle purview of the bored housewife. Consumer culture had become an expression of sexual awakening. To transform buying stuff from a materialistic act into one of feminist solidarity was revolutionary.

Williams truly believed a business could serve as a source of empowerment, as a paragraph from her mission statement shows: "We seek to encourage women to take responsibility for their own sexuality, honor the sacredness of sex, and clearly understand that bodily pleasure and spiritual joy are one, and an inalienable right."[454] Yet as sincere as her statement was, at the end of the day, she was urging women to "honor the sacredness of sex" and subvert the patriarchy by purchasing mass-produced objects made by male-run corporations that denied that their vibrators were used for female masturbation.[455]

Although feminists were wary of Eve's Garden, sex educators were less so. Williams began attending sex research conferences, and it was there where she got to know prominent sex educators, including Dr. Wardell Pomeroy of the Kinsey Institute and Dr. Mary S. Calderone of the Sexuality Information and Education Council of the United States, who informed Williams that there was a large, untapped nationwide market of the sexually frustrated female patients of doctors and sex therapists.[456] Williams began selling vibrators to physicians, with a pamphlet she created titled "Helping Your Patient to Help Yourself." It wasn't just a sales pitch, though. It also offered genuinely good advice, such as telling doctors to actually listen to their female patients and let their patients know that their sexual responses and genitals were normal.[457]

Meanwhile, Williams expanded her advertising for Eve's Garden to other feminist journals, including *Big Mama Rag, off our backs,* and *New Women's Times.*[458] This time, she had the budget to actually bring her advertisements out of the classified ghetto and into the main advertising section. Her ads now featured illustrations, usually a drawing of an apple, and a message that was bolder than her earlier ones: "Now is the time to declare your sexual independence or share it with a vibrator! Why not? A feminist-owned business."[459]

Thanks to Eve's Garden, women could get their hands on vibrators without fear of harassment from male customers, and they were very appreciative. "I know I would never go into a store to buy a vibrator, but thanks to you I don't need to," one woman wrote to Williams on April 5, 1975.[460]

While Williams's store was groundbreaking, it didn't change entrenched attitudes about sex toys overnight. For starters, it was only one small showroom and a mail-order outlet in a sea of hundreds of Sturman stores. Most Americans had probably never seen a sex toy, and those who had had seen them in porn stores. But even women who had the first orgasms of their lives thanks to the vibrators that Williams sold were conflicted. In 1975, one of these women, a woman from Athens, Ohio, was so awed by her Prelude vibrator–induced orgasm that she wrote a poem about it and sent in to the store. After describing her masturbation experience as "sink[ing] into the warm sweet cave that is me," she described her orgasm glowingly as an "orange tingling spasm" and concluded with the sentence: "I AM POWERFUL." But she followed this stanza of new-found self-confidence with one that was full of ambivalence about vibrators.

> I rejoice in finding a part of me
> lost since birth. In a horrible age of
> machines it is in a paradox that a machine
> led me to rediscover my offended birthright.

The vibrator transformed her life, but she still viewed it as a part of the "horrible age of machines" that she lived in. In the final stanza she ended with this goal: "One day . . . I will again look to find intimacy with another human being."[461] Vibrators were a stop along the journey to a relationship with another person, not an end in and of itself.

The development of a business centered on vibrators was in some ways in opposition to the 1970s-era counterculture mind-set wary of technology, the belief that natural was always better. Therefore it made sense that some women during this era felt ambivalence toward vibrators. Sex therapist and masturbation advocate Lonnie Barbach argued in her 1975 sex-advice book *For Yourself: The Fulfillment of Female Sexuality* that "Some women who object to the technological computer-instant-freeze-dried orientation of society may classify vibrators with frozen TV dinners, tape-recorded answering services, and microwave ovens. These women generally prefer a return to the more natural, slower, less complicated human functions. Thus, philosophically, they might be unwilling to use a vibrator."[462] Similarly, anthropologist Margaret Mead wrote in a 1976 issue of *Redbook* that vibrators were an unnatural technology that dehumanized sex: "We have invented [vibrators] to substitute for what is natural. Machines alienate people from their bodies and their emotions."[463] Women's sex manuals of the time, addressed these concerns: "If you see the use of a vibrator as unnatural, perhaps you can try thinking about it as an extension of yourself."[464]

(*)

Four years before Williams launched Eve's Garden in an attempt to change the world by selling sex products, two men in North Carolina were trying to do the same. Instead of selling vibrators, however, they were selling condoms.

Phil Harvey and Tim Black were likeminded, despite coming from completely different backgrounds. In the mid-1960s, after graduating from Harvard with a degree in Slavic Languages in Literatures, Harvey began working for the antipoverty organization CARE in India, where he helped feed malnourished Indian children in a school lunch program. After five years there, he felt like his work wasn't making much of a difference. "Not only did I experience a very clear object lesson in the futility of shipping American food to India to feed a growing number of kids," Harvey said. "But in the process it became quite clear to me that it would be more useful to provide Indian couples with a means of controlling fertility, which was very high at the time."[465] So he returned to the United States in 1969, where he enrolled in a master's program in family planning administration at the University of North Carolina–Chapel Hill and met Tim Black.[466]

Black was a physician who had spent time in Papua New Guinea and Nigeria. While working in these countries, he had been dismayed to discover that contraceptives just weren't available to most women. Hospitals and clinics couldn't provide family planning services, Black discovered, because they were so overwhelmed by taking care of people who had medical emergencies that they had little time to do anything else. Like Harvey, Black was determined to get contraceptives in the hands of women worldwide.[467]

When Black and Harvey met, they immediately bonded over their similar goals. "We said what we've got to do is find a way of promoting birth control outside of the clinical and medical networks in developing countries," Harvey said. One way of working around the medical networks to distribute birth control had recently been tried in India two years earlier: social marketing. "The idea was to provide contraceptives that are packaged and branded just like any other consumer goods product, heavily advertised through mass media, and made available through commercial distribution and retailing networks, but at very low, subsidized prices that everyone could afford," Harvey said. In other words, Harvey and Black were going to act like brand marketers instead of typical NGOs.[468][469] They were going to package and distribute condoms through bodegas as if they were any other consumer product and place them alongside Coca-Cola.

But Harvey and Black didn't just want to help abroad. They wanted to address the issue of teen pregnancy at home in the United States. Black was familiar with the condoms-by-mail programs that were popular in European countries, and he suggested this approach to Harvey. When they began researching a condoms-by-mail program, they were surprised that condoms weren't being sold this way in the United States They soon discovered why. Thanks to 19th-century censor Anthony Comstock's law, selling condoms in the United States directly to consumers remained illegal. However, there was a recent Supreme Court decision—*Griswold v. Connecticut* (1965)—that made selling condoms to married people legal. This was the opening they needed. Although they couldn't be assured that only married people were buying their condoms, they did possibly have some sort of cover. They were taking a serious legal risk, however. Harvey and Black contemplated whether changing the world was worth the prospect of enduring jail time. Black had two young kids and a wife at the time. He was risking a lot. But they decided it was.[470]

So, in 1970, Harvey stayed in the United States to start their condoms-by-mail business in North Carolina, which they called Population Planning Associates (PPA), while Black flew to Kenya to start the social marketing nonprofit with help from USAID.[471] Instead of combining advocacy and capitalism into one entity as Williams had done with Eve's Garden, Harvey and Black decided to break it up into two separate organizations. It was a bold choice, and there was no guarantee it would work.

PPA took out their first ads for the condom business in college newspapers, then moved on to national magazines like *Stag* and *Penthouse*. The orders started flooding in. "The fact that nobody was selling condoms by mail made it very easy to make money doing it because no one was doing it," Harvey said.[472] Since neither Black nor Harvey had ever taken a business course, they weren't sure how to proceed. "Tim and I sat down one afternoon and said, 'Well, there seems to be more money coming in than going out. I guess that's called profit and maybe we should pursue [the business],'" Harvey explained later. Their success took them by surprise. "The profit-making business was almost accidental," Harvey said. The condoms-by-mail business wasn't necessarily meant to be long term. Harvey's goal was, after all, helping women with family planning in the developing world. But he talked to Black and they decided that if the business kept going at the same rate, perhaps some of their profits could help fund the nonprofit.[473] "The thought of a Robin Hood business selling contraceptives and sexual accoutrements to the relatively wealthy citizens of the United States in order to generate funds to subsidize the sale of contraceptives in poor countries struck us as marvelous," Harvey said.[474]

In 1972, a change in the U.S. law occurred. Women won the right to contraception whether they were married or not, thanks to the Supreme Court decision in *Eisenstadt v. Baird*. This was great news for American women, but it also meant that Harvey and Black were probably going to start having competition. They decided to expand by selling other products, starting first with books and magazines about sexual physiology and reproduction. It wasn't a particularly successful part of the business, as few people were interested in dry books on sex. Then, one day they added "erotic magazines with soft-focus nudity" to their inventory—and, according to Harvey, "sales took off."[475]

Although their erotic magazines were a success, not everything they tried was. Their venture into selling ship-building kits, digital clocks, and leather belts failed. Consumers seemed to only want sex-related products. So around 1973 they sought out a different product to add: vibrators.[476] But they didn't advertise their vibrators as sex toys, even when they were placing ads in *Playgirl*, a newly created sex magazine for women. They sold their vibrator as a "health and beauty aid" that was "perfect for every part of the body: scalp massage, facial toning, penetrating spot massage."[477] It wasn't too different than the vibrator ads from the early 1900s. Sold this way, the vibrators ended up faring about as well as the sex physiology books. Perhaps the advertising was to blame or it was that 80 percent of their customers were men. Maybe men either didn't want to buy vibrators for their girlfriends or didn't think they could use vibrators themselves.[478] But PPA did continue to keep vibrators in their inventory.

That same year, in 1973, Harvey and Black had a new thing to worry about, as obscenity law was redefined once again in the Supreme Court case *Miller v. California*. Before *Miller*, a work was considered obscene if it was "without redeeming social significance" and it violated national community standards of obscenity. After *Miller*, a work was obscene if it "violated community standards," "depicts or describes, in a patently offensive way, sexual conduct specifically defined by the applicable state (or federal) law," and "taken as whole, lacks serious literary, artistic, political, or scientific value." Fear of prosecution was magnified by *Miller* because a national company could be prosecuted based on the community standards of a conservative locale. Producers of obscenity could be prosecuted in multiple locales, greatly increasing the legal fees. Because most sex-toy companies had to distribute their wares via nationally distributed erotic catalogs, they were also at great risk. This meant that a sex-toy ad prosecuted as obscene in Texas might be considered legal in California.

Around the same time, Harvey and Black expanded their nonprofit, Population Services International (PSI). In 1974, Black moved from Kenya to London to start a European branch of PSI.[479] A year later, Black learned that the famed birth control clinic founded by female sex pioneer Dr. Marie Stopes in 1921 was struggling and entering bankruptcy. He contemplated moving PSI's headquarters to the historic location where Dr. Stopes had founded the first birth control clinic in London. Although Stopes had been a eugenicist (as was common among birth control pioneers at the time), she was also ahead of her time. Stopes believed that both wives and husbands should have orgasms during sex, an idea she spread in her 1918 sex advice book, *Married Love*, which became a bestseller.[480] Black didn't want to see Stopes's historic clinic disappear. So, he; his wife, Jean; and Phil Harvey decided to purchase the lease together in November 1975. In January 1976, they reopened the space and renamed their organization Marie Stopes International, in honor of the birth control pioneer.[481]

(*)

As Black and Harvey were selling porn and condoms with the hopes of bringing contraceptives to millions of women worldwide, Reuben Sturman was in Europe selling the same stuff with grandiose but very different goals. While Black was across the pond to start his nonprofit, Sturman was there to stash his profits away from the prying eyes of the Internal Revenue Service. All obscenity charges from the 1968 case against him, his ex-wife, and his brother Joe had been dismissed.[482] [483] But, spooked by the indictment, Joe had left Sturman's company to start his own smelting business, leaving Sturman one man short.[484] Despite the promise he made to his wife that he would never allow his children to work in the business, Sturman sent his son David to work with Braverman in Europe.

Although Sturman had escaped prosecution, his relationship with the government remained contentious. There were numerous raids on his warehouses, followed by those obscenity charges. At some point, Sturman decided that the government didn't deserve to get any of the fortune he was making from his hundreds of businesses, and he stopped paying taxes on a big chunk of his income. Sturman figured it would be easy; if you want to avoid taxes, it helps to be amassing a large portion of your fortune in quarters, which Sturman was with his peep-show booths. "That was his downfall," said his son David. "He thought he could get away with it."[485]

Aware that he was being monitored by the U.S. government, Sturman became paranoid. He set up closed-circuit cameras outside the company headquarters for his Sovereign News in Cleveland, built a barbed-wire fence, and created an imposing fortress. But he wasn't aware that he was being monitored overseas also. The FBI had assigned an agent, George Grosz, to work full-time on Sturman's case in December 1973, and soon the IRS hired Richard Rosfelder, another man whose goal was to take down Sturman.

This wasn't Sturman's first trip to Switzerland. He had been hiding his profits there for a while and also moving his cash to banks in the Cayman

Islands and the Bahamas. Switzerland was a great place to stash earnings because the Swiss had strict nondisclosure laws. But in October 1974, Sturman made a mistake. He opened account under a fake name—Paul Bekker—with his fake passport. Swiss officials soon discovered what was going on and arrested Sturman in Zurich. Sturman was sentenced to a month in prison and banned from Switzerland for three years.

Then he made another mistake. Sturman sent his son David and a lawyer to withdraw funds from another Swiss bank where they were stashing profits. Per Sturman's instructions, they tried not to leave a paper trail, withdrawing the $400,000 in cash and twenty-two gold bars, which they carried out on a cart and transferred to a new bank.[486] But the FBI was documenting the monetary transfers, and Swiss authorities immediately alerted Grosz and the IRS to Sturman's money transfers.[487]

Meanwhile, Sturman gave his associate Ron Braverman an even bigger responsibility in 1975: running the fifteen London adult bookstores Sturman's company owned. Braverman had learned about England's sex-toy scene, and Sturman and his employees had used Braverman's insights to improve Sturman's sex-toy business at home. They decided to create a brand for the sex toys and lubes they were selling and hire more women to work in their stories.[488] That was the positive side. The negative: Sturman got Braverman involved in laundering money. In September 1975, using the pseudonym John Hastings, Braverman deposited a check for $95,000.[489] That deposit would come back to haunt him.

While Braverman managed Sturman's stores in London, the FBI cracked down on Sturman in Cleveland. In 1975, agents raided Sturman's Sovereign News warehouse. It was finally time to get their man. They used a sledgehammer to batter down the steel-plated door. Once inside, they seized a huge amount of Sturman's corporate records.[490] The documents held the secrets to Sturman's complex web of porn and sex-toy stores, including all the corporate names, bank account details, and tax ID numbers.[491] The records revealed the enormous scope of Sturman's empire. The government later claimed that Sturman was selling either porn or sex toys or both to every state in the United States and in forty foreign countries. Not only was he selling to a huge number of stores, but he also owned many of the stores he was selling to. He was making money twice: on the sale to the store and on the store's sale to the customer. And it wasn't small amounts of money either. In Southern California alone, the porn and sex-toy business was estimated to be $70 million annually, and Sturman virtually controlled the industry there. He had become a very rich man.[492]

Yet the richer he became, the warier he became. He began keeping a loaded handgun in an office drawer. He employed the National Polygraph Company to conduct lie-detector tests to ensure that his prospective employees weren't federal agents. There was a major irony in this. Because he demanded loyalty, he ended up persuading many of his employees to lie for him. Sturman refused to give interviews to the press and didn't want his picture taken. It was no wonder. The less information people had about him, the better.[493]

(*)

As Sturman focused on becoming a rich man, his biggest supplier of sex toys, Marche Manufacturing, was giving them away to charity and constructing them for researchers. One day in 1975 or 1976, Dr. John Money, a sex researcher from Johns Hopkins, contacted Ted Marche with a request: could he make a "juvenile-sized" artificial penis for a little boy born with a microphallus? Marche was accustomed at that point to fielding calls and letters from doctors all over the country. If a doctor needed a prosthetic limb for a patient or even a prosthetic breast or testicle, they could easily obtain one from a medical supplier. However, if they wanted a prosthetic penis, they had to come to Marche. "Almost unbelievably, there is also no source of artificial penis, except the hit-and-miss, mail-order business on the semi-pornographic market," wrote the authors of *The Report of the Commission on Obscenity and Pornography* in 1970.[494] Doctors were in dire need of artificial penises for their patients, who needed them for a variety of different reasons, from being born with misshapen genitalia to injuries sustained during war. Doctors were trying to find ways for patients to have satisfying sex lives or for children to have normal lives. Marche went to work creating the boy's prosthetic penis.

Dr. Money's patient was lucky that Money had suggested an artificial penis and not a sex reassignment, as was Money's default treatment for children born with microphallus, a disorder defined as the penis being "two or more standard deviations below the norm" of the average penis.[495] In fact, around the same time that Dr. Money was commissioning Marche to create a special prosthetic penis, he was also treating another patient named Bruce Reimer (later called David) who had an "abnormal" penis. Instead of prescribing an artificial penis for Reimer, Money had decided on a different, more dangerous course. Unlike the boy with the microphallus, Reimer had been born with a normal penis. But when he was a baby, nearly all of his penis was cut off during a botched circumcision. Reimer's parents took their son to Money for a consultation, and he suggested they raise Reimer as a girl.

In retrospect this seems crazy, but Money so strongly believed that gender was learned and not innate that he thought Reimer's parents could raise him as a girl and he would come to be one. Money convinced Reimer's parents that their son should have his testicles removed via surgery. And they did indeed raise Bruce as Brenda. Money heralded the Bruce/Brenda case as proof of his gender theory, penning a 1972 book about the case. He probably would have made the same suggestion to the parents of the boy with the microphallus if they had taken the boy in to see him when he was a baby. He even hints at this in his article about the boy, writing that when the boy was a baby there was "no record

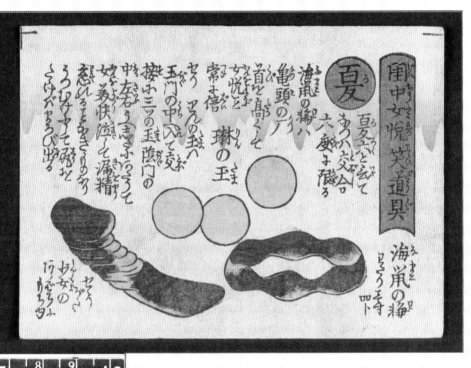

✻ "Sex Toys for Women's Pleasure in the Bedroom. Summer Sea-cucumber Ring, Jewel Balls, Small Dildo," by Japanese artist Keisai Eisen. A print from the early 19th century depicting specific sex toys intended to be used during the four seasons of the year.
[© The Trustees of the British Museum.]

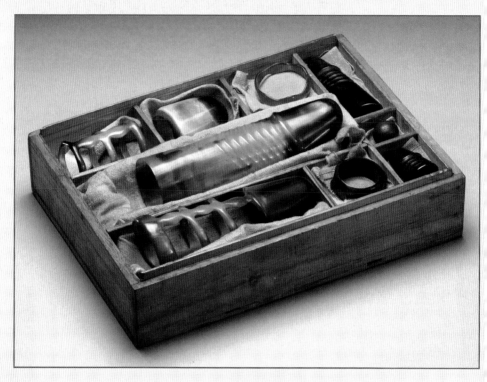

✱ A sex aid kit from late 19th century/early 20th century Japan.
It included six different dildos and penis "supports," as well as two rings and a
Ben Wa–type ball. All items were made of horn and metal.
[© The Trustees of the British Museum.]

✱ Patented in 1892, Young's dilators were some of the most widely advertised
rectal dilators available. [A Gift of M E Vaill, Division of Medicine & Science,
National Museum of American History, Smithsonian Institution.]

✱ Young's Dilators were sold via ads that appeared in both medical journals and popular health magazines in the early 1900s. Here is an ad that appeared in *Health* in 1904. [Reprinted with permission.]

✱ A 1912 advertisement for Hamilton Beach's New Life Vibrator, where some run-of-the-mill ailments—like indigestion—are made to look sexy. [Reprinted with permission from *The Des Moines News.*]

* The "White Cross Electric Vibrator Girl" as pictured in a 1911 "Health and Beauty catalog. [Courtesy American Medical Association Archives.

* Hamilton Beach Type C Vibrator Promotional Booklet circa 1920.

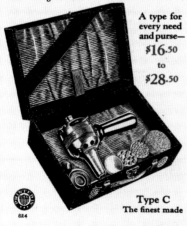

Hamilton Beach Vibrator

A vibrator represents such a small outlay in comparison with what it does to build up run down tissues and give tone to all the vital organs, that everyone can afford the best. Because of its inbuilt quality and fine workmanship, the Hamilton Beach has achieved a reputation for full value and life time service. Made by the world's largest producer of household motors, naturally it is better—*and guaranteed.*

A type for
every need
and purse—
$16.50
to
$28.50

Type C
The finest made

824

Why miss the Super-pleasures of life

✱ An ad promoting a December 1959 event with Ted Marche and his ventriloquist doll Georgie. [Courtesy of *Press-Courier*, Oxnard, CA.]

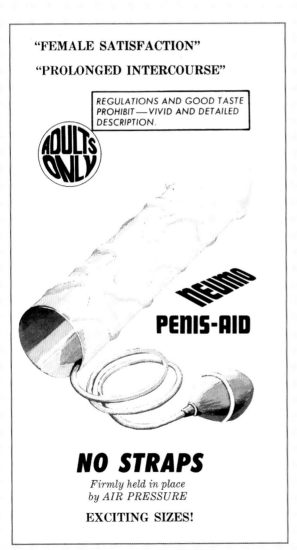

✱ A Neumo Penis-Aid, likely made by Marche sometime in the early 1970s. [From the Kinsey Institute's Sex Aids Dealers collection (U.S. 20th Century 1960). Courtesy of Kinsey Institute.]

✱ Small silver or brass balls meant to be worn inside the vagina, Ben Wa balls date back to at least the 1800s in Japan and likely earlier. They were introduced to the U. S. market in the 1970s. [Courtesy of Doc Johnson.]

✱ Image of "Jake" with hand-lettered text from the first Pleasure Chest catalog, circa 1971. [Courtesy of the Pleasure Chest.]

HERE'S JAKE WHO'S INCREASING THE SIZE OF HIS DONG WITH THE OSIRIS SIZATOMETER, A SAFE VACUUM DEVICE THAT PRODUCES AN ERECTION, LENGTHENS AND ENLARGES THE PENIS, AND BRINGS A NEW DIMENSION TO THE ART OF MASTURBATION. OR, AS JAKE SAYS, "IT GIVES YA A HARDON, MAKES YOUR COCK BIGGER, AND MAKES JERKIN' OFF MORE FUN!" THE SIZATOMETER IS LIGHT-WEIGHT AND VERY EASY TO USE: JUST SLIP YOUR TOOL INTO THE VACUUM CYLINDER, PRESS THE SOFT RUBBER GASKET AGAINST YOUR BODY, AND START PUMPING. YOU'LL BE AMAZED AT THE RESULTS. WE'VE HAD ELEVATOR SHOES, PADDED SHOULDERS, FALSE TEETH, AND TOUPEES; NOW - FOR THE FIRST TIME - YOU CAN ADD INCHES TO YOUR COCK. AND THE SIZATOMETER IS COMPLETELY SAFE AND BUILT TO LAST. IT'S EXPERTLY ASSEMBLED BY HAND CRAFTSMEN FROM THE HIGHEST QUALITY ACRYLIC TUBING, BRASS, AND STAINLESS STEEL. IT'S EVEN GOT THE GOOD HAND-HUMPING SEAL OF APPROVAL. JAKE SAYS HE WOULDN'T BE CAUGHT SOFT WITHOUT IT. GET YOURS AT THE PLEASURE CHEST NOW - IT'S ONLY $24.95. REMEMBER, YOU GET MORE OUT OF A SIZATOMETER THAN YOU PUT IN IT.

⋆ Betty Dodson selling vibrators at NOW-NYC Women's Sexuality Conference, July 1973. [© Betty Dodson Foundation.]

⋆ Farley Malorrus of United Sales and Ben Wa Novelty Corp. in 1976. [Courtesy of Farley Malorrus.]

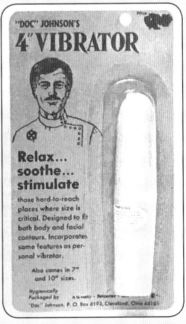

⋆ An ad for a 4" vibrator from the first Doc Johnson catalog in 1976. The hanging display packaging was a marketing innovation in sex toys, as was the use of an advertising mascot. [Courtesy of Doc Johnson.]

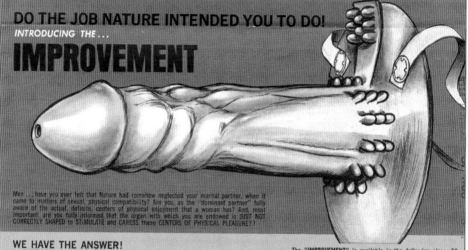
★ An advertisement (circa 1977) for the Coital Training Device, a dildo kit similar to the one sold by Ted Marche and Fred and Farley Malorrus. This device featured a clitoral stimulator. [From the Kinsey Institute's Sex Aids Dealers collection (U.S. 20th Century 1960-1979). Courtesy of Kinsey Institute.]

THERAPEUTIC SEX AIDS

Penile Prostheses and Sex Aid Devices developed and manufactured by a paraplegic for use by paraplegics and quadriplegics and their mates.

Technical assistance given by women and men who are medical doctors, psychologists, social workers, physical therapists, paras and quads.

PENILE PROSTHESES

Size:

No. 1, 1 3/8 x 6"
No. 2, 1½ x 6"
No. 3, 1 5/8 x 7"
No. 4, 1 3/4 x 6"
No. 5, 1 3/4 x 7"
No. 6, 1 3/4 x 8"
No. 7, 2 x 6"   (State Waist and
No. 8, 2 x 8"   Hip size)

No. 1   No. 2   No. 3   No. 4
$19.95 $25.95 $25.95 $29.95   No. 1.
                                    ..Feels like flesh!
No. 5   No. 6   No. 7   No. 8
$29.95 $35.95 $39.95 $39.95

Colors: Caucasian, Mulatto, Negroid, Black.

Kit Includes: Penile Prosthesis, Body Harness and Lubricant.

  Therapeutic Sex Aids as featured in Gosnell Duncan's catalog, circa 1975. [From the author's personal collection.]

* Joyce Farmer, "Cover," in *Tits & Clits Comix*, no. 3. Laguna Beach, Ca.: Nanny Goat Productions. [© Joyce Farmer 1977.]

✶ An artificial vagina, likely one sold by Malorrus's United Sales in the 1970s. [Courtesy of Kinsey Institute. Sex Aids Dealers (U.S. 20th Century, 1960-1979.)]

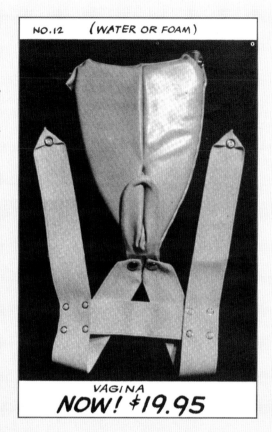

NO.12   (WATER OR FOAM)

VAGINA
NOW! $19.95

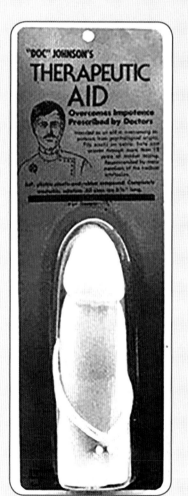

"DOC" JOHNSON'S
THERAPEUTIC AID

✶ "Doc" Johnson Therapeutic Aid. According to the package, it "Overcomes Impotence" and is "Prescribed by Doctors." Doc Johnson catalog, 1981, p. 13. [Courtesy of Doc Johnson.]

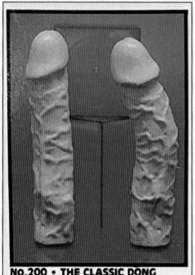

NO.200 • **THE CLASSIC DONG**
Life-like firm, fleshy replica of 8" penis.
#200, white. #201, black. #202, brown.

NO.204 • **THE BENDER**
Dong with pliable insert curves & bends.
#204, white. #205, black. #206, brown.

* Typical dildos from the 1980s. Doc Johnson Catalog, 1988, p. 26. [Courtesy of Doc Johnson.]

* Duane Colglazier (left) at a Pleasure Chest Party in West Hollywood in the early 1980s. [Courtesy of The Pleasure Chest.]

* Doc Johnson's Ron Braverman in the company's catalog, circa 1981. [Courtesy of Doc Johnson.]

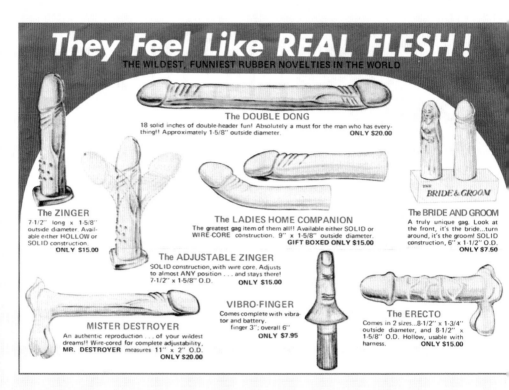

✷ United Sales' Ladies Home Companion and Mister Destroyer Dildos (among others). The dildos are referred to as "the wildest, funniest rubber novelties in the world." Circa early 1970s. [Courtesy of Kinsey Institute.]

✷ A picture of Joani Blank (center) from a Good Vibrations catalog circa 1990. [From the author's personal collection. Courtesy of photographer Jill Posner.]

photo by Jill Posener

Top (l to r): Anne, Roma, Karen, Mariane; middle: Mikki, Laura, Meadow; bottom: Carol, Joani, Cathy

The Magic Wand by Hitachi

The MAGIC WAND is known the world over as the "Cadillac" of vibrators for its precision-made quality, durability and versatility. Originally marketed specifically for body massage, women everywhere began to discover how joyfully pleasurable it was for masturbation. And, with it's flexible soft-vinyl head the MAGIC WAND is just ideal for two since it can stimulate both persons simultaneously! This handsome pleasure-instrument has a grip-contoured ivory plastic body, operates on AC 110-120 V 6 hp, 20W, weighs only 22 ounces, and operates on both "low" and "high" speed control. Now, at last, a MAGIC WAND that will truly transport you to heaven. UL Approved.
(HV250) $39.00

✱ The Hitachi Magic Wand—"the 'Cadillac' of vibrators"—as featured in a 1989 Eve's Garden Catalog. [From the author's personal collection. Courtesy of Dell Williams Estate.]

✱ Happy Penis Massage Cream, a favorite of some home-party companies. [Courtesy of Lubezilla.]

✱ A photo of Dell Williams in 1989 from the Eve's Garden catalog of that year. [From the author's personal collection. Courtesy of Dell Williams Estate.]

✳ A Pocket Rocket—one of
Doc Johnson's most popular items.
[Courtesy of Doc Johnson.]

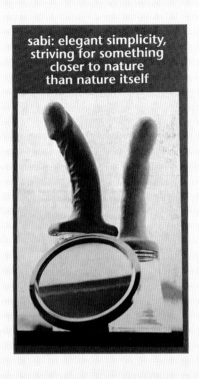

sabi: elegant simplicity, striving for something closer to nature than nature itself

* An advertisement for Gosnell Duncan's dildos from the November/December 1989 issue of *On Our Backs*. [Photograph by Honey Lee Cottrell.]

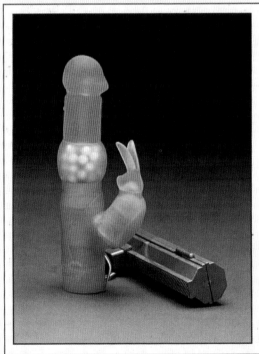

Rabbit Pearl

The first of its kind, the Rabbit Pearl has rotating "pearls" in the middle of the gyrating shaft to give extra delight. The rabbit ears work magic in this winning combination for sheer satisfaction.

* The first iteration of the famed "Rabbit" vibrator as pictured in the 1997 Vibratex print catalog. [Courtesy of Vibratex.]

✳ The first page of *Girls Turned into Vibrator Zombies* , from Weirdo #8.
[Reprinted with permission. © Robert Crumb, Dori Seda and Terry Zwigoff 1983.]

of whether or not the appropriateness of sex reassignment as a female was considered."[496] Money's theory that gender is 100 percent learned was proved false, at least in the case of Brenda. Brenda always felt that she was a boy. It wasn't until more than a decade, when Brenda was an adult, that she transitioned into a man, changed her name to David, received testosterone injections, had a penis constructed and married a woman. But he'd struggled his whole life with this gross medical mistake. He eventually killed himself at age thirty-eight.[497]

Money's choice to fit the boy with microphallus with an artificial penis instead of a sex reassignment quite possibly saved his life. But Money, the boy, and his parents didn't know this at the time. The boy was a foster child whose agency had sent him to Johns Hopkins endocrine clinic after noticing the small size of his penis shaft (1 cm/0.4 inches) when he was nine months old. No treatments were started at the time, and "the boy was lost to follow up," Money later reported in his records. A few years later, a couple went to the foster home looking for a child and they fell in love with the toddler at first sight. The agency told the couple that the boy's penis would grow larger over time. By the time he was nearly two years old, his penis hadn't grown, so they took him to Johns Hopkins.[498]

Money began the boy's treatment with a prescription for testosterone cream. After two months, his penis had grown from just over a tiny 0.4 inch (1 cm) to just under a full inch (2.4 cm). Then the growth stopped. Money had to find a different form of treatment.

When the boy was seven, Money broached the idea of him wearing an artificial penis, and the boy seemed to be open to that. But Money waited two years to bring the penis up again. "What do you think about wearing a prosthetic phallus?" Money asked him when the boy was nearing ten years old.

"I would be better off," the boy reportedly replied. When he came home from the doctor's office, he excitedly declared to his father, "I am going to have an artificial penis!"

Money contacted Marche to design and produce a smaller model of his dildo. Marche, according to Money, was "exceptionally cooperative and enthusiastic." Four weeks later, Marche finished the dildo and shipped it to Money. The boy came with his parents to pick it up and began "smiling and jumping about the office" with joy.

His parents modified the dildo to place a hole in it so that their son could urinate while standing up. They also attached the artificial penis to a jockstrap so he could wear it all the time. He began wearing it most days of the week, all day long. After a year of wearing the device, he said "it feels good" and he "feels happy about it." Although Money was critical of the artificial penis for not being "ideal in either size or flesh-colored tint," he said it undoubtedly was "therapeutically beneficial" for the boy, "enhancing his self-esteem and self-confidence as a male." Based on this experience with the boy, Money suggested that other young boys with microphalluses should be fitted with artificial penises early in their lives, so that they could be incorporated into their body images.[499]

Money believed that it was the taboo surrounding prosthetic penises had led young adults with microphallus and transsexual disorders to not use them. As he wrote in 1977, "All who may benefit from using an artificial penis need time and counseling in order not to feel stigmatized by reason of using a device that, for the most part in our society, is scorned as freakish, bragged about as a joke, or reviled as immoral."[500] The taboo against sex toys was actually hurting the most vulnerable members of society, Money noted: little boys with "abnormal genitals" and those who didn't fit neatly into the standard gender roles.

Marche was not outwardly the type of pioneer as, say, Harvey, Black, or Williams, but his open-mindedness and desire to help people led him to put compassion over profits. Marche's philanthropic spirit meant that he ended up donating a lot of artificial penises to children's hospitals and

HALLIE LIEBERMAN

medical companies, like Medical Sales Associates. "Dad would give away more schmucks and vaginas that you could shake a stick at," said his son. This ended up hurting their bottom line, but his son made sure that they actually could make a profit or at least a successful barter. One of the items they frequently traded their devices for? Per'Als Cheesecake, which was manufactured next door to the Marche factory. It was more than worth the cost of a few strap-ons.

Marche's work with Money was par for the course for him. "Many doctors would call and say, 'Teddy we have this client, and we need it some certain size for a patient,'" his son said. Marche insisted on using his dildos to improve lives. Marche made all his dildos to medical-grade specifications, even though there was no real incentive to do so.[501] The industry was not regulated by the FDA at the time.[502]

Although Ted Marche was generous, he must not have been giving away too many of his dildos. By 1976, the Marches had sold nearly five million of them. They were also producing or distributing 350 other sex products. "Sales [at Marche Manufacturing] have risen an average 28% each year since 1970," reported *Time* magazine in April 1976. "These toys have saved more marriages than all the preachers in the world," Marche's son told *Time*.[503] After a decade in the business, Marche Manufacturing had come to dominate the U.S. sex-toy industry. It seemed as if there was no stopping them.

(* TEN)

Doc Johnson and Sisterhood

The Marches weren't the only ones raking in the profits from their dildos. Reuben Sturman was, too. His Sovereign News was distributing nearly all of Marche's sex toys and many of the Malor-ruses'.[504] While Marche had gone virtually ignored by the federal government, Sturman was being hounded continuously. Obscenity charge after obscenity charge was thrown at Sturman, but none of them stuck. He always emerged from court victorious. With his triumphs over the government and the huge amounts of money from his distribution business, stores (which numbered around three hundred), and peep-show booths, Sturman was becoming cocky. He was living large in his Tudor mansion in the swanky Shaker Heights neighborhood of Cleveland, dating a series of young women who worked for him, smoking fancy cigars, and tooling around town in a Mercedes.[505] And he wanted more.

Sturman saw how successful the Marches were becoming, how their sales were increasing year after year, and he wanted a part of it. Even though Sturman controlled the sex-toy and porn distribution and retail business in the United States (and was influential in Europe too), it was not enough. Sturman preferred to control every aspect of his business, from production to distribution. Vertical integration was what he was after. So in 1976, when Braverman returned from running Sturman's stores in Europe and realized that he loved merchandising sex toys, Sturman saw an opportunity.[506]

Depending on who you ask, either Sturman or Braverman decided to buy out their biggest supplier, Marche Manufacturing. The details on this sale are murky. Sturman's son claims his father bought Marche Manufacturing, while Braverman's son says his father bought it. Why did the Marches sell the business? Marche's son hinted that the equipment for the factory, like the automatic lines, was getting too expensive. The Malorruses were able to buy factory equipment on the cheap, he said, because Sturman was purchasing industrial equipment at a discount and then selling it to the Malorruses. However, Sturman wasn't offering the same lower-priced machinery to the Marches.

How much Marche sold his company for or what the conditions were will probably never be known. Braverman soon moved out to L.A. and began running the Marches' company in 1976. While most of Marche Manufacturing's thirty-two employees stayed on, Ted and his son left the sex-toy business entirely. Was this a condition of the deal, that they would never compete with Sturman? It very well could have been. Soon after selling Marche Manufacturing, Ted went back to being a ventriloquist, and his son started a new career as a hypnotist. Their debut was "a double gig at the L.A. athletic club." It may seem like a weird move, to go from designing dildos to lulling people into a hypnotic state, but Ted's son made the transition well. He was a skilled enough hypnotist that he paid his way through the California State University–Long Beach on gigs alone.[507]

Now that Sturman's company owned Marche Manufacturing, Sturman controlled both the production and distribution of most of the sex toys in the United States, and he owned the bulk of the retail outlets where sex toys were sold. He and Braverman began to revamp the sex-toy industry. Braverman says that, in the mid-1970s, sex toys were virtually ignored in adult bookstores. Most of the toys were kept in a glass case by the register, without any names or packaging. Marche's dildos sat alongside Malorruses' United Sales Company sex toys and those of smaller companies. Even though Marche or

United Sales would create lines of hundreds of products, each store would only carry a few. In a typical adult store, there were "five or six [sex toys] wrapped in frosted plastic bags" in the case "and somebody really had to know what they want to get," Braverman said.[508] There were only a few styles of vibrators or dildos. Most of the vibrators were ivory "flesh-colored" hard-plastic phallic shapes.[509] And even the few available sex toys were not ideal. Many of the dildos in the stores were huge because when men buy sex toys they are thinking of only one thing: size. Nearly half of all men think their penises are too small, and they assume that women do too.[510] "The basic understanding was that if the guy was six inches his significant other wanted eight inches," Braverman said. "The common thinking was that people wanted something bigger, wider, stronger, larger."[511] At the time, most adult stores "were about the 25-cent machines, magazines, paperback books, and eight millimeter," Braverman said.[512]

Those peep show machines were a problem: They were preventing half of the population from coming to adult stores, aside from Eve's Garden and the handful of Pleasure Chests. Anywhere there was a so-called 25-cent-machine, women stayed far away. They didn't want to be near the masturbating men in the little wooden booths. "It was an all 100 percent male business," Braverman said. "There were no females coming into the stores. There were no couples coming into the stores." Braverman wanted to change that.[513]

If Sturman had treated Marche Manufacturing like the porn companies that he bought, he would have simply folded it into his empire with little impact on the sex-toy industry. But Reuben Sturman, his son David, and Braverman decided to do something different. They decided to create a sex-toy brand that appealed to both men and women. In retrospect, this seems to have been an obvious thing to do. At the time, however, it was revolutionary. Although Marche had designed sex toys with women in mind, he didn't have a brand. Reuben and David Sturman were going to change that.

Since Sturman was still being regularly indicted on obscenity charges, they needed a brand that was not very sexual. They brainstormed for a while and came up with the name "Doc Johnson." A number of myths have emerged around the origins of the name. Some believe that Johnson was chosen because it's a euphemism for penis, while others say that it was an homage to the Johnson commission's obscenity report. But Braverman said that neither story is true. Braverman just wanted a familiar name. "He didn't really want to call it doctor, but he wanted it to be a little more friendly . . . like the neighborhood doc . . . a nickname," Ron's son Chad Braverman said.[514]

Following the model of McDonald's and other prominent brands, Braverman and Sturman decided to create a fictional character to embody their brand. The character had to legitimize sex toys and telegraph a sense of trust. An upright penis with a stethoscope hanging from its neck just wouldn't cut it. They came up with a genial, mustachioed male doctor, wearing a 1950s-era-style doctor's coat with a Nehru collar and barely a hint of a smile on his face. "You go in to buy toothpaste, you don't say toothpaste, you say 'Crest,'" Ron Braverman told *Forbes* magazine in 1978. "We want people to say 'Doc Johnson.'"[515] Although in the UK and Germany, mainstream sex-toy brands had been named after women—Ann Summers and Beate Uhse—in the United States this was not to be the case. Perhaps it was because a woman's name conveyed feminism and niche markets.

Choosing a male doctor to represent a line of sex toys and other products made sense not only because it conveyed authority but also because giving sex toys a medical sheen is an old American tradition dating back to the 19th and early 20th centuries when butt plugs, vaginal dilators, and vibrators had been sold as medical devices as a way to get around obscenity prosecutions.

Sturman and Braverman wanted Doc Johnson to be mainstream because their goal was to get sex toys into all sorts of retail environments, from supermarkets to drugstores, where vibrators were already being sold, albeit not as sex toys. "I was hoping my products would go everywhere. I was hoping that the audience would go beyond the men in these stores," Braverman said.[516] Doc Johnson saw their main competition as Hitachi with the Magic Wand that feminists loved, as well as General Electric, which sold a line of vibrators, and Water Pik.[517] One way to get more retail stores to carry Doc Johnson was to sell them in carded packages that could hang from the wall, so they could be prominently displayed.

Another way Braverman and Sturman made sex toys seem more socially acceptable was by referring to them as "marital aids." Doc Johnson wasn't the first company to call their sex toys marital aids, but they were the most prominent company to do so and the first to create a real brand around the idea. Unlike Eve's Garden's liberatory vibrators, which were meant to free women from relationships with men, Doc Johnson marital aids were framed to keep women tightly connected to their male partners. Although it's hard to imagine a nine-inch vibrating dong being bought to improve matrimonial bonds, Doc Johnson's strategy worked.

Even though this was the supposed era of porno-chic, the culture was still conservative, at least when it came to female sexuality and gender roles. In 1976, when Doc Johnson was founded, it had been only four years since unmarried women were legally able to access birth control, and only two years since women were able to open a checking account without a man cosigning. It is not surprising that, throughout their first catalog, Doc Johnson nodded to marriage and sexual convention, while also selling the unconventional. The cover featured a naked man and woman embracing on the beach during the sunset. Underneath the couple, the words "Marital Aids" was placed in bold type. While Betty Dodson was telling women that sex toys could drive them to sexual independence, Doc Johnson was telling them the opposite. If the cover didn't send the message clearly enough, then the inside of the catalog did. On the third page was a silhouette of a male and a female face with the text underneath reading, "Sit by my side. Let us view the ways of love together. Discover our fantasies. Create our future."[518]

Sex toys soaked up the meanings of whoever was promoting them. In one context, they embodied liberationist radical feminist values, while in another, they symbolized traditional gender and sexual roles. Feminists championed them for masturbation while traditionalists promoted them for monogamous heterosexual sex. Sex toys symbolized gay liberation in the Pleasure Chest and disability rights through Gosnell Duncan's newly renamed company Scoprio Products. Sex toys were always political, but the politics they embodied was up for grabs.

Good capitalists that they were, Braverman and Sturman crafted the Doc Johnson brand to appeal primarily to the widest demographic: monogamous heterosexuals. As their catalog read, in the section on penis extenders and French and German ticklers, "Doc Johnson has devoted many years to creating . . . devices for the purpose of bringing diversification to the monogamists."[519] That's not to say that they didn't sell products for gay men, but those were a smaller part of their inventory, and they were marketed in gay magazines like *The Advocate*.[520]

Soon after the purchase of Marche Manufacturing, Sturman and Braverman began opening more adult stores in the United States and overseas. These were the first chain stores devoted to sex toys and porn in America; the nation's first sex supermarkets. Like other chain outlets, Sturman's stores were uniform, with similar layouts, peep-show booths in the back, and shelves lined with porn videos, and Doc Johnson dildos and vibrators. Nevertheless, the stores were not always popular with the neighbors. In London's Soho neighborhood, they caused consternation because of the "men in dirty trench coats, and occasionally a woman" who browsed their wares.[521] Doc Johnson wasn't just about the rebranding of Marche's sex toys; it also involved the rebranding of some of Sturman's adult bookstores. According to FBI notes about one of the early meetings at Doc Johnson, it was decided that the first store "will be a pseudoscientific type of establishment (white coats, etc.) More rubber goods. More professional-type advertising; bondage-type clothing and items."[522]

Thanks to Sturman and Braverman, Marche Manufacturing had finally overtaken their nemesis the Malorruses. Fred Malorrus was none too happy about this. Years later in an interview with the *Wall Street Journal*, Malorrus attributed Doc Johnson's success to Sturman's "near-monopoly on distribution."[523]

(*)

It wasn't just the Malorruses' company, United Sales, that was facing tough times. Farley Malorrus was too. Around the time that Marche Manufacturing became Doc Johnson, Farley Malorrus found out his wife was a lesbian. The blow to his ego was enormous. Even after they divorced, he found himself unable to manage his blow-up doll company, Bosko's Oso, and it started to fall apart. He shut down the company and came limping back to his father at United Sales. Fred took his son back; he needed the help because he had a formidable competitor on his hands in the form of Reuben Sturman.

Malorrus's relationship with Sturman's company was complicated. Through Doc Johnson's wholesale catalog, Sturman was distributing a wide variety of United Sales products, from their bogus Spanish Fly Sugar to their dildos. But now that Sturman was in the manufacturing business, he had become a direct competitor.[524]

Fortunately, Farley had an idea for a new product he wanted to introduce to the American market. It would be new to the United States, but it was actually one of the oldest sex toys around: ben wa balls. Farley suggested they add the new toy to their line. Malorrus said they were too expensive to import.

Farley told Fred they could do it on the cheap by gold-plating ball bearings. "They won't chime, but we'll put them in a jewelry box, cost us a dime to gold plate them, a nickel for the box," Farley told his father. "Wholesale them for two bucks and retail them for twenty."[525] Because ben wa balls rarely gave women orgasms, they weren't an ideal sex toy from a woman's point of view. But from a man's point of view, they were a good toy. They came in a nice gift package and they weren't threatening. No woman was going to replace her man with two small balls that sat in the vagina like weights.

(*)

When it came to vibrators, there was some reason for men to be concerned. Their fear was not completely unfounded. As one customer wrote to Eve's Garden, "P.S. My lover is afraid a vibrator will replace him—he may be right!"[526]

Did vibrators cause women to end their marriages? At least one letter to Dell Williams points to yes. Can the vibrator be solely to blame? Probably not. As Louis C.K. says, "No good marriage has ever ended in divorce." But vibrators may have offered the push to get women to open their eyes to another world of sexual possibility. Vibrators did change women's lives for a very simple reason: They gave women the first orgasms of their lives. These weren't teenagers either; they were women in their thirties and forties. A first orgasm is memorable at any age, but to have one after years of sexual relationships is even more profound. These women began to question why, after decades in a relationship, they had never felt sexual satisfaction. And they began to wonder what else their lives had been lacking, which led them to question the gender roles that had defined their lives.

"I am 40 and left my husband of 20 years recently. I might add, I left him after masturbating to orgasm for the first time in my life," a woman in Texas wrote to Williams in 1976. The woman said that she had stayed sexually unsatisfied for twenty years because she was waiting for her husband to "turn a magic key and all my sexuality would be reborn, my family would not condemn it, neither would the church, nor society. It would be ACCEPTABLE!" When that magic key never appeared, her sexual frustration mounted, and it led her to become "bitter about him, my role in marriage, and the whole world in general." Yet she stayed married, even as she realized that "keeping a spotless house and doing all the expected and 'proper' things simply didn't cut it—something was ghastly, horribly wrong." Her revelation had echoes of Betty Friedan's "problem that has no name," the dissatisfaction of being a housewife, but her epiphany that she would no longer settle for these stultifying gender roles came not from a political awakening but from an orgasmic one. It was only when she "started masturbating to orgasm" that her "new life began." Not only did she leave her husband; she was in no rush to get a new one. "I have had a lot of overtures from men," she wrote, "but I'm determined that I will never have another man if he doesn't love and desire sex like I do."[527]

Not all women who bought vibrators wanted to leave their relationships. Others were trying to save them. Barbara wrote to Eve's Garden out of desperation because her hysterectomy had left her unable to have an orgasm and the hormones her doctor had prescribed didn't help. "I have a husban [*sic*] that don't want to be marry [*sic*] to me anymore because of my condition," she wrote. "I still love him but can't please him, please send me your catalog or some advice."[528]

Williams, though, was not as interested in saving marriages as she was in enlightening women. So even though Barbara was writing to Williams for advice on how to fix her marriage, Williams suggested that Barbara purchase books on masturbation along with a vibrator. Ignoring Barbara's plea for advice on how to "please" her husband, Williams implied that Barbara should become orgasmic for her own sake, instead of her husband's.[529]

Williams wasn't against women using vibrators to improve relationships, but it wasn't her main goal. Like Marche, she received multiple letters from customers who claimed vibrators had salvaged their marriages. "Thank's [*sic*] to you my marriage is back together. I love you all so much," a woman wrote to Eve's Garden.[530]

Eve's Garden didn't just cause women to reevaluate their relationships. The nonjudgmental pro-sex message of the store and catalog also inspired women to explore their sexual orientation. Though Williams herself was bisexual, Eve's Garden's catalog wasn't overtly bisexual or lesbian focused. Yet Williams made sure that lesbians knew they were welcome by advertising in lesbian magazines like *off our backs*.[531] And lesbians made up about half of Eve's Garden's customers.[532] "I still remember, (when I was first coming out of the closet) out of curiosity ringing the bell to the first Eve's Garden," wrote K.C., a New York City–based woman, to Williams in 1977. As the store moved locations around New York City, K. C. came to visit, becoming progressively comfortable with sex toys and her sexuality. "You have helped me realize [my] coming out everywhere," she wrote, adding that she could now purchase a "Magic Wand without any embarrassment." For K.C., masturbation, sex toys, and sexual identity were intimately intertwined. Because Eve's Garden helped her to shed the shame surrounding sex toys and masturbation, she was also able to come to terms with her lesbianism. "You helped me hang up the heterosexual rules and made my life the happiest it's ever been," she said.[533]

Other newly out lesbians who were struggling with feelings of isolation saw Eve's Garden as a beacon that gave them a sense of community and acceptance that they were unable to find elsewhere. A woman named Debby wrote to Eve's Garden to share how sex toys had allowed her to finally have an orgasm after years of struggle. An incest survivor with multiple sclerosis, Debby "had no [sexual] feeling for close to three years." She was also struggling with her newfound openness about her sexual identity. "I've just come out two years ago and am proud to say so," she said. However, in spite of her openness about her sexuality (or because of it) she was "very lonesome." The Eager Beaver vibrator she bought from Eve's Garden did not alleviate her loneliness, but it did bring her sexual pleasure, which was revelatory. "I had the most beautiful flow of feeling and warmth I never thought possible [sic] my love goes out to you all."[534]

These letters proved to Williams that sex toys could possibly lead to social change—that the tagline on the buttons that she sold in her store, "Orgasmic Women Can Change the World," might actually come true someday.[535] She decided it might be time to spread Eve's Garden throughout the nation. If Sturman could create a successful chain of sex-toy and porn stores for men, surely there was room for a female equivalent.

Williams needed to find someone to open a second retail store, and she knew just who to ask: Lynette Brannon, who lived in Austin, Texas. Williams had met Brannon a few years earlier, and they had become fast friends; Williams had taken Lynette with her to Dodson's workshop. Brannon loved it. She too was transformed by Dodson's class. Williams adopted Brannon into the progressive feminist sex fold. "I unlearned a lot of the negative messages about my sexuality that I grew up with," Brannon wrote. Inspired, Brannon decided that she wanted to make a difference too in women's sex lives; she just wasn't sure how.[536] So when Williams suggested she open Eve's Garden in Austin, Brannon saw it as the perfect opportunity.

Unlike the Sturman stores, Brannon's store was planned as intimate and low-key. Brannon set the store up in her apartment in late 1976, as Williams had done a few years earlier. The setup was minimal, and it seemed to only involve hanging "a golden brown batik bedspread" from the ceiling "to separate the kitchen from the boutique."[537] Williams then sold Brannon sex toys to stock her store with, and in January 1977, Brannon opened up the first Eve's Garden franchise, Eve's Garden Austin. Like the first Eve's Garden, it was for women only, so Brannon took out advertisements in local women's papers and hoped for the best. Williams had one major stipulation: that Brannon not process any mail-order sales, because that would compete with Williams. But Brannon pleaded with Williams that she needed to at least sell one product by mail to stay afloat, Dodson's *Liberating Masturbation.* "I make so little on the other books [that I sell in store], that I would like to do this one thing," Brannon wrote to Williams.[538] Williams gave in and let her sell Dodson's book. Brannon also began holding sex therapy workshops in the store, where she focused on topics including lesbian sexuality, erotic art, and masturbation. Her workshops had one big difference from Dodson's: the women remained fully clothed.[539]

In her catalog, Brannon also gave her store a catchy nickname, the Good Vibration Store, perhaps in homage to one of her inspirations, a sex educator named Joani Blank, who'd written two books that Brannon adored: *A Playbook for Women About Sex* and a more recent book about vibrators, *Good Vibrations*, which Brannon sold at Eve's Garden Austin.

(*)

Meanwhile, more than a thousand miles away, Joani Blank had spent years teaching women to masturbate. Born on July 4, 1937, in a Boston suburb, Blank was born to a mother who grew up in an Orthodox Jewish family from Lithuania and a father of German descent whose paternal grandfather was a Torah scribe. Although both parents were raised religiously, they chose not to raise Blank that way.[540] After Blank graduated from college, she trained as a public health educator. She bounced around the country working in Michigan, New Hampshire, and West Virginia, before moving to San Francisco in 1971.

By the time she moved to San Francisco, the sexual revolution was well under way, and Blank began working at Planned Parenthood.[541] One of the first women she met in the city was Maggi Rubenstein, a professor, sex thera-pist, and bisexual activist who urged her to join the new consciousness-raising group she had started. At the time, Rubenstein was working as a nurse and medical school instructor at the University of California–San Francisco, but within the next five years Rubenstein transformed the Bay Area into a sex-positive mecca, cofounding three seminal groups in rapid succession: San Francisco's Sex Information Hotline (1973), the San Francisco Bisexual Center (1976), and the Institute for the Advanced Study of Human Sexuality (1976).[542] Her influence on Blank was profound, as she inspired Blank to begin her sexual advocacy, installing Blank as one of the first volunteers at SFSIH, where she dispensed sexual advice to local callers.

Like Williams had, Blank also attended one of Dodson's workshops and became inspired—so inspired, in fact, that she even let Dodson draw her labia for her book *Liberating Masturbation*.[543] Blank began working as a sex therapist with Dr. Lonnie Barbach at UCSF, who was a codirector of the Human Sexuality Program. Barbach had created a series of sex workshops for inorgasmic women, and she went on to publish a successful book based on her workshops in 1975.[544] In the ten-week courses that Blank cotaught with Barbach, the two would teach women to orgasm through masturbation. Although they were similar to Dodson's workshops, these courses had one main difference: Participants did not masturbate in front of one another; mas-turbation was their homework. After completing their homework, they would return to the group and discourse on whether or not they had orgasms and describe what their orgasms had felt like.[545]

For women who struggled with having orgasms, vibrators were not the first recourse. "Now we didn't start out with vibrators for very good reason. We did not want people to use the vibrator as a way to avoid touching them-selves. We wanted them to practice with their hands first," Blank said. Only if other methods did not work did Barbach and Blank recommend vibrators.[546]

Although they did not suggest vibrators as a first step, Barbach and Blank were both strong advocates of vibrators. Barbach overcame women's objections to vibrators by using a transportation metaphor: "A vibrator may be equivalent to using training wheels to learn to ride a bicycle. You get the feeling of what the experience is like and then, if you want to, you can practice without the machine. However, there is no reason to stop using a vibrator, either alone or with a partner if you enjoy it."[547]

Vibrators were a new technology to most of the participants. "Very few of them had tried any sex toys. If they had, they had tried perhaps a dildo. They were trying to simulate intercourse and they weren't touching their clitorises necessarily. So needless to say, they weren't coming," according to Blank. And the course worked. "Virtually everybody who went through the groups starting having orgasms," Blank said. In fact, they stopped calling the participants "inorgasmic" and started calling them "preorgasmic."[548]

These women wanted to know where to buy vibrators, and Barbach and Blank just did not have a good answer. The only female-friendly store was Eve's Garden in New York. According to Blank, she asked her friend and fellow therapist Toni Ayres to start a vibrator store. Ayres declined, encouraging Blank to start a store instead. Blank seriously considered the prospect. Yet as a self-proclaimed anticapitalist "commie," she hesitated. She wanted to further her career, spread her knowledge of sexuality wider, but she wasn't sure a vibrator store was the best way to do so. After weeks of indecision, she decided that instead of starting a vibrator store, she'd form a publishing company.[549]

In 1975, she opened Down There Press, a publisher devoted to women's sexuality. A few months later she came out with her first book, *A Playbook for Women About Sex*. *Playbook* was a workbook that focused on masturbation, body image, and partnered sex. There were only a few mentions of sex toys, in a checklist of things to masturbate or have sex with and in the myths section.

Weirdly, the one sex-toy "myth" she mention was that "Vibrators are stupid." The reader was supposed to check one of the three boxes listed next to it: "True," "False," or "I dunno."[550] Although there were a lot of myths about vibrators, this wasn't really one of them. *Playbook* sold fairly well for a small-press workbook focused on masturbation, but not enough for her to quit her day job. However, she discovered that she loved publishing. Maybe that was the best way to share her sexual expertise, she thought. A year later, UCSF restructured their program and required all their counselors to have PhDs. Although Blank had two master's degrees in public health, these weren't enough and she was laid off.[551]

Dejected, she flew to New York City to visit Williams and Eve's Garden. Although the store was small, Blank was impressed with its inventory. In addition to vibrators, Williams was stocking a series of books: Blank's former co-teacher Lonnie Barbach's book *For Yourself*; the Boston Women's Health Collective, *Our Bodies, Ourselves*; Dodson's *Liberating Masturbation*; and a variety of feminist books. But Blank insisted that, at the time, Eve's Garden was a "showroom" and not a store. This was a key distinction that was important to Blank. She flew back to California and wrote another book, *Good Vibrations: The Complete Women's Guide to Vibrators*. In this hand-lettered book, she discoursed on the variety of vibrators on the market and suggested that readers buy their sex toys from Eve's Garden.

In the meantime, in October 1976, two women opened a feminist store that sold vibrators in San Francisco and called it Old Wives Tales. Although primarily a bookstore, Old Wives Tales wasn't shy about their sex-toy inventory. Started by Carol Seajay and Paula Wallace (who were lovers), Old Wives Tales was situated in the middle of the lesbian and lefty-centric Mission Dolores neighborhood on Valencia Street, an area populated by a lesbian bathhouse, hairdresser, and café.[552] "A lot of customers were very pleased to buy vibrators in a women-focused, women-safe environment," Seajay said.[553]

Although Down There Press was doing well, it wasn't enough to support Blank, so she thought back to the idea for a vibrator store. A vibrator store could help support her press, she mused. It wouldn't take much capital.[554] In March 1977, a month after the Eve's Garden's Austin branch opened, Good Vibrations opened its doors. "[Williams] was my inspiration," Blank said. "I gave Dell all the credit for giving me the idea." Williams's business model was spreading across the nation. She should have been pleased. Sisterhood and all that. But Williams felt otherwise. She felt betrayed. Why? Well, Williams has a different story.

Williams claims that she suggested that Blank start an Eve's Garden in San Francisco and that Blank had rejected the idea. According to Williams, Blank said she wanted to focus on education instead. This is a story Blank disagrees with: "I'm absolutely sure that I would have remembered that if she had asked me and I said no."[555] Blank said that Williams sent her a postcard with one sentence on it: "I always knew someone would copy me but I never thought it would be you." What's the truth? It's hard to know. According to Blank, when she showed Williams the postcard, Williams said, "I can't believe I wrote that."[556] One thing is for sure: Blank, like Williams, wanted to make the world a better place, and she wanted to do it through teaching men and women about their sexuality.

First she had to struggle to find an appropriate space because even in San Francisco most people did not want to rent space to a sex-toy store, no matter how educational it was. Her first choice of a location was in the Noe Valley, a location in central San Francisco full of hip boutiques. Blank found a good space but was turned down because the landlord did not approve of her business. With $4,000 in capital, Blank opened up her store in the edgy Mission District in San Francisco, an area replete with punk clubs, in March 1977. The tiny, two-hundred-square-foot space she rented gave the store a sense of intimacy that larger commercial sex-toy stores owned by Sturman did not have. An oriental rug adorned with pillows covered the floor, and macramé and ferns hung from the walls. Initially, she carried eighteen items and filled up the rest of the space with her antique vibrator collection. She had only two employees.[557]

Blank claims that hers was the first real woman-owned sex-toy store. "I wouldn't really call [Eve's Garden] a store," Blank said, insisting that Eve's Garden's first store was a showroom. Blank says that Williams also didn't consider it to be a full-on retail outlet. This issue of who was the first never really was settled between them. "For a long time she didn't even credit me as being the first," Williams said.[558] Blank disagreed: "I gave Dell all the credit for giving me the idea for opening Good Vibrations."[559]

Another thing that distinguished Blank's store from Williams's was a try-out booth. ("But I don't encourage real masturbation trips here," she was quick to reassure the *Berkeley Barb* in an interview.) Her store functioned both in opposition to the male-focused adult bookstores dotting the Bay Area at the time and also as a feminist homage to them. Instead of having peep-show booths that encouraged masturbation, she had a try-out booth that discouraged it.[560] She painted the store chocolate brown in homage to the plain brown bags that sex toys were usually sold in, installing a "plain brown cabinet" to top off the look. A home bar served as a sales counter, and a display cabinet rounded out the space, which melded the do-it-yourself hippie ethos with an aura of sex education.[561]

Blank was facing an uphill battle, though, as the very term "feminist adult bookstore" would have been considered an oxymoron among a large swath of San Francisco feminists, as two months after Good Vibrations opened, members of the group Women Against Violence and Pornography and Media (WAVPM) engaged in a "'May Day Stroll' through the city's North Beach district to protest adult bookstores, as well as massage parlors, go-go bars, and XXX cinemas."[562]

The centerpiece of her store was the display case featuring four different plug-in vibrators. The plug-in vibrator was already a feminist symbol thanks to Dodson and Williams, and its central location in the store alerted customers to the ethos of the store. Placing non-phallic vibrators front and center made a statement that the store was about women's pleasure, not men's idea of how women should experience pleasure. Among the vibrators were the Hitachi Magic Wand, a Wahl vibrator, and a square-headed General Electric model. All had been sold as nonsexual massagers by the corporations that produced them.[563] In addition to the prominently displayed plug-in vibrators she also sold a handful of cheaper, less powerful vibrators: phallic eight-inch battery-operated vibrators, bullet vibes, and egg-shaped vibes.

The store was gaining in popularity, but Blank had committed a cardinal sin according to some feminists: She allowed men to shop in Good Vibrations. To these feminists, it was beside the point that only a few men ever stepped foot in the tiny, vibrator-packed store. Just the fact that men were welcome was enough to make them shun Good Vibrations. On one occasion, a male customer's presence led the female customers to pointedly ask Blank: "What is *he* doing in here?" She told the customers that he was shopping, just like they were, but he was embarrassed and quickly fled the store. A few weeks later, Blank discovered that Good Vibrations was left off a map of women-friendly businesses. When she asked why, they told her that they'd overlooked it. But the creators of the map were well aware of the store. She suspected it was her male-friendly policy that left her off the map.[564] What she didn't realize at the time was that this was only the beginning of her battles with the feminist movement.

To be sure, not all feminists were opposed to her store. But the antipathy to it meant that she struggled to get publicity, which wasn't a huge problem for Blank since sales were always secondary for her. She was a bundle of contradictions: an anticapitalist with a business, a saleswoman who was philosophically opposed to advertising. In this sense, she was Williams's opposite. Williams was a former ad agency executive who wholeheartedly believed in marketing, and she used her skills to promote her business, while Blank adhered to a philosophy called "marketing without advertising," a philosophy co-opted from her association with the Briarpatch Network, a business group founded in 1974 to promote ethical community-focused businesses. Inspired by Stewart Brand of *The Whole Earth Catalog*, Briarpatch believed that businesses should avoid traditional advertising because good businesses didn't need to use gimmicks or hard-sell techniques.[565]

Instead of spending a lot of money on advertising, Blank threw parties, told all the progressive San Francisco organizations about Good Vibrations, and ran seminars. "You must remember, I was running this business on a shoestring. So buying advertising? You've got to be crazy," Blank said. One of her most effective techniques was soliciting her customers to send her lists of the names of their friends who would not be "in the least offended to receive an explicit, honest and comprehensive sex-toy catalog" in exchange for a ten-dollar discount.[566]

She wasn't too worried about generating business because, like Williams, Blank was not in the sex-toy business for profit. In that way, Blank was the opposite of Sturman and the other owners of adult bookstores who would sell sex toys at 800 to 1,000 percent markups. In other words, they would buy a plastic vibrator for a dollar and sell it for eight to ten dollars to the consumer, which explained why Sturman's profits were so large. In contrast, Blank would sell the same dollar vibrator for two dollars. She made far less money, but she thought that giving consumers affordable prices was important. "I didn't give a damn about making any money," Blank said.[567] While Sturman was a millionaire, Blank barely got by.

In other ways too, Good Vibrations was the polar opposite of Sturman's store. Where Sturman hid his businesses' financial information from everyone and did most of his business in cash, Blank's store had open books, meaning any customer, employee, or competitor could take a look at her books. She would even share information with her competitors about the cheapest sex-toy suppliers to use.

Her antibusiness attitude extended to her day-to-day running of the store. "I never pushed product sales," Blank said, "particularly to someone who came in and said I'd like to get a vibrator for my girlfriend or my wife." Men coming in to buy sex toys on behalf of their wives was a surprisingly common occurrence. Even after the sexual revolution, women still felt uncomfortable discussing sex. "For [every person] doing free love and free sex, there were [ten to twenty times more] women [who] wouldn't even talk about sex [even to their partners]," Blank said. Instead of asking the husband a series of questions about what he thought his wife would like, and then selling him a vibrator, she would say, "Do you think your wife would be willing to come in here with you?" If he answered in the affirmative, she'd say, "Take the catalog, go home, buy the book on vibrators or not, have a conversation with her, and if she's still too embarrassed to come in here, come back and get what she says she wants." It was the opposite of the hard sell.[568]

Even though she'd send customers away empty-handed, and the markups were small, Good Vibrations made enough money to keep its doors open and hire a few employees.

(*)

With Good Vibrations on the West Coast and Eve's Garden in New York and in Austin, women's sex-toy stores were beginning to spread throughout the country. Still, they comprised only three stores out of the thousands of adult bookstores in the United States. Sturman and the traditional adult bookstores for men were king. It didn't have to be that way.

In Germany, the women-owned contraceptive and sex-toy chain Beate Uhse had more than twenty-five stores by the mid-1970s, and it had been in existence since 1948, more than a quarter century longer than Eve's Garden.[569] Braverman had seen Beate Uhse stores when he was in Europe, and soon after they founded Doc Johnson they began distributing their sex toys at her stores. Founded by Beate Uhse-Rotermund, a former Luftwaffe pilot and mother of four, Beate Uhse started as a mail-order company like Eve's Garden and primarily sold contraceptives. Uhse-Rotermund avoided scrutiny from the government because she mostly didn't advertise and instead gained business through unsolicited direct mailings to customers. Uhse built her first store, the Sex Institute for Marital Hygiene, in Flensburg, Germany, in 1962.[570]

Why did it take so long for a Beate Uhse–type store to open in the United States? "We probably won't see any stores like Beate Uhse here until the Papal Estates come to terms with Margaret Sanger, and Ralph Ginzburg is elected Chairman of Lady Bird's Beautifying Campaign," wrote *The East Village Other* in 1967.[571] The publication had a point: Stores only gained a foothold nearly a decade after they wrote that, and nearly a quarter century after Alfred Kinsey published his first report on sexual behavior. In fact, Kinsey's ideas had influenced Beate Uhse more than they influenced sex-toy stores in the United States. For example, Uhse's catalogs from the 1950s emphasized the necessity of female orgasms and explained how products offered for sale would provide them. American sex-toy companies didn't make such claims until the mid-1970s.

Why were Americans so slow to accept women's sex-toy stores but accepting of men's porn and sex-toy stores? It's most likely due to Eve's Garden's and Good Vibrations's unabashed focus on female sexuality, particularly masturbation. Focusing a store on female masturbation was radical, and it meant the store owners had to deal with the taboos surrounding it that were much greater than the male-masturbation taboos. They had to deal with the guilt and the shame that women felt about masturbating and about using a device to do so. Hence, the eight-page brochure Williams created for women to both explain how to use vibrators and to help women get over their shame and fear. "As you begin this process of self-pleasuring, you may experience feelings of self-doubt and guilt," she wrote. To overcome these thoughts, she told women to "Speak to yourself internally or out loud with the following affirmation; I am not bad, I do not need to feel guilty, and I (insert your name) have a right to pleasure."[572] It's difficult to imagine such an affirmation being placed at the front of a porn store for men. Even though she was selling her sex toys in such a different way than Sturman, she did have a connection with him. Doc Johnson was one of her sex-toy suppliers.[573]

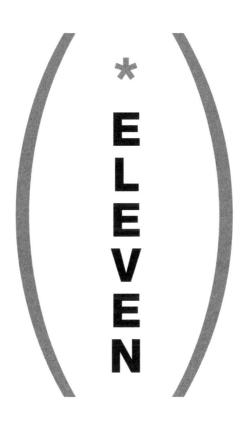

* ELEVEN

Dildo Debates

Doc Johnson sex toys were now being distributed virtually everywhere sex toys were. "From day one, we were the biggest suppliers for Pleasure Chest, Good Vibrations, and Eve's Garden,"
Braverman said. And they were working together. The stores "were asking us
for specific sex toys," Braverman said. "And we were asking them how things
were merchandised. . . . We had a constant campaign of calling to find out
why certain things sold."

One thing the Pleasure Chest, Good Vibrations, and Eve's Garden had
in common that differentiated them from Sturman's stores: They didn't have
peep-show booths. "Any store that opened in those days without the 25-cent
machines were far more inviting to the masses than the stores with [them],"
Braverman said.[574] The peep shows represented a big part of income for Sturman's company. Would he have to jettison them to sustain his success?

Braverman realized that Sturman's businesses had to serve women too.
With the rise of Helen Gurley Brown's *Cosmopolitan,* women were beginning to ask for what they wanted. "We responded to the fact that [women]
wanted something different from what their husbands were bringing home,"
Braverman said.[575] As Braverman and Sturman's sex-toy business was taking
off, IRS agent Richard Rosfelder had a new assignment: to jettison all his
other responsibilities and focus solely on Reuben Sturman.

(*)

Meanwhile, as Doc Johnson flourished, Gosnell Duncan's dildo business was floundering. He'd finally developed a high-quality dildo for disabled people only to discover that either the market wasn't there or he just didn't know how to properly tap into it. The ads he was taking out in disability publications weren't keeping sales afloat. His basement was filled with unsold dildos and vats of multicolored silicone just waiting to be molded into pliable artificial penises.[576]

Then, one day in the late 1970s, Duncan was scanning the classified ads of *The Village Voice* when he came upon an ad for Eve's Garden. Duncan dialed the number and spoke with Dell Williams.[577] He told Williams about his newest invention—the silicone dildo—but Williams wasn't especially impressed.[578] She only carried vibrators in her store, for good reason: The dildo was highly controversial in the feminist movement. While vibrators symbolized liberation and a break with men, dildos did not have the same associations. Criticisms of dildos stemmed from a philosophical divide about what a dildo actually was. The debate was whether or not dildos represented penises. And if dildos were penis representations, the question remained: Did using one represent a submission to the patriarchy or a subversion of it?

If the personal really was political, then the devices that you used during sex were a reflection of your deepest political beliefs. If you fought against the patriarchy during the day but came home at night and fucked yourself silly with a bulging, beveined artificial dick, then you were betraying the movement. Like the antiporn feminists, the antidildo feminists perceived male sexuality as violent and domineering and the dildo as a symbol of maleness and penetrative sex. Using a dildo was an admission that women needed a phallus to be fully sexually satisfied. How could a feminist strap on a dildo in good conscience with Andrea Dworkin calling the penis "a hidden symbol of terror"? As she said in *Pornography: Men Possessing Women*, "Violence is male, the male is the penis."[579] And why would a feminist want to use a dildo when women weren't even supposed to get much pleasure from penetration because, as Anne Koedt argued, the vaginal orgasm was a myth perpetuated by Freud?[580] "[Men] assume that women masturbate with phallic objects (as in *The Exorcist*), and that Lesbians use dildos," Barbara Starrett wrote in the *Amazon Quarterly*. "Like Freud, they assume that women need penetration, body domination, for sexual fulfillment."[581]

Dildos were especially controversial devices among lesbians, one of Williams's target markets. Lesbians were offended by assumptions that they used dildos during sex. "A lot of people can't figure out . . . how we make love without a penis," wrote prominent lesbian feminist Sue Katz in her essay "Smash Phallic Imperialism." "A lot of boys have these ideas of dildos and bananas. Sex as an institution is so totally tied up with the penis . . . boys assume there must be some poor substitute for their noble item."[582] Another feminist argued that only the "maladjusted" lesbians "sported dildoes," and imitating men was not the way "the modern Lesbian should present herself to the world."[583]

But the fact that many feminists disapproved of dildos didn't mean that none of them used dildos—it just meant that they didn't talk about it. "Anyone admitting to using a dildo today would probably be verbally castigated for enjoying 'phallic' pleasure," wrote Karla Jay in an October 1974 issue of *Lesbian Tide*. "Verbal criticism has FORCED some sisters into a second closet."[584]

Not all lesbians were antidildo. Those who saw the dildo "not as a penis representation, but as an object for vaginal stimulation"—as the Nomadic Sisters, authors of a lesbian sex manual, did—advocated using dildos, both during masturbation and partnered sex.[585] While some praised their sex manual, *Loving Women*, for giving "a new sense of respectability and desirability" to dildos, others were critical.[586] A reviewer in *Big Mama Rag* thought that since "most women" associated dildos with penises, redefining them was impossible. She also had two other objections to dildos: that they were artificial and that they were made by men.[587] Both of which were valid criticisms. Most of the dildos in the 1970s were made by men.[588] But most men were not like Gosnell Duncan.

(*)

Although the dildo debates had led Williams to refrain from stocking them, something about Duncan's voice on the phone made her consider changing her mind. Some time in 1977, she told Duncan to come to the store to make his pitch. As he swung open the doors to Eve's Garden and wheeled himself through the entrance, West Indian–born Gosnell Duncan became the first man to enter the store since Williams's brother stopped in years earlier to help with the store's interior design.[589]

Duncan started in on his pitch. Silicone dildos retain body heat and felt more flesh-like than the older models, he told her. They could be shared between partners because they could be easily sterilized. Williams wasn't completely swayed by these arguments. Like other feminists, she took issue with the hyperrealism of the dildos on the market.

"Why did a dildo have to look like a cock at all, I asked Duncan," Williams wrote in her memoir. "Did it have to have a well-defined, blushed-pink head, and blue veins in bas-relief?" Williams wasn't sure that her customers would buy dildos, no matter what they looked like. Her mail-order business was, after all, a haven for lesbians and others in the women's movement who had been fighting for their independence from men. While non-penetrative vibrators symbolized liberation and a break with men, dildos did not have the same associations. The very presence of a realistic replica of male genitalia in the catalog could have been enough to turn away customers.[590]

She sent out a customer survey asking her patrons what they would want in a dildo. Williams's customers said that it wasn't about size; it was about substance. They wanted "something not necessarily large, but definitely tapered. Not particularly wide but undulated at its midsection. Something pliable and easy to care for. Something in a pretty color."[591]

Duncan hadn't manufactured nonrepresentational dildos before, but he wasn't opposed to them. He got to work in his lab and created the "Venus" dildo. Modeled in pale pink and chocolate brown, the dildo looked more like a large crooked finger than a penis. The Venus became the first feminist dildo available to the American public.[592]

When he poured his first vat of liquid silicone rubber into a penis-shaped mold, Duncan did not think of his dildo-making as a political act. He was seeking to solve a problem that he—and thousands of other disabled men and their lovers—had faced. But in the 1970s, dildos were imbued with politics, so to enter the dildo business was to make a political statement. Duncan could have refused to design nonrepresentational dildos in fanciful colors like blue and purple. But he chose to hear Williams out.

Like all tools, sex toys are imbued with meaning that reflects the society they are created in. Designing nonrepresentational dildos in traditionally feminine colors allowed women to literally and symbolically corral male sexual power. A feminized dildo made a statement that the natural penis was unsatisfying, that women could easily co-opt the last bastion of maleness. Williams made sure to clarify in her catalog that "we don't think of dildos as imitation penises" and that a dildo could only bring a woman to orgasm "psychologically."[593] Yet the Venus didn't end the dildo debates. One feminist dildo could not overturn the pervasive antiphallicism in the feminist movement. But it was a start.

(*)

Around this time, Williams decided that she was ready to open up a bigger store in New York's Midtown East district at 246 East Fifty-first Street.

Although her showroom and office on Fifty-seventh Street also operated as a store, it was on a high floor hidden among offices. This new store was different: It was street-level, within a view of passersby. Even though the store's sexual and gender politics were radical, the design of it was traditionally feminine. The garden theme ran throughout the store. Williams commissioned her brother Lorenz to paint a "trompe l'oeil of a garden in the store—flowers in pinks and mauves, and lush greenery."[594] The carpet was faux grass, and the store window showcased plants and books, not vibrators. Although Williams didn't know it, this was a step backward in the merchandising of vibrators. In the early 1900s, electricity shop windows were stocked with vibrator displays, proudly showing off their wares. Yet, in 1978, her vibrator store hid the merchandise.[595] The use of traditionally feminine colors and symbols was ironic, as the store's ethos was to push women away from the strictures of their gender and into a new world of sexual possibility. Yet feminizing Eve's Garden was a clear way to distinguish the store from the existing sex stores, which were decidedly masculine.

Williams feminized the store also by maintaining her banishment of men. Her continued refusal to let men enter emerged, she said, "not out of an overriding ball-busting, man-hating, feminazi philosophy, but to create an environment where women would be free to explore their sexuality in privacy and safety."[596] Although she and her brother were proud of her store, not all of Williams's family would have been happy about it, had they known it existed. "My mother would have disapproved," Williams said. "She was against masturbation."[597]

(*)

As Williams was opening her ground-level store, Sturman was getting indicted again in Cleveland. This time, it was for sending obscene materials over state lines. After hours of deliberation, the jury declared at the 1978 trial that Sturman's porn magazines were not obscene. And they went even further, arguing that the law itself was flawed. "The average person . . . cannot have a morbid interest in sex," declared the jury in a letter to the U.S. District Judge presiding over the case.[598] Their decision suggested that social mores were more progressive than obscenity laws. Sturman was free again. When Sturman won the case, he hosted a three-hundred-person victory party for his employees and their family and friends.[599] But the more successful he became, the harder the federal government tried to shut him down.[600]

The fact that Sturman kept winning obscenity cases emboldened the government to get him on tax evasion. Rosfelder continued to amass evidence, especially as he saw that Sturman's business were swimming in cash. Sturman's sex-toy line was flourishing. By this point, Doc Johnson's sales were $2.5 million a year.[601] The idea to make sex-toy and porn stores more appealing had come to fruition. "Under Sturman, the adult bookstore has become a clean, well-lighted place," wrote James Cook in *Forbes* magazine in 1978.[602] The king of the peep show was cleaning up the way sex toys were sold.

(*)

Meanwhile, the Pleasure Chest was also growing, expanding in 1975 for the first time outside of New York City. It was back to L.A. for Colglazier, who opened up a new retail location on North La Brea Boulevard in the heart of the gay district of West Hollywood. (It later moved to Santa Monica Boulevard.) It was there that the Pleasure Chest really crossed over into the punk and rock 'n' roll scene. Thanks to its new location and the fact that the Pleasure Chest was now making leather gear, the store became a cultural touchstone. The Runaways' Joan Jett shopped at the Pleasure Chest for her friend Sid Vicious of the Sex Pistols. She bought Vicious his iconic metal-ringed leather belt there, which he wore while he was on tour in the United States in 1978. Jett also posed in front of the L.A. store for a picture. It was a bold move for a woman in the 1970s to be photographed at a sex-toy store.[603] Freddie Mercury of Queen incorporated the store into his 1978 song "Let Me Entertain You": "If you wanna see some action/You get nothing but the best/The S&M attraction/We've got the Pleasure Chest/Chicago and New Orleans."

The taboo surrounding S&M drew punks to frequent the Pleasure Chest, as did their new line of leather jackets and jumpsuits, which the company made itself, soon after they started making their own leather cock rings and strap-on harnesses when they had difficulty securing suppliers. Their leather gear became so popular that they set up a workshop on Eleventh Avenue in New York just to produce it.[604] They also sold razor blades and "Nazi insignia jewelry," which was like catnip to punks.[605] Much to the dismay of their parents, teenagers liked the Pleasure Chest's S&M gear too. Although they weren't allowed in the store, they would "stand outside and delegate an older friend" to buy them spiked collars and studded jewelry.[606]

(*)

By the late 1970s, the Pleasure Chest had spread across the nation. Its stores existed in nearly every major city: Atlanta, Philadelphia, Chicago, Miami, New York (where there were two locations), New Orleans, and L.A. They even opened a Canada branch in Toronto.[607] The Pleasure Chest stores were well-lit, inviting, and popular with women.[608]

Sex toys remained controversial, however, and the Pleasure Chest took pains to legitimize itself in its 1978 catalog. "We have tried through clean, well-appointed shops, courteous personnel, and quality merchandise at reasonable prices," the catalog stated, "to bring sex out of the realm of pornography and into the realm of erotica." Even though they wrote that "all persons have a right of sexual freedom," they followed this statement with a warning to unsuspecting people who picked up their catalogs. "Those who believe sex is for reproduction only have a right to that belief and should not be forced to view things or photos that they find objectionable." Such statements made the Pleasure Chest acceptable to antiporn censors, as the store was one of the few that the censors in New York found acceptable.[609]

By this time, the Pleasure Chest had dialed down its gay themes. Yet they didn't abandon their gay male customers. Far from it. They opened all their stores in gay areas of cities, and much of their catalog was comprised of gay products. Still, they worked to make their catalogs more appealing to heterosexuals. Their first catalog in 1971 exclusively featured toys targeted to the gay-male market and drawings of gay men only. Seven years later, the catalog including five varieties of artificial vaginas and pictures of breast-baring young women.[610] They sold lingerie and sex-toy kits featuring images of a man and a woman embracing. The one thing missing was lesbian imagery, unless you count the pictures of naked women wearing strap-on dildos.

By 1981, one of the Pleasure Chest's catalogs even veered into heterosexual porn territory with its images of the female porn star Annie Sprinkle dressed as a character named Ms. Tittiewhite who seduces her male student using the Pleasure Chest's products. One scene featured her completely nude student Steven bending over with his legs spread, ankles tied together. She has one hand on his balls and the other above his ass, which is adorned with anal beads. "Count them one at a time," she instructs Steven, "when they go in and count them quickly when they go out." Other scenes feature her teaching Steven to show off the "three different studded cock rings," assuring readers that "the girls love them too!" Like their first catalog, with hand-drawn gay men, this catalog worked on its own as a piece of erotica.[611]

Targeting heterosexuals was a smart move. By the early 1980s, sales at the Pleasure Chest were $10 million a year.[612] And the fact that they sold sex toys in boutique style stores meant they could open up stores in upscale neighborhoods. In 1981, for the very first time, there was a Pleasure Chest in the nation's capital in the tony Georgetown neighborhood of Washington, D.C., where Duane Colglazier's cousin Cynthia opened up a branch of the store.[613]

(*)

As the Pleasure Chest made a move to the mainstream, Eve's Garden followed. In 1980, an investor from Schooner Capital approached Williams and told her he could make Eve's Garden a national chain, and he was willing to fork over the cash to do so. Eve's Garden Austin never really took off, so Williams was willing to listen to Schooner Capital's pitch.[614] The company told Williams that she would continue to be president, but Schooner executive Marilyn C. Carten would be in charge of financials and management. The company's plan was to expand Eve's Garden to Boston, as well as to promote the store more prominently nationwide. The idea of gaining partners to share the responsibility of running Eve's Garden appealed to Williams. After thinking it over, Williams decided that expanding Eve's Garden to reach more women was a good idea, and that, at fifty-eight years old, it was time to let younger people have a hand in the company. She was also having trouble managing the finances of Eve's Garden. So she agreed to the deal.[615]

Carten and another board member told Williams that the way to make Eve's Garden more palatable to the American public was to eliminate its sex education aspects and deemphasize sex toys.[616] Instead, Eve's Garden should focus on selling lingerie, bath oil, and feathered masks, they advised. The board was essentially telling Williams to get rid of everything that made the store revolutionary. Naturally, she was hesitant to heed their advice since vibrators and sex education were woven into Eve's Garden's DNA. But Carten argued that this change in focus would soon lead to a million in sales and that was just what Williams needed to hear. She agreed to shift the focus from masturbation and vibrators to string bikinis and satin teddies.

Now that the radical aspects of Eve's Garden were gone and sex toys were no longer the focus, major national magazines accepted their ads. For the first time, *Redbook, Self,* and *Brides* were carrying Eve's Garden advertising. Williams was thrilled. Eve's Garden had finally hit the mainstream. Carten wrote to the president of the razor manufacturing company Gillette to share the good news with him. "It sounds as if you are achieving your initial goals of acceptance in upright women's magazines," he responded enthusiastically.[617]

Along with Schooner Capital executive Bernice Bradin, Carten rented a beautiful, large office space in Boston and hired four new employees. Eve's Garden now had locations in two major cities, and Williams saw her dream coming to fruition. But, in one moment, it all changed for the worse. The investors called for a vote about whether to keep Eve's Garden's New York stores open. This was an unbelievable move on their part. The New York stores were Williams's babies; they were the stores that had started it all. She was floored by the suggestion to shut them down. She voted no, of course. But the two other women on the board overruled her. The stores were going to be closed. Williams couldn't bear to close both of Eve's Garden's New York stores, so she told them she was going to keep the Fifty-seventh Street location open with her own money.[618]

Meanwhile, the new focus of Eve's Garden may have been a hit with the advertising departments of major women's magazines, but not so much with American consumers. The investors had miscalculated. A store focused on lingerie and fashion wasn't necessarily a bad idea. In fact, a new lingerie store named Victoria's Secret had opened in Palo Alto, California, in 1977 and was soon a hit, quickly expanding to numerous locations. But lingerie was not what feminist customers wanted. The Boston store may have had Eve's

Garden's name on it, but it didn't have its ethos and it struggled to gain its footing.

After failing to increase sales after a year of trying, Carten resigned in 1981. Bradin followed a month later. Williams rented a car, loaded up her dog Honey, and drove to Boston to see what was going on. What she found was "an entire echoing floor of an enormous warehouse stocked with merchandise and no one there shipping it out."[619] She learned that Schooner Capital was planning on closing Eve's Garden. They suggested she file for bankruptcy. It probably was the right financial decision, but she couldn't bear to do it, even after she learned that Carten hadn't been paying withholding taxes and Williams would be on the hook for thousands of dollars.

All she had was $600 in the Eve's Garden bank account. She could barely keep the doors open in New York. The warehouse was hemorrhaging money; it was full of stuff that her customers didn't want to buy. So she decided to sell off all the lingerie and masks. Even after selling a chunk of the merchandise, Williams was still left financially strained. "July is dropping dead and I am actually in a terrible panic," Williams wrote to her friends. "I just spoke to my psychiatrist on the phone. It helped a little." She could afford only to take out one new advertisement, and she was scared that she couldn't go on running Eve's Garden. "Perhaps Eve's Garden is still not acceptable in the general market," she wrote. "Or to introduce it to the mass market you really need to pour in a lot of money."[620]

Williams ended up having to do what the investors asked her to do from the beginning: to close down Eve's Garden in New York. But she couldn't bear to walk away from Eve's Garden entirely. She still had a stock of the Eve's Garden brand electric vibrators, as well as a stack of catalogs. So she decided to return Eve's Garden "back to basics: quality sex toys and instructional books to go with them."[621] She moved to Boston to run the store and worked out a deal with the IRS to pay back taxes in monthly installments.

In March 1983, she closed the Boston store and moved back to New York to reopen her store there. Later she said about the experience that "Eve's Garden was raped by venture capitalism."[622] Eve's Garden never expanded again.

(*)

As Eve's Garden was struggling, the adult bookstore business as a whole was booming. By 1981, there were more than twenty thousand adult bookstores in the U.S., which together brought in more than $3 billion of revenue.[623] Sex toys were a growing part of this business, and not just in the United States. Sturman and Braverman continued to have a hand in the overseas business, distributing Doc Johnson toys at London's Ann Summers's chain and Beate Uhse.[624]

But Sturman's tax investigation had intensified, and in September 1981, Braverman was called to a federal grand jury in the Northern District of Ohio to testify about his involvement in Sturman's businesses. Since the government's end goal was to get Sturman, they granted Braverman immunity from prosecution. On December 2, 1981, the government's attorneys asked Braverman a simple question: "Have you ever handled any sort of financial transactions for Reuben Sturman?" Braverman responded by saying, "Outside of minor personal ones, no." When asked to give specifics, he said, "I know I bought him some cigars a couple of times, and everyone [sic] of these personal things have always been reimbursed." Through testimony that lasted two days, he continued to answer questions, admitting that he did have Swiss bank accounts but he had used them for himself, not for Sturman.[625]

(*)

Around the same time as Braverman was testifying, in the early 1980s, the still-single Sturman was living in a condo in Los Angeles. A friend asked if he could set Sturman up with a twenty-one-year-old singer from Hawaii named Naomi Delgado.[626] "Are you out of your fucking mind?" Sturman reportedly said. "Do you know how old we are?" Sturman was in his late fifties, more than twice Delgado's age. His friend wouldn't take no for an answer. "She wants an older man," he said. Sturman refused to meet her, but his friend tried again six months later, and Sturman finally said yes. Their first date, at a restaurant in Los Angeles, ended in sex, and after that they were inseparable. Insecure about their age difference, Sturman got a facelift. He was also constantly on a diet and always ate a lunch of only fruit to maintain his weight. Soon Delgado found out she was pregnant, and Sturman married her. They named their baby girl Erica.[627] He and Braverman had also given birth around this time to a new business idea: Tupperware-style in-home parties.

(*)

When home parties for sex toys started in the late 1970s and early 1980s, it wasn't the first-time sex-toy companies had come directly into people's homes. In the early 1900s, traveling vibrator salesmen would go door-to-door selling their plug-in vibrators to those lucky enough to have electricity in their homes. And in the 1940s the Rural Electrification Administration even promoted the vibrator to encourage people to electrify their homes.[628]

Home parties helped spread a pro-sex-toy message throughout middle America. These were mainly women-only parties, although some parties were solely for men. The parties should have been seen as a positive development by feminist sex-toy pioneers. But Blank and Williams weren't enthusiastic. And they had good reason for not being so: Home party companies were going after the same demographic as Good Vibrations and Eve's Garden. They too were peppering their sales pitches with sex education. "The parties purport to provide access to products women would otherwise have difficulty obtaining," Blank wrote in *Good Vibrations*. "Unfortunately the sales reps are often poorly informed about human sexuality." But her criticisms weren't just based on a sense of competition. "The manner in which the products are presented . . . reflect a very traditional attitude about sex," Blank wrote. At the parties sex isn't "talked about except in a joking or sensational way." Another critique was that the parties were more focused on "what turns on men" and that they ignored lesbians and bisexuals.[629]

Other feminists' reactions were also mixed. While NOW was supportive of the parties, prominent feminist Susan Brownmiller was horrified by them. Author of *Against Our Will*, Brownmiller was famous for her argument that rape was about power, not sex. Brownmiller told the *Washington Post*, 'I think [home parties are] just absolutely appalling. It seems to me the purpose of sex is two bodies relating. I find the prospect of paraphernalia ghastly. I think it has to do with the whole consumer society where there's a gadget for everything."[630]

Echoing Brownmiller was a woman on the opposite end of the political spectrum: Patricia Fordem, a leader in the national conservative Christian group Concerned Women for America. "I think it's sick. It's sad that society allows [sex-toy parties] . . . something like that breaks down family unity," Fordem told the *Los Angeles Times*. "Those people have to be looking for kicks outside their marriage. They can't be very happy with their partner." Even psychologists who said that "artificial sex devices" have a place warned women against purchasing sex toys at home parties because the toys "can replace true human values." Given the controversy, it makes sense that some women who attended the parties lied to their husbands about where they were.[631]

Despite the taboo, the parties were occurring across the country: In California, the Midwest, and on the East Coast. In New York alone, the sex-toy party company Just for Play had one thousand consultants. The main suppliers of their sex toys? The Doc Johnson Company and Fred Malorrus of United Sales, of course.[632]

Malorrus saw sex-toy parties as the wave of the future. "The average person won't walk into an adult bookstore. And he's not on the mailing list of most of these places," Malorrus said. "This way they get to look at the stuff with their next-door neighbor. That way they get over the shock."[633]

Even the Pleasure Chest joined the fray with home parties of their own.[634] The Pleasure Chest's home parties in the early 1980s were a wild success, with sales representatives selling huge numbers of the company's sex toys in locations where the stores didn't exist, including Minnesota and Alaska. But as the orders poured in, they couldn't keep up. Customers were paying for dildos and ending up empty-handed in return. Naturally, they felt like they were being ripped off.

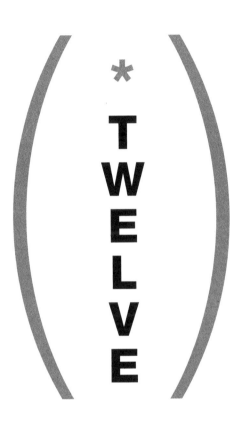

*TWELVE

GRIDS and Good Vibes

When their sex toys never arrived, a few unhappy Pleasure Chest customers who'd attended home parties decided to take action. They tipped off the Federal Trade Commission, which began an investigation and discovered that the Pleasure Chest didn't fulfill fifteen thousand of their orders. In September 1982, the Pleasure Chest ended their home parties.[635] Yet even as they had the FTC on their back, there were soon bigger things to worry about.

While the Pleasure Chest's home parties had been short-lived, their stores were thriving. As their catalogs became less gay, the store in West Hollywood became gayer by fully integrating itself into the gay community with a public event. The Great American Yankee Freedom Band marched, a clown-penis ring-toss game was set up, and shirtless men modeled leather and latex gear. Radiating a playful attitude toward sex, the event attracted a large crowd of gay men who wanted a sense of community in a society that widely shunned them.[636]

Soon such public celebrations of gay sexuality were to become scant. In San Francisco in 1980 rumors began swirling of a strange new disease that was killing young gay men. On the opposite coast, on July 3, 1981, a small story was buried in the *New York Times*: "Rare Cancer Seen in 41 Homosexuals." This cancer was Kaposi's Sarcoma, a disease that had up until this point only occurred in people older than fifty and was now showing up in twenty-somethings. It was fast growing and fatal. Eight of the men who had been diagnosed with it had already died. Nobody knew just how it was transmitted.[637] Many of the gay men who had contracted the cancer were regular users of amyl nitrate (poppers) during sex, which the Pleasure Chest sold. As a result, some doctors thought there could be a possible connection with the drug. Others thought the disease might be caused by anal sex itself. Because so many of the victims were gay, the disease was named Gay-Related Immunodeficiency (GRID). Many began to believe that the disease was sexually transmitted and urged gay men to stop having sex, but some gay organizations thought "these beliefs were motivated by a repressive strategy to return all gay men to the closet."[638] Since GRID implied that the disease was caused by gay sex, the name was controversial from the beginning. Soon gay activists insisted the name be changed to Acquired Immune Deficiency Syndrome (AIDS) in 1982.[639]

A year later, in 1983, HIV—the virus that leads to AIDS—was discovered, and doctors established the routes of transmission: through blood and body fluids. As hemophiliacs got AIDS, it became clear that it wasn't just a gay disease. But the die had already been cast and gay people were seen as vectors. Anywhere that gay sex was public and visible was pointed to as a site for a spread of a deadly disease: bathhouses, adult movie theaters, and sex stores. Bathhouses received the most blame, but sex stores didn't go unnoticed. Being the most prominent gay-focused sex store at the time, the Pleasure Chest was suddenly not just a place for gay sexual liberation but also a store that was promoting a gay lifestyle that had led to an epidemic. Even though it was more heterosexual than it had ever been, the Pleasure Chest was still seen as primarily gay.

It wasn't just heterosexuals who were critiquing places like the Pleasure Chest. Gay Liberation Front founder Jim Fouratt told the *New York Times* on September 22, 1985, that he had disdain for a particular group of gay men: those who owned "sex-related businesses." "The basic motivation was not freedom but profit," Fourratt said in the article headlined HOMOSEXUALS STEPPING UP AIDS EDUCATION. Under the subheading "Ignorance About Spreading AIDS," journalist Jane Gross reported in the same article that "on a recent afternoon at the Pleasure Chest . . . a store that sells sexual devices, the customers included a man covered with purplish lesions associated with Kaposi's sarcoma, a cancer frequently infecting AIDS victims." What was Gross implying? That it was irresponsible to go shopping at the Pleasure Chest if you had AIDS? That by stepping foot in a sex store, the man was planning to spread his disease? In fact, since many of the toys in the Pleasure Chest were for masturbation, the opposite could have been the case: Shopping there could've been presented as the responsible thing to do.[640]

In fact, some health educators suggested to gay men that masturbation with sex toys was a safe-sex practice that could help prevent HIV/AIDS.[641] Masturbation didn't have to occur by yourself either, they told gay men. Mutual masturbation, where two or more men masturbate together, was also promoted. According to a 1984 study by the San Francisco AIDS Foundation, mutual masturbation was the only safer sex practice that had increased in popularity since the AIDS crisis began.[642] Two years later, in 1986, the Gay Men's Health Crisis (GMHC) pushed mutual masturbation as a sexy gay sex act in their "Hot, Horny & Healthy: Eroticization of Safer Sex" interactive workshops.[643]

Some gay men even organized masturbation parties. It combined the best of both words: the safety of masturbation with the community of doing it in a group. These parties had existed before the 1980s, but they became even more prevalent after the discovery of AIDS. Bringing sex toys to the party was just a part of the fun. But sharing sex toys was another story.

While HIV-prevention pamphlets assured people that transmission of the disease was not possible through sharing toilet seats, towels, or toothbrushes, they frequently portrayed sex toys as potentially deadly weapons.[644]

Mainstream experts warned of possible transmission of HIV/AIDS via sex toys, and this advice was passed on by gay health organizations. Using "dildos and other toys" was a form of "unsafe sex," according to the Harvey Milk Lesbian and Gay Democratic Club's 1983 pamphlet, but the message was muddled because on another page it suggested using toys was safe.[645] Even the AIDS Awareness medical trading cards released years later in 1993 claimed that "sharing sex toys such as vibrators may transmit HIV between partners." Such warnings persisted even though no evidence existed of people contracting HIV through using sex toys. For gay men, the message was confusing. Sex toys were safe when used by yourself but dangerous when shared with a partner. Why didn't organizations just suggest that men place condoms on their sex toys when sharing?

This irrational fear of sex toys arose in part from their association with gay and lesbian culture. Although sex toys were symbolic of feminist culture, they were also seen as symbols of gay male culture, and like the members of this culture, sex toys were thought to carry disease.

While arguments occurred within the gay community over whether gays should tone down their sexuality or should focus on eroticizing safer sex, lesbians and feminists weren't too worried about the disease. Through the mid-1980s, AIDS was still considered a gay disease, and no women-to-women transmission had been documented, although women's safe-sex pamphlets also advised that "sharing 'sex toys' can be dangerous."[646]

But sex was a topic of controversy among feminists at the time, and there were raging debates going on that culminated in the Barnard Sex Conference (officially known as "Scholar and the Feminist IX Conference: Towards a Politics of Sexuality"), held on April 24, 1982, in New York City. One person who watched the Barnard conference closely, from afar, was the pioneering lesbian erotica photographer and part-time Good Vibrations employee, Honey Lee Cottrell. Her lover Amber Hollibaugh traveled there as a key speaker.

Organized by Columbia University professor Carole S. Vance, the conference's goal was "to expand the analysis of pleasure, and to draw on women's energy to create a movement that speaks as powerfully in favor of sexual pleasure as it does against sexual danger."[647] The conference was controversial thanks to Vance's and other organizers' pro-sex views, particularly their positive attitudes toward pornography, sex toys, and S&M. What especially irked antiporn feminists was that Vance and others had decided not to involve them in the planning of the conference. Sexual pleasure was still a controversial topic within the feminist movement. This was the height of the feminist antiporn wars, and many speakers at the conference were highly critical of the antiporn movement for replicating old gender stereotypes that women weren't interested in sex, and that women had a responsibility to control male sexuality.[648] On the day of the conference, antiporn feminists "picketed and distributed leaflets . . . claiming that the decision to deemphasize pornography silenced a significant feminist presence."[649]

But what was most fraught for Cottrell weren't the debates over pornography and sex toys. It was that her girlfriend had found another lover at the conference and was head over heels for her. Cottrell was heartbroken. She quit her job at Good Vibrations and moved back home to Michigan.

As Cottrell was fleeing the Bay Area, a young woman named Susie Bright had just hitchhiked back to San Francisco from her seasonal job in an Alaskan fishery. She needed a new job and had applied to be a lane-cone changer on the Golden Gate Bridge, a job that "involve[d] standing in weather suits in every kind of weather on the Golden Gate Bridge and moving lanes of traffic through the bridge on the commute." It was a good-paying, solid, union job. But she had just learned through a friend that a new job was opening up working one day a week at a little vibrator store in San Francisco. Good Vibrations is "just so appealing," she thought, because it "put philanthropy first and profit last." She mused over which job would be better. She chose Good Vibrations.[650]

Bright wasn't your average young woman. By her early twenties, when she stepped through the door at Good Vibrations, she had a wealth of lefty experience that belied her young age. She had gone to a communist summer camp, worked for *The Red Tide,* and organized unions. Good Vibrations was the perfect place for her, with its focus that put sex education over profits. "I loved Joani's attitude," Bright said. "We hit it off. After all, it was one day a week. I had to do very little to prove myself."

When she first got to Good Vibrations, the store was truly putting business last. Good Vibrations "hardly had any customers," according to Bright. "I basically did sex therapy all day long." The store's inventory was spotty. "At that time, the vibrator museum took up more room than the stuff we had for sale," Bright said. It wasn't uncommon for Good Vibrations to have no Hitachi Magic Wands in stock.

Soon Bright was working at Good Vibes constantly, and she was promoted to manager. She instructed customers to take vibrators into the "tryout room," which doubled as Good Vibes's bathroom, where there were vibrators plugged into the wall. "The second you touch this [vibrator] to your jeans you will understand whether you like it or not," Bright would tell customers.

Bright and Blank forged a close connection. They began writing books together, including 1988's *Herotica.* With Bright on board, the store became even more of a touchstone for the Bay Area's avant-garde. One day, underground comics pioneers Robert Crumb, Terry Zwigoff, and Dori Seda came into the store with a request. "They wanted to do a photo funny [a comic with pictures instead of drawings] for their next comic book, which was called *Weirdo,*" Bright said. So Bright called up Blank to ask if after the store closed the rabble-rousing comic artists could do their "photo funny where they tie somebody up in vibrators." Blank agreed, and the shoot was on.[651]

Featured in *Weirdo #8,* the finished photo funny was called "Girls Turned into Vibrator Zombies." The plot featured two horny women, Bettie Bidet and Sylvia Silicosis, who decide to visit a sex-toy store.

"Yuck!! These things are gross," Sylvia exclaims in the comic when she sees the vibrators for the first time. But when "the vibrators come alive suddenly," she and Bettie have a change of attitude. They go to the try-out room to use the vibrators, but the store clerk—Vaseline Sally—demands they leave. A fight ensues; Sylvia and Bettie hit Sally over the head with a vibrator, tie her up, stuff dildos in her mouth, and run out of the store with a handful of stolen dildos and vibrators.[652] The theme of the story: Vibrators turn women into sex maniacs who shun men and become criminals. Of course it was tongue in cheek, but it is still telling that this was the underlying message. In fact, this wasn't the first time vibrators had appeared in underground comics in the 1970s and 1980s.

Usually, these underground comics were drawn by women, and women portrayed vibrators very differently. On a cover of her 1976 comic *Tits & Clits,* Joyce Farmer drew three women proudly thrusting their vibrators in the air while participating in a women's liberation protest in front of the White House. "We Shall Overcome" is being sung in the crowd. Farmer presents vibrators as symbols of freedom that unite members of the women's movement by liberating them from men, embodying the feminist mantra of the time, "The Personal Is Political."[653] [654]

Another issue of *Tits & Clits* (1976) featured the story "Fuller Bush Person," written and drawn by Farmer and Lyn Chevli It's the tale of saleswoman Mary Multipary, who drives around town in a "clit-mobile" selling vibrators and contraceptives to housewives door to door. A symbol of female empowerment, the clit-mobile looks like a Volkswagen Beetle, except it has been adorned on the front grille with a large vulva featuring an enormous clitoris. The story begins with Mary arriving at the house of a be-muumuu'd, overweight female customer. Mary removes a vibrator kit from her suitcase and delivers her sales pitch.[655] "No more tedious clit twiddling on weekdays or compulsory cunnilingus on Saturday night . . . I recommend the starter kit with a 4-inch vibrator which prevents primary male jealousy," Mary says as the expectant client looks on.[656] The customer is won over. Later on she arrives at another house, and the woman who opens the door and declares, "Oh, Mary, I hate being married." She talks her into purchasing a vibrator by saying, "A vibrator isn't a substitute for a husband—it's in addition to one."[657] Unlike in Crumb, Zwigoff, and Seda's comic, Farmer and Chevli's comic shows that sex toys do not have to threaten conventional society by destroying male-female relationships. Women can have men and sex toys both.[658] [659]

(*)

Around the time Bright started working at Good Vibrations, Blank decided to broaden the profile of the store. Although she was taking out local ads in the alternative newspapers *East Bay Express* and the *San Francisco Weekly*, her ads were barebones and her ad budget was tiny: less than a third of the amount they were spending on catalog production.[660] After five years in the business, she decided she wanted to go national. It was March of 1982, and there was really only one national feminist magazine to speak of: *Ms.* It seemed like the logical choice for an ad for a feminist sex-toy store, as they had been printing ads for Eve's Garden since 1974.[661]

Because she was only interested in running a small, text-based advertisement, she chose to buy space in the classified section. The ad was simple and to the point: "Good Vibrations: vibrator store and museum: sex toys and books about sex. Friendly, feminist, and fun." Pleased with its straightforward language, she sent the draft of the ad to *Ms.* and waited.[662]

A few weeks later, according to Blank, she received a letter from *Ms.* She opened it, expecting a confirmation of receipt and information about the run date of her ad. Instead the letter said that "they already had too many ads for sex aids in the classified section." Blank was confused. How could they have too many ads for vibrators? Wasn't this a feminist magazine? Weren't vibrators feminist devices? She called the advertising department, insisting that they run an ad for Good Vibrations. The staff acquiesced and agreed to run the ad in June.[663]

When she opened the June edition of *Ms.*, there in the back was a small ad for her store. Nothing fancy, but it was a step toward a national presence for Good Vibrations. Within a few weeks, it had generated nationwide interest. Pleased, Blank sent *Ms.* a check to pay for running the same ad in the July and August issues. A week later, Blank claims that she received her check in the mail, un-cashed, accompanied by a letter from a classified advertising staff person saying, "'The Advertising Acceptance Committee' ha[s] cancelled all vibrator ads from the pages of *Ms.*" The letter also helpfully suggested that she "advertise another product."[664] She didn't understand why *Ms.* had suddenly chosen to change their policy. When they'd refused to accept her ad the first time, they'd told her that they had too many sex-toy ads. Now they were unwilling to carry any ads at all.

Yet Blank was undeterred. Having successfully talked her way into getting *Ms.* to run her ad before, she refused to take no for an answer. She wrote the *Ms.* advertising department back, begging them to take her ad. They declined. So she enlisted her famous feminist friends to campaign on her behalf, to no avail. One of her friends informed her that *Ms.* was publishing a feature article about Betty Dodson. The hypocrisy of not accepting ads for vibrators while featuring a piece on Dodson galled Blank. So she called up staffers at *Ms.* to ask why they would publish an article promoting masturbation but refuse to run ads for a vibrator store, and she was told that "the advertising department and the editorial department have nothing to do with each other."

Blank continued to protest, leading the *Ms.* staffer to declare: "We are not a sex magazine."

For Blank, this answer was not satisfactory. She refused to back down. "You know about Good Vibrations," she said. "You write the ad that has acceptable words to you." *Ms.* balked, said Blank, so she rewrote the ad, using "the most bland words [she] could possibly think of." When she submitted the new ad, the *Ms.* staffer replied by saying, "You can't use your name [in the ad] because it says 'vibrations' in it." For *Ms.* the war was over, but Blank was undeterred.[665]

To be fair, employees at *Ms.* weren't just being arbitrarily prudish. They had logical reasons for rejecting a Good Vibrations ad. The vibrator ads in *Ms.* had been used to undermine the legitimacy of the magazine before. Four years earlier, in 1978, a school-board member in Nashua, New Hampshire, had succeeded in removing *Ms.* from a local high school's library "largely [because] it contained advertisements for 'vibrators,' contraceptives, materials dealing with lesbianism and witchcraft, and gay material."[666] The school-board member's equation of vibrator ads with witchcraft shows how dangerously vibrators were viewed. They were totems that could destabilize society by empowering women to be less dependent on men. The *Ms.* ban was soon overturned by a student who won a class-action lawsuit and got the magazine reinstated on the library's shelves. Yet the belief remained that vibrator ads undermined *Ms.*'s credibility.[667]

Blank had no options left. Her famous friends had not succeeding in convincing *Ms.* magazine to run her ad. Staffers at *Ms.* had refused to write the Good Vibrations ad themselves. They'd even told her that the name of her company, a name co-opted from a family-friendly Beach Boys song, was offensive. So she gave up. The most famous feminist magazine in the United States was not going to accept her ad. That was that.[668]

A few months later, in early 1983, she had been attending a booksellers' meeting on behalf of Down There Press when she happened upon a poster promoting Gloria Steinem's memoir *Outrageous Acts and Everyday Rebellions*. Steinem, founder of *Ms.* magazine, was in attendance, the poster said. Who better to talk to about the rejection of her ad? If she just let Steinem know that *Ms.* was rejecting vibrator ads, she would change the policy, Blank surmised.

Blank made her way to Steinem's table. It wasn't difficult to find. A long line of people stood in front of it, waiting for autographs. Blank patiently took her place in line. She asked for Steinem's autograph, then introduced herself. Blank told the story of the rejection of her ad, explaining that Good Vibrations was a feminist store, and *Ms.* was the perfect venue to reach potential customers. She waited for Steinem's reply, convinced that if anybody at the magazine understood the injustice of rejecting a feminist store's advertisement, it would be Steinem. "Oh yeah, I heard about that," Steinem replied curtly, according to Blank.[669] Steinem says she doesn't remember the incident. If Blank's account is correct, then Steinem shared the same views as Betty Friedan, founder of National Organization of Women, who wrote in 1976, "I didn't think a thousand vibrators would make much difference . . . if unequal power positions in real life weren't changed."[670 671]

Steinem's and *Ms.* staffers' refusal to accept the ad, according to Blank, shows the precarious position that the vibrator occupied in the mainstream feminist movement in the 1980s. While they published a feature article on sex toys and mentioned Good Vibrations prominently, they wouldn't allow their advertising. Another sex-toy company, the Xandria Collection, was allowed to advertise, as was Frederick's of Hollywood. Why not Good Vibrations? "Big corporate advertisers don't want to be seen with us," wrote Bright and Blank in a 1987 edition of the *Good Vibes Gazette*. They asked their readers to start a letter-writing campaign to Pat Carbine, *Ms.*'s publisher.[672]

Their problems with getting advertising accepted hadn't ended. Blank continued to try to get an ad accepted at *Ms.*, but *Ms.* refused unless Good

Vibes used their corporate name, Open Exchange. *Woman's Bookstore News* wryly commented about *Ms.*'s insistence on sanitizing Good Vibrations ads in 1987: "Do we now have to raise a generation of readers who have to refer to the 'v-word.' . . . Woman's liberation to *Ms.* Women's liberation to *Ms.* Come in please."[673]

Ms. wasn't the only magazine that quaked at the thought of offending its readers or corporate sponsors with supposedly salacious Good Vibrations ads. In 1988, an unlikely publication had problems with Blank's ads: the sexy women's magazine *Cosmopolitan*, which required Blank to bowdlerize her ad by removing all mentions of sex from it. Yes, that's right, the magazine whose February 1988 cover featured the headline, THE NUMBER ONE SEX QUESTION: HOW OFTEN? had problems with the word *sex*. Perhaps *Cosmo* was concerned because Blank sold her toys for couples and for masturbation?[674] In one of several changes required, Blank was forced to change the term *sexual playthings* to *sensual playthings*, but allowed to keep the word *vibrator*.

So much for the sexual revolution and the triumph of sexual liberation. To be fair, not all magazines had problems with her ads. Some left-wing magazines like *Mother Jones* and *The Utne Reader* let them run as is. But *The Village Voice* required them to remove the word *sex*, suggesting *adult* instead. Blank rejected their suggestion and "reluctantly settled for sensuous."[675] Even the feminist magazine *off our backs* refused the Good Vibes' ad because, according to Blank, "they know our products represent and could be said to support a diversity of sexuality fantasies and activities, including some that they do not consider politically correct."[676]

Good Vibrations couldn't win when it came to advertising. *Playboy* rejected their ads in 1989, including one ad that was for their sexuality books. The magazine was particularly upset about a book they were advertising called *Period.*[677] Men's magazine *Penthouse*, though, was willing to run their ads. Yet some customers weren't too happy about Good Vibrations taking out ads in a men's magazine. "I don't know why you pay money to a magazine that exploits women, particularly lesbians," one customer wrote. "You say you are for liberating women's sexual freedoms." It was a valid point. Why would a feminist company advertise in *Penthouse?*

After much debate, Blank and the other employees decided to keep running the ads in *Penthouse.* And they wrote back to the customer with a solid, articulate defense. "While such magazines' depiction of human sexuality is regrettably limited, unappealing, and even flawed, in this sex-education starved nation, they are often the only place that people can think of to turn to when they need information about sex," the staff wrote. "When 'feminist' publications such as *Ms.* and *off our backs* refuse our ads, while 'sexist' magazines such as *Penthouse* run them—and when *Penthouse Forum* frequently and enthusiastically supports our business in its editorial sections—you start to wonder who's really committed to, as you put it, 'liberating women's sexual freedom.'" Feminists, it seemed, still were not unequivocally in favor of sex toys. Men, however, were beginning to coming around.[678]

(*)

As Blank struggled to get her ads in *Ms.*, Honey Lee Cottrell and another employee were waging their own battle with Blank, trying to get her to carry dildos. They succeeded in convincing Blank to stock dildos, but their victory was halfhearted because Blank insisted on hiding them. She kept the dildos secreted away in a cabinet because she "didn't want to scare away the people who were not wanting to look at dildo-y things," she said. "There were still lots and lots of lesbians who wouldn't use them." The only women who got to see the dildo inventory were those brave enough to ask if the store carried "anything else." Only at that point would Blank ask, "Are you inquiring about dildos?" If they did, she'd finally show them the wares.[679]

Blank had her reasons, both ideological and practical. The dildos she sold weren't exactly up to her standards. This wasn't by choice, however. The only supplier of dildos she knew about was Sturman, and, at the time, Doc Johnson dildos were low quality, hard to clean, porous, and full of bubbles. As Bright described them, one of the dildos was a "bullshit Caucasian-colored soft latex" extremely long dildo "stuffed with nothing but foam" with a small vibrator, run by one AA battery, inserted in the bottom. "It was like grabbing a piece of foam that just vaguely vibrated," Bright said.

Blank would pick up these and her battery-operated vibrators at warehouses in sketchy areas of San Francisco. "We were both like Ms. Betty Angry Consumer Reports about the novelty business," Bright said. The people running Doc Johnson "were like, what's a nice girl like you doing in a place like this? And I'm like why are you making such crap? And why don't you make something like this that women could get off on? Oh my God, they thought that was hilarious." It wasn't true that Doc Johnson didn't care about women's sexual pleasure at all, but they were trying to primarily appeal to the men's market, so it's understandable why Bright felt that way.[680] But no matter how crappy Bright and Blank thought the novelty industry's products were, Good Vibrations persisted in selling them.

They really had no choice. Doc Johnson was the largest distributor of sex toys in the United States. More than 70 percent of the sex toys sold in the United States were made by Doc Johnson.[681] Sturman controlled the industry through his Byzantine system of eighty-five nationwide distribution centers. These centers purchased sex toys in bulk from Doc Johnson and then sold the toys to the more than fourteen thousand adult books stores in the country, many of which Sturman owned. Not only did Sturman control Doc Johnson, but he also distributed nearly all the other sex-toy brands in the United States Sturman had his hand in every aspect of the sex-toy business: production, distribution, and retail.[682] For a sex-toy company to be profitable, they had to go through Sturman.

But not everything was going well within the Doc Johnson empire. Braverman's earlier claim that he never did business for Sturman overseas—a statement he made under oath—was now being questioned. The government accused Braverman of lying. They also said that Braverman had lied about depositing $600,000 from the sale of Doc Johnson's Amsterdam stores in a Swiss bank account. Braverman had been granted immunity in exchange for his testimony, but the deal didn't cover perjury. He'd also claimed that David Sturman was not involved in any of Sturman's overseas business, but Sturman's son was, in fact, an officer of two of them and supposedly helped launder more than $7 million for his father.[683] In March 7, 1984, Braverman's testimony came back to haunt him. The government indicted him for seven counts of perjury. While returning from a trip to find new sex toys in Hong Kong on March 20, 1984, Braverman was arrested at the Los Angeles International Airport. He faced a potential thirty-five years in prison and a $70,000 fine. If he served his full sentence, Braverman wouldn't get out until he was in his seventies.[684]

Now that the government had gotten Braverman, they were closing in on Sturman himself. Rosfelder had been amassing a large dossier on Sturman, and he felt that they finally had enough evidence to convict the porn king for tax fraud, a charge much easier to successfully prosecute someone on than obscenity. On June 28, 1985, while overseeing the Doc Johnson sex-toy factory and headquarters in Los Angeles, Sturman was arrested and charged with sixteen counts of tax fraud. The government claimed that Sturman had secreted $7 million in overseas bank accounts. His thirty-three-year-old son David was charged as well, in addition to four others, including the general manager of Sovereign News, Melvin Kaminsky.[685] Sturman faced up to seventy-five years in prison and $10 million in fines. His bond was a prohibitively expensive $3 million. His lawyers protested, but the judge refused to reduce the bond because they found the passport of a dead man in his desk and assumed that Sturman was planning to flee. Sturman was able to scrounge up the money for his bond with the help of fellow pornographer and First Amendment advocate Larry Flynt, who provided $400,000 of it. On July 10, less than two weeks after going to jail, Sturman was free—at least for the time being.[686] David's bond was set at $200,000; that was paid by his mother, Esther, who had begged Reuben not to bring the children into the business. It must have been heartbreaking for her to use her $200,000 condominium as collateral for his bond.[687]

The government alleged that, between 1979 and 1982, Sturman had systematically hid his earnings. They claimed that in addition to his Swiss bank accounts, Sturman had secreted money by setting up corporations in Lichtenstein, Panama, and Liberia. Those three countries all allowed corporations to hide the names of their officers and other corporate information. The Swiss banks could not be compelled to reveal details of customers' accounts, with one exception: If a foreign government was trying to get information about the head of an organized crime ring, the Swiss would hand over names. So the U.S. government told Swiss officials that Sturman was in charge of a mob-like organization. And Sturman did indeed have some connection with the mob. The mafia ran a lot of the porn industry beginning in the 1970s. *Deep Throat*, for example, was funded by a $25,000 loan from mobster Anthony "Big Tony" Peraino.[688] But despite Sturman's connection with some unsavory figures, it was certainly an exaggeration to describe Sturman as a mob boss.

After eight years of chasing him, the IRS case agent Richard Rosfelder had gotten his man. The arrest was so monumental that President Reagan's attorney general, Edwin Meese III, announced it at a news conference. A little while after Flynt paid Sturman's bond, in 1986, Braverman pled guilty to six of the perjury counts. He was sentenced to 366 days in prison and fined $60,000. Braverman appealed, arguing that he had inadequate legal representation.[689] The case went all the way to the Supreme Court. On March 21, 1988, the Court made its decision: the sentence would stand. Braverman ended up spending only six months in prison.[690]

(*)

As the Sturman empire was crumbling, Bright got a thick envelope in the mailbox from a man named Gosnell Duncan. "He had mechanical drawings of all his different devices, and I could tell he was a big nerd, the kind of guy who reads *Popular Mechanics*," she said.[691] "At first I thought, is he kooky, because of the long letter. I could tell he was obsessed." She wrote back asking him to tell her more about his products. A little while later Bright received a box in the mail. When she opened it, she gasped. His dildos "were so beautiful," she said. "They were island colors. The colors in sex toys were just so fucking ugly and here he had this creamy vanilla color, and these pale lavenders, and these pinks that weren't Barbie pink, it was cool pink, and this mysterious grey," Bright said. Even though they were different than the dildos she had seen before, she couldn't simply begin stocking them in the store and putting them on display without Blank's approval.

Yet Bright thought she could win Blank over because, she thought that Duncan was "the kind of person Joani would love [since] he is making something with his own hands in his garage that he came up with because he's disabled." Blank and Bright had been inspired by "movies like *Coming Home*, where Jon Voight plays the disabled vet in a wheelchair who seduces Jane Fonda. Jon Voight eats her out and she comes for the first time, and it's like this big Hollywood movie." Movies like this promoted the idea that "men who can't rely on their penis have learned there's a lot [more] going on [during] sex [than just intercourse]."[692]

Yet when Bright urged Blank to sell dildos openly, Bright was met with resistance. "Eww. I don't want to put them on the shelf, icky. Ugh," Blank said. Dildos remained a political minefield: representative of masculinity and patriarchy for some and symbolic of female usurpation of male power for others. To be sure, some feminists simply viewed dildos as innocuous pleasure tools. Yet the politics of the sex-toy movement remained fractious.[693] Blank was antidildo in part because she thought that women were falsely informed through popular culture (romance novels and movies) that penis-in-vagina intercourse would give them orgasms. They needed to learn about their clitorises, Blank argued. Selling dildos would continue to perpetuate the false romantic myth. Bright agreed that many women "needed the clit message." But she told Blank that "most of the dykes are already past that stage, and we can't just treat everybody like they are in kindergarten. [Many lesbians] know what gets them off, understand their clitoris backwards and forwards, and they also want vaginal and anal penetration." Finally, she convinced Blank to carry Duncan's dildos even though, as Blank said, "so many lesbians would feel they were betraying the movement if they were buying dildos."

Soon, Bright proudly placed Duncan's dildos on display in Good Vibrations. Two factors made Duncan's dildos likely to not sell well: They were expensive, and he had trouble keeping up with demand. But they were a hit, and these factors turned his dildos into status symbols. "The elite sex people in San Francisco were like, 'I want dibs on the next one that comes in. I don't care how much it costs,'" Bright said.[694] Why was it so hard for him to keep up with demand? Not only was he making dildos and butt plugs by hand, but he was also making them to customers' individual specifications. And it wasn't just women writing him. Both men and women sent him requests for handmade sex toys. Men sent him their orders for butt plugs, complete with mechanical drawings. One man sketched out a 7-inch-long by 3½-inch-wide butt plug in either a black or violet color.[695]

Bright began consulting with Good Vibrations customers to discover the types of dildos they wanted. In addition to the probe-like Venus, customers were interested in having a dildo that looked like a minimalist penis, with a defined head but no veins. Duncan and Bright even designed a dildo together that he named after Bright.[696] The Suzie was a simple, abstract phallus, 6 inches long and 15/8 inches in diameter. It retailed for forty-two dollars at Good Vibrations and was available in pink, cream, and lavender colors.[697] Suzie later made its cinematic debut in 1988 in Monika Treut's punk feminist film *Die Jungfrauenmaschine* in a scene where Bright, as Susie Sexpert, shows it off to the main character and mentions that it's silicone that makes it unique.

Detailed back-and-forth discussions with individuals ranging from widows to prominent members of the lesbian community ensued with Duncan over sex-toy design.[698] One lesbian activist even gave him important insights about why she liked the Suzie dildo. "Well, most of why I like it is because it is short and wide," she told him. This was news to him, as well as many men who believed that length was all that was important in a dildo or a penis. Penises are spoken of in terms of one dimension: The longer the better. Porn stars are known for their nine-inchers (or thirteen-inchers in the case of John Holmes). In fact, girth was more important to her and her friends. "Most of the women I play with like thickness." she said. She asked him to increase the girth of some of the dildos from 1¼ inches to 1½ inches. Without any negative judgment, Duncan took notes, adjusted the sizes, and sent new dildos back to her a few months later.[699] She thought the new, thicker dildos were much better, but she still asked for more changes, including making them shorter and less curvy.[700] That Duncan, a heterosexual man, was willing and eager to work with gay men and women and help design toys to suit their needs was groundbreaking.

When Good Vibrations created their first newsletter, the *Good Vibes Gazette*, in 1985, Duncan's silicone dildos were featured prominently. "Before Scorpio Products came along, dildos came in two sizes: huge and ridiculously huge," said the *Gazette*. "They were not well made, were ugly, and impossible to clean." But Duncan's dildos, the article said, contained "a wide range of sizes and colors that are attuned to our customers' desires."[701] That same year, Good Vibrations created their first mail-order catalog, and now they were real competitors with Eve's Garden.

Even with Duncan's new designs, dildos remained contentious, however, as Bright noted in the inaugural edition of her 1984 lesbian erotica magazine *On Our Backs*. "The facts about dildos aren't nearly as controversial as their famous resemblance to the infamous 'penis' and ALL THAT IT REPRESENTS. The political, social, and emotional connotations of dildos have many unhappy lesbians in a stranglehold," Bright wrote. "Ladies, the discreet, complete, and definitive information on dildos is this: Penetration is as heterosexual as kissing!"[702] Not all feminists agreed with Bright. *On Our Backs* was a jab at a certain faction of the feminist movement, its title a take on the popular feminist magazine *off our backs*.

"I don't want to be part of a movement that has a sense of priorities that says, 'Sticking a dildo up my vagina is more important than [fighting] pornography as an institution of sexual abuse for women,'" antipornography activist Andrea Dworkin declared in the December 1985 edition of the *Gay Community News*.[703] Customers writing to Eve's Garden reflected Dworkin's viewpoint. For example, a lesbian contemplating ordering a dildo wrote to Eve's Garden: "I feel like I want something huge packed up me . . . even if [my female partner] thinks if you want a dildo you might as well be heterosexual."[704]

Bright soldiered on, undeterred by Dworkin and others in the mainstream feminist movement. But dildos remained fraught for some lesbian feminists, as Bright witnessed when they came into Good Vibrations. "I would have women tearfully tell me, 'I'm a lesbian this is my lover, we're like wives. We're completely satisfied with each, but we're both curious about dildos,'" she said. "They're like, is something wrong with us? Are we not really gay?" She'd reassure them. "I'd be like, 'Of course you're gay.'"

Bright turned out to be a very skilled sex-toy saleswoman. Because she was on commission, she was making enough money to live comfortably. "I suddenly wasn't living paycheck to paycheck, so I was thrilled, and a lot of people were coming in and asking for me," Bright said. There was one person who this didn't sit well with: Joani Blank. At least that's what Bright thinks. She thinks that Blank got uncomfortable with Bright's earnings because Blank "never thought [Bright's] commission would be more than paltry." Around this time, Blank hired a business advisor and demoted her from the position of manager. "For me he represented a man who came to cut my wages in half," Bright said. Insulted and upset to see herself replaced by business managers, in 1986 Bright finally quit Good Vibrations.[705]

Meanwhile, women-owned sex-toy stores sprouted up throughout the country in the 1980s, their shelves lined with dildos. In New York, Come Again opened its doors in the tony Upper East Side of Manhattan in 1981.[706] By 1987, women-friendly sex-toy boutiques also existed in Bellevue, Washington; Albuquerque, New Mexico; and Boulder, Colorado.[707]

In 1989, Bright declared victory in *On Our Backs*. "Now the dildo wars are over and guess what? We won. So stick it in and enjoy it."[708] Yet Bright continued to be attacked for her advocacy. Many feminists acknowledged that using a dildo did not make a woman less of a feminist. Yet for other feminists, dildos would always be patriarchal symbols. One feminist in particular, Sheila Jeffreys, railed against Bright in her 1993 book *The Lesbian Heresy*, calling

Bright a "lesbian sex industrialist" for Bright's selling of dildos in Good Vibrations new venture: in-home sex-toy parties. By 1986, Blank had changed her mind about, as Bright called them, "fuckerware parties" and decided if you can't beat 'em, join 'em.[709] Criticizing Bright, Jeffreys later wrote, "As lesbian feminists, we had to counter the sexological lie that lesbians really wanted to be men and could not do anything with each other without an imitation penis. It is ironic that it is now lesbian sex industrialists who see it necessary to cure lesbians of an inability to admit the dildo, a penis substitute."[710]

Bright was not just focusing on winning the dildo fight. She and Blank had also turned their attention to what Good Vibrations could do to help with the new disease hitting the gay community in San Francisco. In July 1984, Bright lent her assistance to the Gay Men's Health Crisis sex-toy booths at both the East Bay and San Francisco gay days.[711] The disease was soon to become an epidemic, and the sex-toy business was caught in the middle.

* THIRTEEN

Meese and Masturbation

Thanks to the sex-toy parties and the VCR, by the mid-1980s, sex was moving into the home. Now viewers didn't have to leave their houses to watch porn, and they could buy a dildo at a party with friends. With pornography spreading throughout the United States, President Ronald Reagan convened a Commission on Obscenity and Pornography headed up by Attorney General Edwin Meese. Similar to the obscenity commission created under the Johnson administration, the so-called Meese Commission set out to find the danger in obscene materials. Reagan was determined to create a commission that would come to the opposite conclusion as Johnson's, which found that porn wasn't harmful, and recommended the repeal of all obscenity laws. Although Nixon (who was president when the first commission released its report in the 1970s) hadn't heeded the commission's advice, it remained the most important federal government work on obscenity. Reagan was hoping to supplant it.[712]

To get the results he wanted, Reagan stacked the deck by placing such figures as an antisex conservative Catholic priest on the commission. In 1986, the Attorney General's Report on Obscenity and Pornography released its report. It concluded that porn was dangerous and led to crimes ranging from rape to child abuse, and most erotic materials were harmful. Just one type of material wasn't declared obscene—the vibrator—though that wasn't for a lack of trying. Some members of the commission, including the commission's executive director, Alan Sears, "repeatedly sought to ban the sale of vibrators and sexual devices even though there seemed to be little evidence the products were harmful."[713] "We'd vote down the idea, but it would keep coming back and coming back," reported a panelist to the *New York Times*. A doctor on the commission had the final say with his declaration that "the ordinary vibrator is no more obscene than the Washington Monument."[714] Although the commission hadn't suggested outlawing vibrators and dildos, anti-sex-toy laws continued to exist in some states.

(*)

A few years prior to the Meese Report's release, Colglazier and Rifkin learned that they had contracted HIV. In the early and mid-1980s, there was not much that could be done to treat HIV or AIDS. When they were diagnosed with the disease, treatments were scant in part because President Reagan had basically ignored the disease. The first AIDS drug, AZT, wasn't approved by the FDA in 1987. Although it ended up helping people live longer, the drug could have nasty side effects.[715] The life expectancy for those who contracted HIV in the early and mid-1980s was not long. Sometime during the mid-1980s, Rifkin died. (As in the case of so many other victims of the AIDS crisis, there's no existing record about an obituary or a funeral to point to the precise date.)

Even though he was gravely ill, Colglazier somehow managed to hide his sickness from his family back in Holyoke, Colorado, who didn't know that he was gay. Colglazier worried about the Pleasure Chest continuing without him. He had spent more than a decade and a half building up the Pleasure Chest. It was his baby; he didn't want to see it fall into disarray. His partner was no longer living, so he needed someone else to leave it to. By 1988, Colglazier had full-blown AIDS and was hospitalized. He had two choices: Continue to hide his sexuality from his family and die without seeing them, or come out of the closet. He chose to come out. Colglazier flew his siblings and his parents out to New York City in February, and they said their goodbyes to him as he lay in his bed at St. Vincent's Hospital.[716] He was only forty-three years old when he died.

In spite of everything Colglazier had done for the gay community and demolishing sexual taboos, he didn't receive an obituary in the *New York Times*. He only got an obituary in the *Holyoke Enterprise*, which devoted two paragraphs to his jobs at Dempsey-Tegeler and driving an ice cream truck. There was only one sentence about his most important accomplishment: "Duane was the founder of the Pleasure Chest line of boutique stores with locations in five cities." There was no hint of the true nature of his life's work.[717] The Pleasure Chest continued without Colglazier, but it wasn't the same.

According to his nephew, Brian Robinson, Colglazier decided to leave the Pleasure Chest business, and the multiple stores he'd created, to his parents. But when he asked them if they would take over the business, they said, "Duane, we've lived our lives, we're retired. We can't do anything with these," according to Robinson. "So he ended up leaving it to his three siblings: my aunt, my uncle, and my mother. And my mother stayed in the Seventh-day Adventist religion so she didn't want anything to do with the business." Robinson said that his mother wanted to sell, but Colglazier's aunt and uncle, who were no longer Seventh-day Adventists, hoped to hang on to it. And they each wanted 100 percent control over the Pleasure Chest. But they each refused to sell to each other, so they entered a stalemate. According to Robinson, since Colglazier's siblings couldn't agree on running the Pleasure Chest, his lawyer had to run the company.[718]

(*)

By the time Colglazier passed away in 1988, the lesbian community still wasn't overly concerned with HIV and AIDS. There was reason for this cavalier attitude. No definitive proof existed that HIV had been transmitted through lesbian sex. Although AIDS had already decimated huge portions of the gay male community, lesbians had been less affected, and therefore they were more cavalier about safe sex. Pamphlets about women and AIDS barely mentioned lesbian sex. But some lesbians, notably Susie Bright, believed it was time for the lesbian community to start taking HIV and AIDS seriously. "Lesbians have to pull their heads out of the sand (and stop thinking) that [HIV/AIDS] doesn't happen to them and that we're some pure race that it can't affect," Bright told the Associated Press in 1987.[719]

Good Vibrations stepped up and began educating women about AIDS, suggesting women use condoms during sex, as well as when sharing sex toys. In addition to educating their customers about AIDS, they also sold discounted condoms that they received at a nominal price from the AIDS Foundation. But Good Vibrations's founder Joani Blank didn't believe that fear of partnered sex during the AIDS era increased the use of sex toys. She thought that "for every person" who had turned to sex toys because of a fear of AIDS, another person had "given up sex altogether."[720]

Blank and Bright educated lesbians and straight women on the fact that they were vulnerable too. Yet they were playing a balancing act: They needed to keep sex sexy while also conveying a serious life-or-death message. And sex toys made this task even more difficult because they were cast both as vectors of HIV and as devices that could help prevent its spread. Surprisingly, masturbating with sex toys was rarely promoted as an anti-AIDS measure to women, as it was with gay men. Sex toys were once again primarily presented as couples devices, as objects meant to be shared. For example, the 1988 "Women, Sex and AIDS" pamphlet asked the question "What is risky behavior?" The usual suspects were listed: sharing needles, sex, oral sex. The pamphlet didn't stop there. It warned readers that "Even sharing sex toys can be dangerous."[721] Other pamphlets gave similar advice. One suggested placing condoms on the toys or disinfecting sex toys with bleach or rubbing alcohol.[722]

Bright participated in safe-sex events in California to educate the public about sex-toy safety. She was a part of Santa Cruz AIDS Project's 1988 "Feeling the Heat" program, which was designed to teach women about safer sex and raise money for AIDS, because, as the AIDS Project's director wrote, "the Federal Government has yet to provide adequate funding for the care of those with AIDS." In the conference's program, Bright included a warning to women about the dangers of sex toys: "Anyone who has ever shared a dildo or vibrator knows how easy it is to pass a yeast infection, let alone herpes or AIDS." To prevent passing diseases, she instructed women to use condoms on sex toys instead of "boiling dildos in your spaghetti pot."[723]

It wasn't until a few years later that Dell Williams joined Bright in the safer-sex push. After moving Eve's Garden again, this time to the fourth floor of the same building on 119 West Fifty-seventh Street, Williams developed an increased focus on safer sex, instructing customers to use condoms on dildos and vibrators.[724] An offshoot of the Gay Men's Health Crisis, the Lesbian AIDS Project contacted Williams with a request. They were making a safer sex booklet for lesbians and they wanted to know if she would be willing to lend vibrators, butt plugs, dildos, latex barriers, and lubes for their photo shoot. Williams agreed, and soon a Hitachi Magic Wand, Duncan's Scorpio dildo (lavender colored), latex sex gloves, and a smattering of other products were being photographed in the service of reducing AIDS transmission. Once again, the personal was political. And sex toys had now become another tool in the fight against AIDS. It was a heavy load for a silicone rubber penis to bear.[725]

And those masturbation parties that had become popular thanks to AIDS? Women wanted in. "A few brave, curious women pestered their gay male friends for entree to one of their now-regular jackoff events," wrote Carol Queen and David Steinberg, in a 1991 article in *The Realist*. And on November 7, 1987, a new type of party, a Jack-&-Jill-off party, was born. Queen went to the first party at a loft in San Francisco with some trepidation, thinking "nice girls don't go sniffing like beasts around warehouses full of men with erect cocks." Although Queen had given herself permission to "just watch" or "to leave if [she] felt too uncomfortable," she ended up staying for hours, even orgasming eight times in ten minutes, and when she was done, she saw gay men "marveling that women really can do that," Queen wrote. (Queen & Steinberg, "The Jack-and-Jill-Off Parties," Jan/Feb, 6.)"

Queen enjoyed the Jack-&-Jill-off party so much that she became an organizer. A recent San Francisco transplant, she was enrolled in the doctoral program at the Institute for the Advanced Study of Human Sexuality. One of her instructors suggested that she get to know another woman who was interested in masturbation: Betty Dodson. After meeting Dodson in New York City, Queen went to one of Dodson's parties in San Francisco, and at the party was none other than Joani Blank. Several months later, the phone rang, and it was Blank asking Queen "if she was available one day a week" to work at Good Vibrations. Queen was familiar with Good Vibrations from attending their Erotic Reading Circle. She said yes.[726]

(*)

While the progressive sex community in San Francisco was keeping safe sex sexy with masturbation parties, Sturman continued to fight his indictment on tax evasion. In 1987, Sturman showed up to his pretrial motion hearings in a Groucho Marx disguise and mocked the waiting reporters. After winning every obscenity trial he'd been subjected to, he'd become cocky.[727]

As Sturman faced a possible conviction, he began selling off his companies and shredding important documents to hide evidence from the government. Much of the adult bookstore industry fell into disarray. The largest porn magazine distributor, purported mobster Robert DiBernardo, was missing and feared dead. Violence erupted elsewhere in Sturman's empire. Three people were shot and killed outside an adult bookstore in Shelby, North Carolina, on January 17, 1987, an incident that was thought to be connected to Sturman. In Houston, the house of one of Sturman's associates was set on fire, killing her maid. Another woman who worked for Sturman was subjected to a murder attempt in Chicago. Then Sturman faced a new indictment. Under the federal RICO racketeering act, which only a few years earlier had been expanded to cover obscenity violations, Sturman was brought up on charges in Las Vegas related to his Talk of the Town bookstores and his shipping illegal porn videotapes.[728]

During the chaos, his employees remained loyal, at least in the beginning. After they were subpoenaed they either lied or pled the Fifth. But there was only so long that they could hold out. Soon a few employees told the truth and began assisting the FBI, revealing where his documents proving his tax evasion were. They were hidden in an unlikely place: his housekeeper's basement. Sturman realized that his luck may have run out. The government may have actually won this time. So in October 1988, facing a likely conviction and prison sentence, Sturman divorced Delgado, allegedly in order to protect her. But they continued to live together in his five-thousand-square-foot Cleveland mansion.

On September 14, 1989, Sturman's trial finally began. It was the moment of truth. Could the government finally put Sturman away? On November 17, 1989, the answer came: Sturman was convicted on sixteen counts related to tax fraud and misusing foreign bank accounts.[729] Sturman wasn't the only member of his family facing prison. Even though his lawyer had argued that he was not "a knowing, intentional conspirator," his son David was convicted of one count of conspiracy.[730]

On February 12, 1990, Reuben Sturman entered the Cleveland courtroom for his sentencing hearing clad in a blue cowboy hat, matching blue aviator sunglasses, and one of those face masks to prevent germs. He was sentenced to ten years in prison and $2.46 million in fines. His life was in disarray. He also was awaiting trial on a Las Vegas RICO case, where he could face an additional seventy-five years in prison.[731] His son David was sentenced to four years. Both Sturmans appealed their convictions and were released on bond.[732]

(*)

Sturman wasn't the only one in the industry facing legal trouble. By the mid-1980s, Phil Harvey's company—now called Adam & Eve—was thriving, mailing out eight million catalogs yearly. Condoms were still their bestselling product, but vibrators had gained in popularity. They still didn't make any of their products themselves, but they were distributing huge amounts of them. The company now had seventy-five employees, and Harvey was beginning to get rich.[733]

Then on May 29, 1986, they got a rude awakening. Thirty-seven law enforcement agents burst into their Carrboro, North Carolina, warehouse with a search warrant, directing them to seize videos, magazines, and sexual devices on the hunt for obscenity.[734] Nobody was arrested, but more than one hundred employees were subpoenaed.[735] Adam & Eve's parent corporation, Phil Harvey Enterprises (PHE), and Harvey himself ended up being charged with nine felony counts of obscenity for magazines and videos. "The penalties, laid end-to-end, totaled forty-five years in jail, plus fines," Harvey wrote.[736]

The government, it seemed, was nearly as uncomfortable with sex as it had been two decades earlier when it began going after Sturman for obscenity. This time, however, the government was targeting a company whose founder was a well-liked and respected philanthropist. Phil Harvey prepared for the fight of his life. Even though the obscenity charges were for the so-called pornographic magazines and videos only, when the case went to trial in March 1987, out came "Prosecution Exhibit #123," which was a "foot-long double dong" that the prosecutor had ordered from the company. Although Harvey expected his lawyers to object, they did not. And the dildo was entered into evidence. The dong, along with brochures and magazines, was passed around by the jury. "They wanted to convince the jury that we were dirty dogs, and the double dong was something that they could ask the jury to pass around and feel in their own two hands, which you can't do with a video," Harvey said. "I think they just felt it would make it more convincing that we were a dirty, disgusting company." Later, the prosecution left the dong "in one of the attorney's recess rooms, quite possibly on purpose, to remind the defense team just what pernicious products their client sold."[737] But instead of the dong giving the defense attorneys second thoughts about Adam & Eve, one of the defense attorneys, Wade Fox, put the dildo in front of his crotch and exuberantly waved it around in front of his defense team.[738]

Seventeen days after the trial began, Harvey and PHE were found not guilty by the jury. It was cause for celebration, but it was only the beginning. That same day, the U.S. attorney for the Eastern District of North Carolina, Sam Currin, said that the federal government was going to continue to investigate Adam & Eve for obscenity in North Carolina and in Utah. In fact anywhere that Adam & Eve sent their products could be possible grounds for a prosecution. Adam & Eve was the target of the Department of Justice's 1987 Project Postporn project, which was a new strategy of engaging in "multi-district, simultaneous prosecutions of major mail order obscenity distributors." Known as a process called "forum shopping," these simultaneous prosecutions would usually occur in the most socially conservative locations in the United States, areas like the Bible Belt, where the community standards would presumably be so conservative that they would surely declare adult videos obscene.[739]

In the meantime, Currin interviewed Adam & Eve's employees to intimidate them and make them question their loyalty, telling one "that mailing any kind of pornography was like mailing a snake or a gun."[740] Although the government was going after the pornography side of Adam & Eve, "the case was about sex. Our company, Adam & Eve, sold sexually oriented merchandise, everything from condoms to massage oils, from lingerie to erotic videos, from vibrators to books and magazines with sexual themes and content," said Harvey.[741]

Indictments came down in Utah and Washington, D.C., in 1990. There was one way to avoid the nightmare of prosecutions: Plead guilty and pay the government a large sum of money (about $750,000, according to negotiations between Harvey's lawyers and Currin's office and prosecutors in Utah). Harvey and his lawyers contemplated accepting a settlement. But they just couldn't do it: The First Amendment was at stake.[742]

(*)

As Harvey was being prosecuted all over the country, Sturman was appealing his sentence. He continued to assert control over his empire, in a sometimes violent fashion. The owner of Pleasure World in Phoenix, Arizona, experienced this violence firsthand. When the original owner passed away in 1991, his wife took over the business and she noticed something suspicious: Her husband had been writing $10,000 checks to Reuben Sturman but there were no bills in sight. She decided to stop sending Sturman the checks. Big mistake. Sturman called her and explained that he owned part of the store. This was not convincing to her. She refused to be bullied. But then Sturman dispatched some criminals to destroy peep-show machines in her store to show her who was boss. She continued to send checks to Sturman soon thereafter.[743]

Emboldened by the success of his violent approach to dealing with adult bookstore owners who were delinquent with their payments, Sturman stepped up his tactics. In March 1992, when owners of Chicago and Milwaukee bookstores stopped making what Sturman called mortgage payments but the FBI insisted were extortion payments, he used a similar tactic to get them to pay up. He hired four men to bomb the stores to scare them. However, the people he hired made some mistakes. Their first was to use a Visa card in their own name to rent a car to plant a bomb at a Chicago store. They then accidentally set the bomb off within the car. One of the men was killed, and the other two turned themselves in.[744]

On June 10, 1992, Sturman's lawyer plea-bargained so the Las Vegas case didn't have to go to trial. He was sentenced to four years in prison, a $1 million fine, and forfeit of his businesses in Las Vegas, San Francisco, and Reno. The judge said he could serve it concurrently with his other sentence.[745]

In July, he had exhausted his appeals on the main tax evasion case and finally began serving his sentence in a minimum-security prison in Kern County, California. As far as prisons go, his wasn't bad. It was a white-collar jail for criminals with a low flight risk. But Sturman wasn't doing well. He was sixty-eight years old, and he desperately missed his young daughter, Erica, who was living in Encino with his ex-wife Naomi. On December 10, 1992, at 9 p.m., guards at the Boron Federal Prison Camp were doing a head count at the vehicle maintenance yard, where Sturman worked, when they noticed someone was missing. After only five months in jail, Sturman had escaped on foot.

"Everyone is speculating that he's out of the country," a federal agent told the *Los Angeles Times*. "With his unlimited funds and contacts around the world, he could be anywhere."[746] Yet the true story was more mundane: He was en route to see his ex-wife and daughter in Encino, with a stop at In-N-Out burger on the way.[747] According to his son David, this incident was the result of "early onset Alzheimer's dementia. . . . [My father] decided to see his daughter and walked away."[748]

Whatever the case, Sturman was not traveling throughout the world to hide from authorities. On February 9, 1993, two months after he escaped, he was caught. By then, he also faced trial in Chicago for attempted murder.[749] His future looked bleak. Even his son David was cooperating with the government.

(*)

With his father in jail in the early 1990s, David Sturman continued in the sex-toy industry, controlling most of the Northern California stores. But there was an area not dominated by Sturman: San Mateo, where one man, Harold Spielberg, owned thirteen stores, which he'd bought in the 1960s. Spielberg never finished high school, but he didn't need to. He had a natural affinity for business, and his stores did well. They were typical of the adult bookstores of the time: They catered to men and had a mix of pornography and sex toys. "At the time it was always men buying this stuff," said Spielberg's daughter Shay Martin. Spielberg's stores sold sex toys "that no woman really would want," she said. The vibrators Spielberg sold "looked like uncooked hot dog[s] with veins all over, really unappealing." One day in the late 1960s, Spielberg's friend introduced him to a Japanese nurse named Suzi. They hit it off. Soon they were married and Suzi and her young daughter, Shay, moved in with him.[750]

Yet if you were in the adult industry during this time, there was one man you couldn't avoid dealing with: Reuben Sturman, who if he was not running the stores himself was supplying the sex toys. Sturman wanted control of the entire industry. You either had to work for him or with him, which was almost the same thing. The worst thing you could do was to upstage him. He was the head honcho of the erotica business. Spielberg decided the best strategy of dealing with him and his organization was "to not step on toes . . . to stay under the radar and . . . play nicely with the big guys and not piss them off," Martin told me. One way to do this was to not get too big. Spielberg didn't expand beyond his area of Northern California. If he had wanted to be an empire builder like Sturman he probably couldn't have, not without incurring Sturman's wrath. Although Shay grew up knowing Sturman and all the "old-school guys," she learned the important lesson from her father of not making waves.[751]

By the time she was in high school in the late 1970s, Shay was working for her father's company during summer breaks, packaging orders and shipping them. "The topic of sexuality was just normal for me, ever since I was a kid," Martin told *Store Erotica* magazine in 2013. "I kind of grew up with all this stuff around me," she said.[752] Although her father's business was normal to her, not everybody felt that way. One day in high school, while Shay was taking driver's ed, she, her instructor, and a few students were driving down El Camino Real in San Mateo and they drove by one of her father's stores. "Oh, there's my dad's store," she said with pride. "And the guy is like 'That's your dad's store?'" There was silence in the car. "It didn't even dawn on me that it was such a strange thing. I was just so open about it," Shay told me, laughing. "Nobody gave me hard time, which was really nice." Not everybody was so sanguine about Spielberg's stores. In the 1980s, his stores were regularly raided by the police, but "he won all his battles with the police at the time."[753]

In the early 1980s, while Shay was studying biochemistry at San Diego State University, her mother and father found something unusual on one of their regular trips to Japan to visit Suzi's family. It was a vibrator that looked nothing like the vibrators he was selling in his store. It was bright pink and colorful and "it didn't have the same smell as some of these other products had." One of the reasons it looked so different was that "it was illegal to have anything that looked phallic." And it had something even more ground-breaking: a clitoral stimulator and a vibrating phallus together in one product. Each one had its own motor. At the time, vibrators were "either for internal use, penetration, or for external use [clitoral stimulation] but you couldn't do [both] at the same time, so it was like a revelation." Even better: The clitoral stimulator was intricately designed to avoid looking sexual. Some of the vibrators looked like woodland creatures, others like geishas, complete with kimonos and necklaces, and the vibrator was better made than any of the vibrators they had ever seen. He and Suzi decided to import them. But they were taking a risk. Would American men want to buy a vibrator that didn't look like a penis? A vibrator that featured a cute little animal? A vibrator that could stimulate a woman's genitals in a way their penis never could?

When they stocked their stores with the dual-action vibrators, they got their answer: American men would buy this strange-looking Japanese vibrator, and they would buy a lot of them. They came back to the store raving about the new vibrators. "These guys are saying, 'Wow! My girlfriend, my wife, my partner loves them, and [the vibrator] works for her,'" Shay said. Soon other adult stores throughout the United States heard about this new Japanese vibrator, and they all wanted to sell it too. But they didn't have the connections that Suzi and Harold Spielberg had. So the other store owners said, "We know we're your competitors, but would you mind selling these things to us?" The Spielbergs agreed, and, so they had another business on their hands, Vibratex, which they started in 1983. They were both distributors and store owners, kind of like Sturman. They sold to male-oriented adult stores and a few new boutique stores that had cropped up: the Pleasure Chest, Eve's Garden, and Good Vibrations.

As her parents built up a new sex-toy importing business, Shay continued studying for her degree. One day, while studying in the law library she met an engineering major named Dan Martin. They began dating, and when Shay told him about her parents' business, he wasn't fazed. They both graduated, got married, and began their careers, Shay in cancer research and Dan as a groundwater hydrology engineer.[754]

Although Sturman and Spielberg were friends, Spielberg never wanted to sell his stores to Sturman. Then, around the mid-1990s, Spielberg got terrible news: He learned that he had a terminal disease. He asked his daughter Shay if she'd be interested in taking over the Vibratex company. Shay thought it over. She loved her job as a cancer researcher. She'd been doing it for more than a decade. Switching from cancer research to selling sex toys wasn't exactly a natural transition. But her husband, Dan, was willing to join the business too. She told her father yes. Before Harold handed over the business to Shay, he sold his stores to David Sturman. Even though his father was in jail, David was carrying on his legacy.

When Shay and Dan started running Vibratex, one of their first steps was to talk to Good Vibrations and the newer feminist sex-toy store Toys in Babeland to see what they thought of Vibratex's wares. The retailers loved the company's toys, but they also saw room for improvement. They "could see a few tweaks here and there that could make a big difference," Shay said, such as placing the clitoral stimulator closer to the shaft of the vibrator. So Vibratex listened and began asking Japanese manufacturers to make these changes, particularly "telling them what works better for American women because Japanese women are so friggin' tiny" that their vibrators needed to be shaped differently, according to Shay. They developed a symbiotic relationship with the stores. "They're kind of our eyes and ears to the people out there using the products," she said.[755]

(*)

The Martins were entering the vibrator business at just the right time. Duncan's dildos had spread throughout the country, at the new boutique sex stores that had been created in the wake of Eve's Garden and Good Vibrations, stores like In Harmony in Albuquerque, New Mexico, and Majik Moments in Washington, D.C. There was even a store in Norway that carried them.[756] He had started advertising more frequently in lesbian magazines in the late 1980s, including Bright's *On Our Backs*.

On Our Backs worked with companies to create lesbian-friendly ads, and Duncan was more than willing to collaborate with Bright and photographer Honey Lee Cottrell, famed within the lesbian community for her daring erotic portraits of lesbians. Cottrell and Duncan bonded immediately, and Cottrell began coming up with ads for Scorpio Products, Duncan's company, which treated his dildos as art objects. One ad elevated dildos to high art with her photos of Duncan's dildo inspired by photographer Robert Mapplethorpe's calla lily photograph. She also shot an early ad for Duncan's dildos at Tomales Bay in Marin County, where she arranged the dildos like "watery sea creatures."[757] Another ad had a picture of two dildos elegantly displayed on pedestals with the definition of the Japanese word *sabi* written above: "elegant simplicity, striving for something closer to nature than nature itself."[758] The ad was a rejoinder to all those who thought dildos were unnatural.

By the late 1980s, Duncan wasn't the only person on the silicone dildo market—suddenly he had competition from two women-owned companies. Lickerish was founded by a former construction worker named Cindy Burns, who had begun experimenting with silicone and created a few models that were carried by Good Vibrations. The other competitor was chemistry student and sometime sculptor Trilby Boone, who took dildo-making to a new level with her fanciful designs of dildos shaped like cats and corn cobs for her new company Dills for Does.[759] In Good Vibrations's catalog they noted that both companies were "women-owned businesses located here in the San Francisco Bay Area." Although they didn't say that Scorpio Products was male-owned, they didn't have to.

Duncan thought that his gender may have affected his slow-down in business even before he had competition. "In the early '80s, a few articles [were] written about Scorpio Products and they mentioned my being involved it," he said. "[Business] started dropping off because I am a man who was making these items for the woman."[760] There's no way to know if that was the cause of lower sales. Women did continue to work with him and promote his products throughout the 1980s and 1990s.

By the early 1990s, Duncan was taking a more hands-on approach to the advertisements, as Cottrell would send him her photographs and Duncan would write back with notes from his home in Brooklyn. They ranged from the simple: "Arrange [the dildos] so that they don't block the nipples of the model's breasts," to bordering on micromanagement: "The model should hold one of the longer dildos in her hand touching the outside of one of her breasts" or "Add another tripod light to her side away from the camera so that there would not be a shadow." To her credit, Cottrell listened patiently to Duncan and took his requests to heart. She sent back a contact sheet of twelve poses of Jennifer, a topless model sitting in front of a desk, variously grasping dildos, placing them between her breasts and sitting in a serene pose.[761]

By this time, Duncan marketed his dildos in a much less clinical way. For starters, he didn't call them prostheses; they were now "Lil' Pal." And in addition to saying that his dildos were a "therapeutic aid," his sell sheet also said that they were "ideally suited for adults with active sexual imaginations." Although he sold dildos to lesbians in *On Our Backs*, in his own promotions he sold the dildos in terms of heterosexual gender norms. "[Dildos] can be used to fill in when 'The Real Thing' is not available," his brochure said. But Dell Williams's and Betty Dodson's masturbation empowerment rhetoric snuck in. Dildos allow women to be "sexually self-sufficient," Duncan wrote. They don't "get soft afterwards" or "get you pregnant." And dildos are useful for women who have partners, Duncan said, because if "the male partner is unable to satisfy . . . he can use the Penis Device" instead.[762]

He continued to sell dildos to the handicapped community, but he combined his pitches to both communities. "Originally designed and developed to be used by the physically handicapped they are also being used by able bodied adults," said one brochure.[763] And he didn't ignore the gay community.

By 1990 his bestselling products were a small butt plug and the dildo called "Adam's Thing."[764]

As Duncan was helping everybody with their sex lives, his own was suffering. His marriage to Angela was lonely; he yearned for connection with other people. He reached out to Bright, writing her long letters, sharing details of his disappointing sex life. Bright was his muse, and they collaborated with each other. "I said width is more important than length," Bright said.[765]

By 1993, Duncan's business was struggling, and he asked Bright if she wanted to take it over. "Of course I am interested in Scorpio continuing to stay alive," she wrote to him. "I know a lot about SELLING, ADVERTISING and USING your devices, but very little about manufacturing them, or what it takes to run your business, or about the income and expenses," she said.[766]

She declined to run Scorpio Products, but the dildo wars continued, and Bright kept fighting against those who she referred to as "dildo bigots" through the 1990s. Bright now admitted that dildos were political devices. "No matter how irreverently a woman chooses to uses a dildo, she is bound to confront the meaning of such a masculine symbol to her body and desires," Bright wrote. She noted, however, that gay men weren't faced with the same crisis. They "have the Dionysian advantage of enjoying dildos without the 'buy one, get an identity crisis' dilemma."[767]

(*)

Around this time, Joani Blank and Carol Queen transformed Good Vibes into more than just a sex-toy store. They'd moved from their tiny Mission District store to a larger, more prominent location on Valencia Avenue in 1989.[768] By the 1990s, the store had become a hub for sex education, with classes ranging from sexual sign language for the hearing impaired to safe sex in the age of AIDS.[769] In 1992, Blank decided to turn Good Vibrations into a worker-owned cooperative.[770] "Existing employees were offered the option of buying into the company for a nominal sum; those who chose not to do so stayed on as employees," said Queen. Blank considered this not only the socially responsible way of running a company but also the feminist way.[771]

Another aspect to her social responsibility: training other women to open up their own stores for a small fee of $500. Her first intern was Claire Cavanah, a lesbian feminist whose views on sex had flip-flopped between being a part of the "'take-back-the night, rape crisis center, obscenity laws' feminists and . . . the more progressive, much more fun, 'let's have sex, let's get turned on' feminists."[772] Eventually, the "let's have sex" ideology won out and Cavanah went to Good Vibrations to learn the secrets of the vibrator store trade. She took the valuable information she learned back to her hometown of Seattle and, with her best friend Rachel Venning, opened Seattle's first women-owned sex-toy store, Toys in Babeland, in 1993, with the goal of "getting a vibrator on every bedside table."[773]

A year later, another aspiring sex-toy store owner interned with Good Vibrations: Kim Airs. Airs was working at Harvard University for Larry Summers, when she decided to travel to San Francisco to learn the ropes. Her store—Grand Opening!—opened in Brookline, Massachusetts. After the success of both Good Vibrations interns, Good Vibrations cancelled the program. They didn't want to create any more competitors. Capitalism, it seemed, trumped sisterhood. Besides Good Vibrations wasn't making a huge amount of money anyway. Net income in 1994 was $73,678.[774] That was nothing compared to Sturman's empire. And Sturman's company was profiting from Good Vibrations too by selling them their Doc Johnson sex toys.

* FOURTEEN

The Government vs. Everyone

D espite Sturman being in jail (or perhaps because of it), Doc Johnson hummed along smoothly with Braverman at its helm until 1995, when a fire destroyed part of the Doc Johnson building. Nobody knows who did it, but rumors point—perhaps unfairly—to Sturman. Maybe he was trying to assert control. After all, some people believe that Sturman was the one who bought Marche Manufacturing from Ted Marche back in 1976, and, if the company was Sturman's baby, then he possibly didn't want Braverman profiting from it. Although, as journalist Dave Gardetta points out, it is entirely possible that Sturman didn't buy Marche Manufacturing and that Braverman funded Doc Johnson with his European bank accounts that the government discovered. A year after the fire of unknown origin, Braverman was arrested again on tax evasion charges related to Sturman. He ended up serving ten months, five in prison and five under house arrest.[775] With the building burned down and both its founders in jail, could this be the end of Doc Johnson?

(*)

They did have a big competitor on their heels. In the 1990s, Phil Harvey's Adam & Eve company saw that their porn video sales were slumping. It was the beginning of the Internet, and porn was becoming available online. So they began to focus on another line: sex toys. But just like Sturman had,

Harvey continued to be embroiled in obscenity cases through the early 1990s related to porn. First, they were charged in Utah and Washington D.C. in 1990; then they were soon subpoenaed in Kentucky, and an investigation was opened in Alabama. The government planned on bringing charges in multiple states simultaneously as part of their new tactic for going after companies selling pornography by mail order. "When [the government discovered that a] company was selling erotic material by mail in more than one state, which of course all of us do, the government was going in and saying, 'We'll prosecute you in Alabama, we'll prosecute you in New Jersey and in Utah and we'll break your bank,'" Harvey said. "Four or five companies just went out of business, signed plea agreements of various kinds."[776] Adam & Eve decided they couldn't sit back as the government tried to destroy the adult industry, and they decided to fight instead. So they sued the Department of Justice in 1990, arguing that the multiple prosecution strategy was an attempt to "coerce [companies] to cease distribution of sexually oriented materials, including [ones that] . . . are not obscene and are protected by the First Amendment." Nine months later, the court decided that "while the lawsuit was pending," the government wouldn't be allowed "to use its multiple-prosecution strategy against PHE [aka Adam & Eve]." Harvey and his Adam & Eve Company only had to defend itself in one location at a time. The obscenity case was about to go to trial in Utah, but they filed a motion to dismiss the case "based on bad faith and vindictiveness" on the government's part. They ended up getting the case dismissed in 1992. And the government has "never used that multiple simultaneous prosecution strategy again," Harvey said. "With our lawsuit and persistence, we got just enough appellate court judges to question the constitutionality of that approach." But a year after their victory, they were facing more trouble.[777]

In spite of having to spend $2 million fighting the government, Adam & Eve's profits were increasing.[778] Sales were growing, with sex toys being a big portion of those sales, and they decided to expand their headquarters from Carrboro to Hillsborough, North Carolina. But they faced another set of foes. This time it wasn't the government; it was the same groups upset about sex-toy parties in the 1980s: antiporn feminists and evangelical Christians. Both groups joined together to protest the new location of Adam & Eve's warehouse. The Christians were protesting Adam & Eve because they believed that their products "corrupt men, degrade women, and promote crime, homosexuality, and sex outside of marriage." Feminists were just upset about what they say is porn's degrading treatment of women.

The feminist leading the charge against PHE was the staunch abortion-rights supporter Lori Alward, who "view[ed] society as unfairly controlled by white men," according to an Associated Press article about the controversy. Alward must have been unaware that the white man she was fighting had devoted his life to promoting reproductive rights to women of color around the world with the nonprofit Population Services International, which provided abortion services in developing countries.[779]

For a while, the lobbying by conservative Christians and feminists was successful. The Hillsborough Board of Adjustment refused to give Adam & Eve a permit, claiming that the company was an "adult-use business," but Harvey, as he had done with the free-speech battle against the government, just kept appealing and winning.[780] In March 1994, the State Supreme Court decided to refuse further appeals and Adam & Eve broke ground for their 74,000-square-foot warehouse.[781]

(*)

Around the same time, Good Vibrations expanded again, this time to Berkeley, in 1994. It was there that they hit a snag. The leaders at Good Vibrations assumed that opening a store in Berkeley, a liberal bastion of free speech, would be no problem. They thought wrong. Located in a redbrick building that also featured a women's bookstore and an ecology center, Good Vibrations Berkeley was just a week shy of its opening date when the City Planning Department suspended its license. A resident had alerted their local city council member that they believed Good Vibrations had been improperly zoned as a retail and gift store. The resident insisted that it should be zoned as an adult bookstore instead, in part because the presence of Good Vibrations could increase prostitution in the area. Why was the issue of zoning important? "Because, according to Berkeley Municipal Code (23E.16.030), adult bookstores couldn't be "within 300 feet of . . . a residential district . . . or within 600 feet of any public park, health clinic, library, public school or church." In fact, zoning laws are one of the key ways that adult bookstores are regulated.

On Monday, December 13, 1994, just three days before the store was set to open, its future was uncertain. Instead of arriving to an operational sex-toy store on Thursday, December 17, customers were greeted with the option of signing a petition and urged to contact city officials. Hundreds heeded the call. The permit was provisionally reinstated.

The store managed to open just two days late, on Saturday, December 19. But Good Vibes's managers remained uneasy because they lacked a permanent permit. The only way to get one of those was to prove that Good Vibrations was not an "adult-oriented business," which according to the ordinance meant stores that "predominantly engage in the sale . . . of products or materials that appeal to the prurient interest or sexual appetite of the purchaser." In other words, Good Vibes—a sex-toy store—had to pretend that they weren't selling sex. To get their license, they had to prove that more than half their products (51 percent) were "educational materials and gifts." So they made their vibrators barely visible in the store, added "shelves and shelves of books" and sufficiently proved that they weren't too salacious. They got the permit reinstated for good in January 1996.[782]

Even as they expanded, Good Vibrations was in the middle of a financial crisis, and they were suffering losses. Many at the store blamed management. Eighteen years after Blank had founded the store, her tenure at Good Vibrations came to an end in 1996. Blank claims that she was pushed out because she wanted to continue to run the store as a co-op with no hierarchical management, and others disagreed, but the official line was that she retired. "One of the reasons that people were glad to see me leave [was] I think that many of them believed, and they were probably right, that I didn't [try to make the store grow]," Blank said in retrospect. "I was trying not to make a profit. I'm not really a business person. I'm an anti-business person. I am anti-capitalist."[783] After Blank left, Good Vibrations hired a general manager, Cathy Winks, to run the store.

It was the end of an era. The store's problems continued to get worse. According to Good Vibrations's internal history documents, "Morale took an all-new dive as many difficult changes were made." Some employees stopped "showing up for meetings on time or at all," while others worked overtime for free to get the business back on its footing.[784] The business was too big to succeed with the loosely organized structure it had had from the beginning, so they added two departments: one for buying and inventory and one for marketing. The surprising aspect of this was not that they had added these departments but that they had survived for nearly two decades without them.[785]

It's worth noting that Good Vibrations's cultural influence was belied by its relatively small profits, as was Eve's Garden's. Neither store made huge amounts of money. Dell Williams and Joani Blank were both idealists whose goals were never to become super-wealthy, although Williams did aspire to have Eve's Garden become a large nationwide chain.

Instead of creating national chains, Blank and Williams inspired imitators. By 1996, when Blank left Good Vibrations, women-owned sex-toy stores existed all over the country. San Francisco made room for another women-owned sex-toy store, Romantasy. In New York, in addition to Eve's Garden, Toys in Babeland and Come Again had opened. Portland, Oregon, had It's My Pleasure. There was Loveseason in Lynnwood, Washington. In Madison, Wisconsin, there was a Woman's Touch, and Womyn's Ware was in Vancouver, British Columbia.[786] England got Sh! in 1992.

Good Vibrations's cultural influence went beyond the store itself. They declared May National Masturbation Month in 1995 "to protest the firing of then Surgeon General Dr. Jocelyn Elders for stating that masturbation 'was perhaps something that perhaps should be taught' as safer sex information for youth."[787] This was, of course, self-serving for them because it gave them a way to raise awareness of sex toys and therefore sell more of them, but it also made masturbation a topic of national discussion in a positive way, a much-needed change. We can also thank Good Vibrations, Eve's Garden, and Gosnell Duncan for the high-quality silicone sex toys that are the norm today, although it took the adult industry more than twenty years to catch on to silicone.[788]

Why did Good Vibrations and Eve's Garden struggle so much where adult bookstores did not? The founding principles of the stores were radical for the times, even though they were post–sexual revolution times. Williams's store initially banned men from its premises and sold sex toys as tools for awakening female sexuality for the purposes of creating sexual independence. It was the male fear of sex toys realized: a women-only space where women were educated on liberating themselves from male dominance through mas-turbation. And half of the customers were lesbians to boot. Good Vibrations was a little less scary an idea because it welcomed men, but it still hewed to a similar ethos of independence.

Culturally, their influence was to amplify Betty Dodson's radical ideas, and this didn't sit well with a large portion of the populace who remained intimidated by female sexuality and feared female independence. Through the 1990s, Good Vibration's focus was always more on masturbation than couples toys. In 1999, they inaugurated an event to celebrate that focus: the masturbate-a-thon. The way it worked was a participant asked his or her friends to sponsor them for every minute they masturbated on May 7, National Masturbation Day. Good Vibrations donated 100 percent of the proceeds ($8,500) to HIV prevention.[789]

Yet Good Vibrations's cultural influence was not as great as Doc Johnson's, for a very simple reason: The Good Vibrations's brand was much less visible than Doc Johnson's. They had only three stores at their height in the 1990s, and their sex toys were sold only within these stores and via catalog, while Doc Johnson's were sold in almost every adult store in the nation and in several overseas.

(*)

Around the same time Good Vibes was having trouble, in the mid-1990s, another iconic sex-toy store was floundering. Without Colglazier at its helm, the Pleasure Chest had become a shell of its former self. For nearly a decade it hadn't made a profit, according to Colglazier's nephew Brian Robinson. Although Pleasure Chests existed in major cities, only the New York and Chicago stores were still owned by the Colglazier family. Around this time, Robinson was living in New York and working on the TV show *Northern Exposure* as an art director. Although he had a great job, he was working nearly ninety hours a week, and he was looking for a less demanding profession.

He saw that his uncle's business wasn't doing well, and he thought he might have the skills to turn it around. So Robinson borrowed $100,000 from his grandparents to buy out the business from Colglazier's siblings. According to

Robinson, half of the money went to Colglazier's brothers and sisters, and they let him keep half as working capital. Robinson first began overseeing the New York Pleasure Chest in 1996, and the day he started, he said all "the managers quit. There was some malfeasance that was going on that they knew I would discover."[790] The store seemed as if it was "stuck back in time." Although it had an upscale clientele that included a lot of women, the employees working there were "older gay men in black leather vests smoking cigarettes behind the register." Robinson started turning the store around with a small-scale improvement that telegraphed the new style of the store: the store window. Using his skills as a TV art director, he created intricate scenes in the front window that drew attention. Once again, the Pleasure Chest was turning heads. And soon a TV show came that would change the future of the business.

In 1998, two years after Robinson took the helm at the Pleasure Chest, a show about female sexuality premiered on HBO. *Sex and the City* centered on four thirty-something women in New York who were seeking sex and love in equal measure. The show centered on New York sex-columnist Carrie Bradshaw (Sarah Jessica Parker), based on real-life sex-columnist Candace Bushnell, who had written the book upon which the show was based. Not only did *Sex and the City* feature open discussions of sex among women, but it was also one of the first TV shows to present women's sex drive as just as strong as men's. The most sex-positive character was Samantha (Kim Cattrall), who was perhaps the first female TV character to be known for having acrobatic, emotionless sex whenever the impulse struck her. Samantha's antithesis was a prudish character named Charlotte, who couldn't detach sex from love and was frequently shocked by Samantha's escapades.

One of the scripts for the first season involved Charlotte buying her first sex toy and becoming addicted to it. This was boundary-pushing television. Never before had an American TV show episode featured a sex toy so prominently. They needed to find a sex-toy store to film in, and they hit on the

Pleasure Chest in Los Angeles.[791] Staff at the Pleasure Chest also suggested a possible toy for the scene: a Japanese vibrator imported by Vibratex called the Rabbit Pearl. Barbie pink, featuring a dual-stimulating vibrator with a bunny-shaped clitoral stimulator and tiny rabbit ears, the Rabbit Pearl looked decidedly feminine, just like the character Charlotte. "It looked more like a woman's sex toy instead of . . . the uncooked hot dog, [which] would be terrible in that episode," said Vibratex's Shay Martin. "Why would she be addicted to that and not come out of her apartment for a weekend?"[792]

The *Sex and the City* crew shot part of season one's ninth episode, "The Turtle and the Hare," in the Pleasure Chest. In the episode, after Miranda convinces Charlotte she needs a vibrator, the four women tromp down to the Pleasure Chest to seek out toys. The one that stands out to Charlotte is the Rabbit not only because, as Charlotte says, it is "pink for girls!" but also because it does not look like a penis. Notably, the Rabbit appeals to Charlotte because it conforms to typical gender stereotypes, with its bunny shape and traditional female color. Soon, Charlotte has so many wonderful orgasms with her Rabbit that she becomes addicted to it. She masturbates all day long, ignoring her friends' requests to hang out. Her friends finally stage a "Rabbit intervention," with Carrie and Miranda confiscating her vibrator because they want Charlotte to have sex with men instead.

Instead of being an advertisement for vibrators as most news articles presented it, the episode reads like a cautionary tale warning women not to masturbate with sex toys. Vibrators are portrayed as dangerous devices that lead to masturbation addiction, social isolation from friends, and possible future loneliness.[793] Though the message that many people watching the episode got was a lot different: They saw a vibrator that reliably produced orgasms, and they wanted one.

After the episode aired, the Rabbit immediately started selling even better than it had before. Vibratex's Shay and Dan Martin wondered why their sales were increasing. They didn't have HBO, so they had no idea their vibrator had been featured on *Sex and the City*. When the Pleasure Chest called them to tell them about it, Shay said that she asked a customer to send her "a VHS tape of the episode."

In spite of journalists' claims to the contrary, this episode didn't shift attitudes toward sex toys overnight. *Sex and the City* helped eliminate the taboo against talking about sex toys, but it didn't completely erase the cultural taboo against sex toys. In 1998, the same year that *Sex and the City* debuted, legislators in Alabama decided to pass an anti-sex-toy law. Good Vibrations even waded into the fray by offering 10 percent discounts to Alabama residents.[794] This episode was an acknowledgment that women used sex toys, but it was also a criticism of these women.

"The Turtle and the Hare" episode was only the beginning of *Sex and the City*'s sex-toy showcase. HBO wanted to feature more sex toys in their episodes, and they wanted Vibratex's. They sent scripts to Shay and Dan to review for their approval. Before they OK'd how Vibratex's sex toys were being used in *Sex and the City*, Shay and Dan wanted to "mak[e] sure their products weren't going to be run over by a trash truck or whatever." Dan and Shay never signed up for HBO. When an episode aired, they'd just go to a friend's house to watch.[795]

In fact, even in later episodes, *Sex and the City* rarely depicted vibrators as effective masturbation devices. Most of the time when characters use vibrators in *Sex and the City*, they do not have orgasms with them, and when they do there is some sort of punishment. Underlying many of the sex-toy scenes is the belief that vibrators are inferior to sex with men, reinforcing the idea that masturbation is subordinate to regular sex and that a "natural" penis is superior to an "artificial" one.

For example, one episode shows the perpetually aroused Samantha unable to have an orgasm during sex. She turns to her vibrator for assistance, but it also fails her. Her orgasm finally comes later in the episode, when she is having sex with a man.[796] Even the most positive depiction of vibrators in *Sex and the City* show vibrators not as neutral masturbation devices but as machines that cause social upheaval. In one episode, Samantha's vibrator breaks while she is masturbating, thwarting her orgasm. Samantha goes to the Sharper Image store in the mall to replace it. "I'd like to return my vibrator," she says. But the manager insists that the Sharper Image doesn't carry sex toys, and he informs her that her sex toy is, in fact, a chaste massager. Samantha vehemently argues with him, an argument that escalates and draws the attention of the other female shoppers. Samantha capitalizes on this attention and instructs the women in the store about the joys of using the massagers for masturbation.

This scene demonstrates that vibrators continued to be taboo in the late 20th and early 21st centuries, as simply discussing their sexual uses in a store that sells them is shown to cause chaos. The only time that vibrators are depicted as working well in *Sex and the City* is when they are used for non-sexual purposes. The most positive depiction of vibrators is an episode where Miranda's infant son Brady's vibrating chair breaks, and Samantha uses her own vibrator to put Brady to sleep.[797]

(*)

Sex and the City did help to usher sex-toy scenes into mainstream media, including primetime broadcast TV shows and big-studio films. But along with borrowing the sex-toy theme from *Sex and the City*, these TV shows and movies also borrowed the negative attitudes toward sex toys. Sex toys were usually portrayed as shameful, both in the context of the family and the broader community. Stories usually reasserted conventional gender norms.

For example, in *Not Another Teen Movie* (2001), a young woman named Janey lays in her bed and masturbates with a pink vibrator emblazoned with the phrase "My Lil' Vibrator." As obvious sexual arousal becomes visible on her face, her father and brother walk in. "Morning, sweetie," says the dad, as the mortified Janey tries to hide her arousal. "It's her birthday, Dad. What's that buzzing sound?" her brother asks. "Maybe they're still doing the construction next door," responds her dad. Her grandparents arrive in her room in quick succession with a cake. A priest and a bunch of small children follow.

With her entire family in the room, her dog jumps on the bed and rips off the cover, revealing that she is masturbating with a vibrator. She has an orgasm, and the vibrator flies out of the bed and onto the cake, splattering white frosting on her father's face, a "money shot" that uses the frosting as an ejaculate stand-in to symbolize her orgasm. The vibrator floppily spins around in the middle of the cake, a ridiculous device.[798] Janey's vibrator-induced orgasm is tempered by heaping doses of shame and public humiliation brought upon by her family and community watching on in horror. That *Not Another Teen Movie* dared to depict a young woman masturbating with a vibrator is, on the surface, presenting progressive gender and sex norms, but since the scene frames this as a taboo act that destabilizes the community, it actually reinforces traditional gender norms. The scene graphically shows the community attempting to rein in "deviant" female sexual behavior; it presents female masturbation and orgasm as absurd, humiliating, and even immature, as implied by Janey's naming her sex toy "My Lil' Vibrator."[799]

Similar themes appeared in broadcast television shows. In the 2007 "Bachelor Party" episode (season 2 ep. 9) of CBS's *How I Met Your Mother*, a show about four friends navigating their lives in New York, a young artist named Lily is having a bridal shower. Lily's friend Robin buys Lily a vibrator, not realizing that Lily's mother and grandmother are coming to the shower. Robin is mortified to be presenting Lily with a vibrator in front of her relatives, so she puts another partygoer's card on top of the gift. When Lily opens the card, Robin discovers that she has placed Lily's grandmother's card on the gift.

Lily reads her grandmother's card, and then, before Lily opens the gift, Grandma Lois starts in on a soliloquy about the gift's history. "Honey, this handy little device has been in our family for generations. I used it. Your great-grandmother used it. Now, her mother didn't use this one. But she used one just like it. Of course, back then they were made out of wood. Before that you just had to do it by hand. When I was a girl my mother taught me and my sister to use it. We used to have contests to see who could finish faster. It was so exciting! The whole family would gather around to watch. When I was a new bride, this is what kept me busy all those long nights when your grandfather was in Korea. Speaking of your grandpa, though I don't think he'd care to admit this to any of his army buddies, but he'd have a go at it every once in a while. And he enjoyed it. Open it up, sweetie. May this gift bring you as much joy as it brought me." Lily opens up the box to find a vibrator and burns with embarrassment. She refuses to take the vibrator out. "Well, take it out, honey. I want to show you how to use it," Grandma says, expecting that the gift will be an antique sewing machine. But Robin interjects, "Don't take it out, Lily. It's not your grandma's gift. It's mine."

Curious, all the women at the bridal shower gather around and discover the vibrator. An uncomfortable silence ensues that Grandma Lois breaks by saying, "It's just like the one Miranda gave to Charlotte on *Sex and the City*." Lily's mom chimes in with: "So where do I get one of these?" Although Lily's family eventually has a positive reaction to the vibrator, it is a hard-won acceptance that arrives only after Lily is forced to imagine her mother, grandmother, and grandfather masturbating with the device. The vibrator is stripped of any eroticism and is no longer as threatening to traditional gender roles.

(*)

Around the time sex toys became more talked about in pop culture, in 2000, a crisis in the sex-toy world occurred: The Hitachi Magic Wand was nowhere to be found. In February 2000, "a frisson of horror spread through New York's community of female self-lovers," according to the *New York Observer*, as the Wand disappeared from stores all across the country. Thanks to an issue with Hitachi's American distributor, the Appliance Corporation of America, the Wand was nearly impossible to obtain. Dodson, who was still purchasing large quantities of the vibrator for her private clients, began buying up Dr. Scholl's–brand vibrators. On eBay, Wands were going for $300.[800]

The Martins found out through the Pleasure Chest that the store was unable to get any Wands and saw an opportunity to help. "So we thought we're going to try our Japanese connections and see if we can get a hold of Hitachi and find out what was going on," said Shay. They told Hitachi that they were "an American company" that was "owned by a Japanese woman." They asked if Hitachi would be willing to distribute through Vibratex. Hitachi replied that they were already in negotiations with another American company that was going to distribute the Wand and some of Hitachi's other small appliances. The Martins told Hitachi to keep them in mind if the negotiations fell through.

Meanwhile, "a couple months go by and there is still no Magic Wand on the market," Shay said. They called Hitachi again, but this time the Martins had a different strategy. Instead of asking to be Hitachi's distributor, they asked to do a onetime deal with the company for their vibrators that were in Hitachi's warehouse. "We ship all the time from Japan," Shay told them. "So we've already got all those channels set up and we can take that inventory off of your books, and you can continue negotiations with whoever you're working with. But we might as well get the Magic Wand and get some money at the same time." Hitachi agreed. Soon twenty thousand Magic Wands were shipped to Vibratex's headquarters in Napa, California. The demand for

Wands was so high, that within a day they'd completely sold out to retailers. But very quickly the Wand was scarce again.[801]

Shay and Dan didn't hear from Hitachi for a while, until one day, while Shay and her mother, Suzi, were in Japan, Dan got a fax from Hitachi asking if they were still interested in importing the Wands. Apparently, when it came time to sign the import agreement with the other American company, the company had told Hitachi that they didn't want to import the rice cookers and hair dryers; they just wanted the Magic Wand. "Hitachi being a Japanese company . . . the way they do business, it's more based on loyalty and trust," Shay said. "And they just didn't like the way this American company had fooled them all along."

Dan told Hitachi that the two other owners were in Japan and could meet with them. He called Shay to relay the good news. "Can you guys meet Hitachi tomorrow at the offices and negotiate the account?" he asked her. Shay freaked out. "I was like, 'What?!' We were just there visiting family and visiting some of the other smaller manufacturers that we work with, and we're like family with all the other manufacturers, so it's very casual."

Hitachi was a large multinational corporation. You couldn't go dressed in jeans and a T-shirt. Shay and her mother didn't have business suits, and to complicate matters, Suzi had just gotten her hair braided and beaded during a trip to Mexico with a friend. "I'm like 'Oh my gosh, Mom. They're not going to go for the beads there,'" Shay told her. But Suzi said she couldn't take them out because it took forever and was too painful. "I said, 'I'm sorry, Mom. I love your individual style, but this one time we're going to have to quell your little wild look here. It's not like I'm embarrassed, but we really want this account.'" Shay asked her mother to wear a scarf to cover up the beads, and her mother agreed. They put on the only black outfits they had, Suzi placed a scarf on their head, and they called a taxi, hoping they looked professional enough for Hitachi. When they pulled up, they were met with ten unsmiling men in dark suits lined up outside. The men bowed as they came near. Suzi and Shay were intimidated "I don't think . . . they were used to working with women . . . as presidents or vice presidents," Shay said. "Most of the women over there were serving tea and typing letters and stuff and there was not one woman in there in a suit."

The meeting began, and Shay and Suzi discussed their connections with shipping channels in Japan and outlets in the United States Most of the Hitachi executives only spoke Japanese, so they directed their questions to Suzi, who's fluent. Shay was looking at her, hopeful that she "was explaining well to them." After all, Vibratex was a small company unknown to Hitachi, and Hitachi was an enormous international company with a corporate reputation to uphold. All was well and good until Shay saw a "little bead . . . falling out from underneath her [mother's] scarf." The careful sense of propriety they had created was literally falling apart. Alarmed, Shay casually reached over to her mother's hair and tried to "tuck it in" without the Hitachi people noticing. Either they didn't notice or they didn't care because Suzi charmed the Hitachi execs, who invited them out to lunch and dinner afterward. Vibratex got the account. And Dan and Shay became the U.S. distributors of one of the most beloved sex toys in the country.[802]

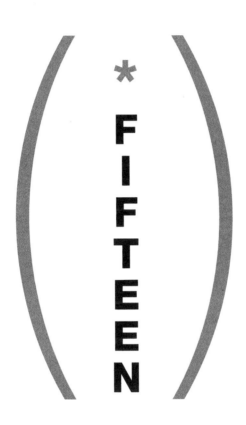

* FIFTEEN

21st-Century Toys

Good Vibrations's bestseller was saved in 2000. That same year, they expanded their website to boost their online sales and share sex information.[803] Also around this time, a new company had decided to enter the online sex-toy sales business, a retailer whose name was synonymous with online book sales: Amazon.com. Amazon could undercut them in price and speed of delivery, and Good Vibrations's online sales declined.[804] The company was in danger of going bankrupt.

This led to Good Vibrations CEO Theresa Sparks traveling to a porn distribution warehouse in San Francisco for a meeting with a member of the Sturman family in August 2007. Sparks took a winding road to get to Good Vibrations. Born in 1949 in Kansas City with an assigned male gender, she served in Vietnam, married and divorced twice, and had three children. She always struggled with her gender identity and even underwent electroshock therapy to try to "correct" her urge to be female. She finally transitioned in 1997 and started working at Good Vibrations at a seasonal holiday job shipping sex toys in 2001. Within a few weeks, she was their chief financial officer. A few months before her meeting in the warehouse, in May 2007, Sparks achieved an extraordinary feat, becoming the first transgender person elected as president of San Francisco's Police Commission.[805]

Which Sturman was waiting for Sparks? It wasn't Reuben. He'd died in prison a decade earlier at the age of seventy-three. It was Sturman's son David, who now ran a number of sex-toy and porn stores in California in addition to

Spielberg's adult bookstores. Joining Sturman's son was another man: an executive of Sturman's business, Joel Kaminsky. Joel's father, Melvin Kaminsky, had been the general manager for Sturman's Sovereign News. A strip-club impresario rounded out the group. They were trying to convince Sparks to sell Good Vibrations to the half-century-old porn and sex-toy distributor based in Cleveland, General Video of America and Trans World News (GVA-TWN), founded by none other than Reuben Sturman. GVA-TWN was now being run by Kaminsky's daughter Rondee Kamins. Good Vibrations, which was founded to counter Sturman's peep-show booth–filled adult bookstores, was now considering becoming a part of them. The fact that it was now headed up by a woman didn't hurt.

"After a long courtship that included tours of sex shops in San Francisco and Cleveland, a trip to Vegas and shared tables at the annual adult film festival awards in L.A., Sparks says she 'drank the Kool-Aid,'" wrote Joel Kaminsky in the *San Francisco Chronicle*. Sparks agreed to sell the company Joani Blank founded forty years earlier to the company Reuben Sturman had founded nearly two decades before that.[806] Good Vibrations was being sold to a company that distributed everything from Doc Johnson sex toys, vibrating women's buttocks, and jelly dildos and vibrators with phthalates, types of sex toys that Good Vibrations had recently stopped carrying.[807]

How had one of Sturman's companies ended up in Rondee Kamins's hands? After Sturman married Naomi Delgado in the 1980s, he sold the company to his friend and associate Melvin Kamins (who had shortened his name from Kaminsky). Then Melvin sold the company to his brother Joel Kaminsky, who had started working for Sturman in the 1960s and spent decades in San Francisco owning and operating adult stores. In the early 2000s, Joel moved back to Cleveland to help out his sick mother and be closer to his daughter, Rondee. Joel then installed his daughter as chief operating officer of GVA-TWN in 2002.

Good Vibrations continued to be owned and run by women. "I like to call it a partnership between the two of us," Kamins told the *Bay Area Reporter* soon after the deal was made public. "Because everything that Good Vibrations is GVA isn't and everything GVA is Good Vibrations isn't. Together we are a perfect fit."[808]

In 2008, a year after GVA-TWN bought Good Vibrations, Rondee Kamins stepped down, and her father, Joel, bought Good Vibrations outright and became the president. Now, one of Sturman's men headed the sex-toy store renowned for its female focus. The most visible women-friendly sex-toy store in the nation was owned by one of the most infamous porn conglomerates in the United States. "It's ironic given his family line to the business is from the complete opposite, the thing we completely resisted and criticized and made fun of," Bright said.[809]

You could lament this turn of events as a sign that the women-owned sex-toy business sold out. And some people certainly have. Two years after the sale, Sparks lamented to the *San Francisco Chronicle* that she regretted the deal.[810] And when customers found out about the sale, not all of them were happy. "In case you were wondering why I don't like to purchase toys at Good Vibrations, it's because they are no longer women owned and operated," wrote Sara J. on Yelp. "They sold their company last year to a mega-sex-toy company that sells sleazy, gross toys. Good Vibrations started as the antithesis to companies like GVA TWN (who they bought out to) making sleazy toys and now they are in partnership with them. Yuck."[811]

The criticism is understandable, but what were the alternatives? Good Vibrations could have gone bankrupt thirty years after its founding. Would that have been better? Some purists would say yes, but the true test is whether the store and website have changed for the worst. And they haven't. Good Vibrations's flagship store in San Francisco is spacious and beautiful. It's stocked with all the high-quality sex toys it was known for: Hitachi Magic

Wands, silicone toys (now from newer women-owned companies like Tantus), and strap-on harnesses. Dr. Carol Queen continues to work there as the staff sexologist, historian, and curator of their Antique Vibrator Museum, which Blank created.

There are a few things to lament, however. Gone is the worker-owned cooperative Blank created, with every employee sharing in the wealth. And perhaps the biggest one: Good Vibrations is no longer a woman-owned business.

(*)

When GVA-TVN purchased Good Vibrations, Sturman's other former company, Doc Johnson, was thriving. Ron Braverman had served his short time in jail for Sturman-related tax evasion, and when he came out, he continued to head up Doc Johnson. But he couldn't shake Sturman entirely. Why? He ended up marrying a woman named Naomi Delgado. Yes, *that* Naomi Delgado, Reuben Sturman's much younger widow. It was Braverman's fourth marriage. He also adopted Sturman's daughter Erica, who currently works at the company as a marketing director. Women now are in positions of power in Doc Johnson. His son Chad Braverman (from his second marriage) is now the chief operating officer of Doc Johnson, even though Chad didn't even really know what his father did until he was about thirteen. He ended up working at the company during the summers when he was in college and loved it. The Bravermans have kept most of the manufacturing of Doc Johnson sex toys in the United States, around 75 percent of their products, which is unheard of for a sex-toy company of their size, which would usually just make everything in China. "The number one thing I think we stand for is being an American manufacturer," Chad Braverman said. "That is really where we stuck to our guns." His father echoes that sentiment: "Because our dildos are made in the U.S. I'm sacrificing profits [but] I believe in America."

Still, they struggle for acceptance among some of the more mainstream magazines that tout sex toys, which are hesitant to recommend purchasing sex toys from a company that sells the All-Stars Porn Stars Gang Bang Set, with eight male masturbators molded from eight different porn stars vaginas. Yet Doc Johnson also sells more than a hundred vibrators, including my first love, the Original Pocket Rocket. For adventurous women they offer a pegging set, a dildo and harness set for women to use to penetrate their male partners during sex. Their range of sex toys is designed to appeal to nearly everyone. And they manufacture close to two hundred different silicone toys from butt plugs to wavy non-realistic looking silicone dildos, like the kind Dell Williams and Gosnell Duncan developed in the late 1970s.

Given that silicone dildos have gone mainstream, it's not terribly surprising that Gosnell Duncan's company Scorpio Products ended its operations on June 22, 2007. It was impossible for Duncan to compete, especially since he was seventy-seven years old. It was the end of an era.

(*)

Meanwhile, in the mid-2000s, the Pleasure Chest was becoming even more female-friendly. While New York had attracted women from the beginning, the Los Angeles store had not. "When I first started working here [in 2001] it was mainly gay," said longtime shipping clerk Walter Fallon.[812] After Robinson bought out the L.A. store in 2005, he made it more female- and couple-friendly and more of a hub for education, like the feminist sex-toy stores. The stores offered free courses every week on topics from blow jobs to sex toys. Robinson even hired an employee from the women-owned store Babeland.

While Eve's Garden continued in New York, it was not as influential as it once was. There was only one store. In 1998, Williams sold Eve's Garden to a company in Boston, but unlike the earlier sale, she didn't move the store there too. She continued to run the business, until about 2000, when she was seventy-six, and began looking for some kind of spiritual guidance. After enrolling in seminary, a year later Williams was ordained at St. John's Cathedral, "the oldest new minister in the class." By this time many other women-owned sex-toy stores had spread throughout the nation. And most people didn't get their sex toys in stores anyway; they bought them online. By 2004, Eve's Garden had set up their own online store.[813][814]

Harvey's Adam & Eve now has a chain of sixty-eight adult stores around the country and a bustling website that focuses mainly on sex toys. They had about $120 million in sales in 2016.[815] Marie Stopes International, the non-profit he founded with Tim Black, is thriving. It provides contraception and family planning services to 120 million women around the world in thirty-seven countries. While Marie Stopes focuses on opening clinics around the world, Harvey used his Adam & Eve profits to found another nonprofit, called DKT International, in 1989. As Marie Stopes International did in its early years, DKT focuses on using social marketing to offer contraception at drastically reduced rates through retail outlets worldwide and creates unique advertisements suited to each culture. Although "PHE Inc. or Adam & Eve has not itself as a corporation had a policy of subsidizing the promotion of contraceptives in developing countries," Harvey said, "it just happens that, I who have a fairly big chunk [of Adam & Eve], have chosen to use a good deal of my proceeds from Adam & Eve to promote DKT international and birth control in developing countries." And along with birth control, DKT also helps distribute another product worldwide that it doesn't subsidize: vibrating cock rings that come packaged with condoms. Harvey and Black succeeded in their goal of changing the world and they are continuing to change it today (even after Tim Black's death in 2014).[816]

Harvey and Black weren't the only sex-toy pioneers whose legacy continues to be felt today. Williams's and Blank's legacy is that nearly all sex-toy companies today target women and make sex toys out of silicone or other body-safe materials. Even though Good Vibrations isn't women-owned anymore, more women head up sex-toy companies than ever before. In addition to Shay Martin of Vibratex, there's Susan Colvin of major sex-toy company CalExotics, Metis Black of Tantus Silicone, who has carried on Gosnell Duncan's legacy and improved upon it (and she introduced me to Gosnell in the first place), and MIT-educated engineer Janet Lieberman (no relation) of Dame Products, who designs couples vibrators that are for all sexual orientations. Innovation has occurred in other ways too. The first masturbation toy for transmen, the Buck-Off, was created by Buck Angel in 2016.

Yet sex toys are socially acceptable enough that they are an estimated $15 billion industry worldwide and a $9 billion industry in the United States, and make up about 80 percent of the revenue of adult bookstores. Around 5 billion dollars' worth of sex toys are sold in home parties.[817] And 60 percent of the sex toys bought in stores were bought by women—a big shift from the 1960s when 1 to 3 percent of customers were women. Famous designers are creating sex toys, which Gwyneth Paltrow promotes through her website *Goop*. Television shows, most famously Lifetime's *Unreal*, have featured women masturbating with vibrators, as if it is an everyday occurrence (which it is). Sex toys are so commonplace that Amy Schumer has a skit where women compete to impress their bachelorette friend by bedazzling vibrators.

(*)

So sex toys are now accepted by American culture, end of story, right? Well, not really. Take E. L. James's *Fifty Shades of Grey* trilogy (first published in 2011), which supposedly made sex toys completely mainstream. Thanks to James, grandmothers now discuss the virtues of buttock whipping over cups of chamomile tea. *Fifty Shades of Grey* "pleasure rings" even showed up in the aisles of Target.

Fifty Shades is a traditional romantic story about a handsome, wealthy BDSM-loving man who seduces a virgin and teaches her about all manner of sex toys. The books and movies have made sex toys more widely discussed than they had been maybe ever been. But why are we comfortable with sex toys in *Fifty Shades*? Because they were portrayed as fitting in with traditional gender and sexual norms.

Fifty Shades's ultimate message is that a woman's sexual awakening comes at the hands of a man. *Fifty Shades* is *Cinderella* with handcuffs. In the film, all the sex toys are usually wielded by Christian Grey, not Anastasia Steele. The film completely ignores the fact that sex toys are primarily used for masturbation. Similarly, the *Fifty Shades* sex toys sold at Target are not for masturbation but for partnered use. To be fair, the *Fifty Shades of Grey* sex-toy line sold elsewhere includes toys traditionally used for masturbation, though they aren't promoted that way. The *Fifty Shades* Charlie Tango Classic Vibrator, for example, which is a phallic vibrator, is touted as "the perfect couples' toy, whether you use it to stimulate each other's erogenous zones, or to pleasure yourself in front of your lover." When masturbation is mentioned as it is in the description of the Heavenly Massage Bullet Vibrator, it is only after assuring women that the bullet is "non-intimidating to share with your lover," which makes it "the perfect supplement to both self-pleasure and lovemaking."[818]

Fifty Shades reinforces the message that sex toys should be used to bind women ever tighter into monogamous, dependent relationships. It strengthens the retrograde idea that women's most intense orgasms come during intercourse, when they usually occur during masturbation. This is the exact opposite of Betty Dodson's message.

When Dodson introduced vibrators to the women's movement, they were tools that were synonymous with women's liberation. She held workshops where she taught women how to masturbate with vibrators as a way of liberating women from stultifying sexual dependence. Vibrators, as Dodson perceived them, were devices that allowed women to become sexually independent, to free themselves from relying on their partners for orgasms. Sex toys were radical tools that threatened conventional gender norms. Although American culture is more comfortable acknowledging women's sex-toy use, it has not become fully accepting of sex toys for masturbation.

In the 1960s and 1970s, sex toys symbolized emancipation from male-imposed sexual and gender norms. Sex toys are now more widely accepted in culture not because our gender and sexual norms have radically shifted but because the meanings of sex toys have. Sex toys no longer necessarily epitomize female sexual liberation from men and are instead promoted as devices that help improve relationships. The idea of masturbation as a powerful act that should be celebrated, and sex toys as being representative of this philosophy, still exists, but it is not mainstream. While Good Vibrations, the Pleasure Chest, Eve's Garden, and other sex-toy stores still promote this masturbatory ideal, it is not the ideal celebrated in home parties and *Fifty Shades*. Female masturbation and women's sexual autonomy remain threatening to gender and sexual norms in the 21st century. As Dodson told me, "If nothing else, the popularity of [*Fifty Shades*] tells us that women have not made one step forward in claiming our sexual power. They are still waiting for that prince. So my work has just begun."

(*)

It's been twelve years since I have sold sex toys, and in that time, sex toys have been legalized in Texas and several other states where they were outlawed. Are sex toys legal across the land? Not quite. As of 2017, sex toys remain illegal in Alabama.[819] Are sex toys safe from government intervention in the future?

Not necessarily. "Male masturbation aids [such as porn and strip shows] are recognized as 'expression' and protected under the First Amendment" and have been since the mid-20th century, wrote law professor Kim Shayo Buchanon. But the opposite is the case when it comes to vibrators, she notes. "The legal treatment of sex toys . . . is marked by a legislative hostility and judicial ambivalence that betrays a fundamental societal discomfort with the nonprocreative sexual pleasure of women and sexual minorities."[820]

Just take a look at the erection-inducing drug Viagra. Why is Viagra covered by insurance but not vibrators? Because erections are considered medically necessary for normal sexual functioning but female orgasms are not. In 1998, the same year that Alabama outlawed sex toys, Pfizer debuted Viagra ads on national TV starring former senator and unsuccessful presidential candidate Bob Dole. Now imagine that a similar ad was run for a vibrator on national TV starring former senator and unsuccessful presidential candidate Hilary Clinton in 2017. Think we'll be seeing a line of Nasty Women vibrators later this year? Unlikely.

Although female politicians don't promote sex toys, sex toys are used as a form of political protest. An artist photoshopped dildos in the place of guns in pictures of Republicans leading up to the 2016 U.S. election. Butt plugs and blow-up dolls were used to protest Donald Trump during his candidacy. The Donald Chump blow-up doll packaging even critiqued his policies with its drawing of a "Chump Resorts" wall spray-painted with "No Immigrants" that adorned the back of the package, and a list of Trump endorsements from the likes of A. Hitler, David Duke, Stalin, Mussolini, and the Ku Klux Klan. To be fair there was also a Hillary Clinton blow-up doll, Horny Hillary. But the doll's package didn't critique Clinton's policies, it just had a Bill Clinton joke on it.

Artists have also been using sex toys to express political discontent. A 3D-printed Donald Trump butt plug was created by Mexican artist Fernando

Sosa in response to Trump's insulting comments to Mexicans. "I'm no rapist and no drug dealer," Sosa said. "I have a college degree in 3D animation and run my own 3D printing business and guess what? I can make you into any shape I want and 3D print you and sell you to others who share a dislike of you. You can threaten to sue me like you have done hundreds of times to others. But you are a public figure and my making you into a butt plug is Freedom of Speech. Welcome to America Mother Fucker!!"[821]

Yet sex toys have made progress: They are now openly sold in more outlets than ever before, including drugstores like Walgreens and big-box retailers like Walmart. Although in the past decade, most legal restrictions have been lifted, societal restrictions have not gone away. In 2010, MTV refused to air a Trojan Vibrating Triphoria commercial unless the word "vibrator" was removed. Even the revamping of the vibrator ad drew complaints to the FCC. "I have seen this new commercial for the 'Trojan Triphoria' female vibrator during the day. . . . It explains how it blows the mind out [of] the woman that uses it, all the accessories, etc," wrote a viewer. "It's a most disgusting commercial and I cannot believe there are these types of commercials during the day."[822] While fairly chaste vibrator ads raise ire, the networks run innumerable explicit ads for erectile dysfunction that go into great detail about how men "may have an erection lasting four or more hours" with very little protest. And vibrator companies insist on promoting the ideal of the monogamous heterosexual relationship in their advertisements.

Dildos still inspire fear. The college student who started the campus dildo carry protest in 2015 received death threats for carrying dildos in public.[823] A few years earlier, in 2012, the U.S. Post Office forced *Vice*'s print magazine to censor a dildo on the cover of a 2012 issue. The magazine covered it up with a sticker with the world "dildo" instead. Although half of all Americans admit to having used vibrators, and 75 percent of young women, vibrators too remain intimidating. Also in 2012, a local grocery store chain in Madison,

Wisconsin, refused to display a copy of the weekly paper *The Isthmus* because it featured a vibrator designed for "post-menopausal women and those recovering from cancer treatment" on its cover.[824]

Where do we go from here? I have some ideas. In a perfect world, the FDA would regulate sex toys so we could ensure that they're safe. Sex toys would be covered by insurance. Boys and girls would be taught about them in sex education courses. And vibrators would be subsidized worldwide by a nonprofit to promote women's sexual health.[825] Pipe dreams? Maybe. But the people who made their indelible marks on the history of sex toys had dreams that were considered ridiculous for their times too.

Sex toys can't change the world on their own. But the people making them, selling them, using them, and talking about them can. At the end of the day, I realized my obsession with sex toys wasn't just about the technology itself, but it was about the meaning of it. Sex toys can mean so many things to so many people, and not all of these things are good. They can be used to promote monogamy or polygamy, repressive gender roles or female independence. Sex toys can be used to help handicapped people have better lives and to help women have their first orgasms. To me, sex toys symbolize hope because what I see when I look at a sex toy is the people who I profiled in this book, the people who woke up one day and wanted to change the world. And they thought to themselves that a dildo was the way to do it. I am one of those people. And I'm no longer embarrassed.

Bibliography

ARCHIVAL SOURCES (ABBREVIATIONS IN PARENTHESES)

American Antiquarian Society, Worcester, MA

    Trade Catalogs (AAS–Trade)

American Medical Association, Chicago, IL

    Historical Health Fraud Collection (AMA–Health Fraud)

The Bakken Museum, Minneapolis, MN

    Artifact Collection and Library Trade Literature Collection

Center for Sex and Culture, San Francisco, CA

    Good Vibrations Collection (CSC–Good Vibes)

Cornell University Library, Ithaca, New York

    Dell Williams Papers, #7676. Division of Rare and Manuscript Collections (Cornell–Williams)

    Susie Bright Papers and *On Our Backs* records, #7788. Division of Rare and Manuscript Collections (Cornell–Bright)

Doc Johnson Corporate Collection, North Hollywood, CA. (Doc Johnson)

Gosnell Duncan Papers, Author's Personal Collection (Duncan)

Kinsey Institute Collections. Indiana University, Bloomington, IN.

Sex Aids Dealers (U.S. 20th Century 1960-1979) (Kinsey–Sex Aids U.S., 1960–1979)

Sex Aids Dealers (U.S. 20th Century 1960–) (Kinsey–Sex Aids U.S., 1960)

Sex Aids Dealers, (United States, 20th Century 1980–1999) (Kinsey–Sex Aids U.S., 1980–1999)

National Archives, Washington, D.C.

Records of the U.S. House of Representatives, 1789–2011, Office of Post and
Office of Solicitor

National Museum of American History Archives Center, Washington, D.C.
(NMAH–Archives)

Division of Medicine and Science, Artifact Collection (NMAH–Med)

Louisan E. Mamer Rural Electrification Administration Papers 1927-2002
(NMAH–Mamer)

Warshaw Collection of Business Americana (NMAH–Warshaw)

Division of Science, Medicine and Society HIV/AIDS Collection (NMAH–HIV)
National Museum of American History Library, Washington, D.C.

Trade Literature Collection (NMAH–Trade Lit)

Pleasure Chest Corporate Collection, Los Angeles, CA (Pleasure Chest)

Racine Heritage Museum Archives, Racine, WI

Hamilton Beach Collection

Science Museum, London, England

Medical Object Collection, Blythe House

Wisconsin Historical Society, Madison, WI

Dorothy Dignam Papers

Ralph Ginzburg Papers (WISC–Ginzburg)

John Sumner Papers

INTERVIEWS CONDUCTED BY AUTHOR

Joani Blank, founder of Good Vibrations, April 1, 2014 & March 23, 2015.

Chad Braverman, COO of Doc Johnson, July 6, 2016.

Ron Braverman, founder of Doc Johnson, December 27, 2016.

Susie Bright, co-founder of *On Our Backs* & Good Vibrations manager,
July 7, 2016.

Betty Dodson, author of *Liberating Masturbation*, January 15, 2014.

Gosnell Duncan, inventor of silicone dildos, August 2 & 3, 2013.

Walter Fallon, longtime Pleasure Chest employee, April 1, 2016.

Phil Harvey, co-founder of Adam & Eve, February 3, 2017.

David Keegan, Adam & Eve FC General Manager, February 13, 2017.

Michael D. Lieberman, physician & former medical staff president, October 10, 2016.

Farley Malorrus, co-founder of Ben Wa Novelty Corporation, October 4, 2016.

Ted Marche's son, September 30, 2016 & October 4, 2016.

Shay Martin, co-founder of Vibratex, September 6, 2016.

Lurline Martineau, Gosnell Duncan's niece, January 10, 2015.

Brian Robinson, owner of the Pleasure Chest & Duane Colglazier's nephew,
    March 23, 2016.

David Sturman, Reuben Sturman's son, December 7, 2016.

Sarah Tomchesson, Pleasure Chest Marketing Director, February 15, 2016.

Carol Queen, Staff Sexologist, Historian & Curator, at Good Vibrations,
    July 17, 2016.

Dell Williams, founder of Eve's Garden, interviewed on November 19 & 22,
    2013; January 9, 2015.

SELECTED PRIMARY SOURCES

"AIDS: A Woman's Health Issue," Whitman–Walker Clinic Inc., Washington,
    D.C., Maryland, Virginia, circa 1990s. (NMAH–HIV)

Altman, Lawrence K. "Rare Cancer Seen in 41 Homosexuals." the *New York
    Times,* July 3, 1981.

Aristophanes. *Aristophanes: Birds. Lysistrata. Women at the Thesmophoria.* Translated
    by Jeffrey Henderson. Cambridge, MA: Harvard University Press, 2000.

Auerbach, Stuart. "Mail Order Company Called Just a Tease; Complaints Cite
    Undelivered Goods." the *Washington Post,* June 4, 1983.

Barbach, Lonnie. *For Yourself: The Fulfillment of Female Sexuality.* Garden City,
    New York: Anchor Books, 1976.

Beltair, Mark. "The Town Crier: Remember the Yanks." *Detroit Free Press*, May 29, 1965, 14-B.

Bennett, De Robigne Mortimer. *Anthony Comstock: His Career of Cruelty and Crime a Chapter from the Champions of the Church*. New York: Liberal and Scientific Publishing House, 1878.

Blank, Joani. *Good Vibrations: The Complete Guide to Vibrators*. Burlingame, CA: Down There Press, 1982.

Blank, Joani. *Playbook for Women About Sex*. San Francisco: Down There Press, 1975.

Blystone, Richard. "Residents Deploy Porno Atmosphere." *Carroll Daily Times Herald*, June 9, 1976.

Boston Women's Health Collective. *Women and Their Bodies: A Course*. Boston Women's Health Collective, 1970.

Bright, Susie. "Toys for Us." *On Our Backs*, September-October 1989.

———— "What a Friend We Have in Dildos." *The Advocate*, September 10, 1991.

Brody, Leigh, and M. Duck, "Two Views on Loving Women." *Lavender Woman* 4, no. 3 (June 1975).

Bumiller, Elisabeth. "Our Bodies, Our Salves; The Erotica Party Comes to Silver Spring," *Washington Post*, May 30, 1980, C1.

Califia, Pat. "In Response to Dorchen Leidholdt's 'Lesbian S/M: Radicalism or Reaction.'" *New Women's Times* 8, no. 9 (October 1982).

Comfort, Alex. *The Joy of Sex: A Gourmet Guide to Love Making*. New York: Simon & Schuster, 1972.

Cook, James. "The X-Rated Economy." *Forbes*, September 18, 1978.

"Designing an Effective AIDS Prevention Campaign Strategy for San Francisco: Results from the First Probability Sample of an Urban Gay Male Community." Prepared for the San Francisco AIDS Foundation by Research & Decisions Corporation. Appendix F, December 1984.

Dickinson, Robert Latou, and Lura Beam. *A Thousand Marriages: A Medical Study of Sex Adjustment.* Baltimore: Williams & Wilkins, 1931.

Dodson, Betty. "Getting to Know Me," *Ms.,* August 1974.

—— *Liberating Masturbation.* New York: Betty Dodson, 1974.

—— *Sex for One: The Joy of Selfloving.* New York: Harmony, 1996.

"Dongs: The Images of Men," Doc Johnson Marital Aids Catalog, 1977.

Dworkin, Andrea. *Pornography: Men Possessing Women.* First edition. New York: Perigee Trade, 1981.

"Electro Thermo Dilators: The Guaranteed Drugless Cure." *Electro-Surgical Appliance Co.* brochure. Los Angeles, Circa 1895. (NMAH–Warshaw)

Ellis, Havelock. *Studies in the Psychology of Sex, Vol 1.: The Evolution of Modesty: The Phenomena of Sexual Periodicity, Auto-Eroticism.* Philadelphia: F. A. Davis Company, 1910.

Epstein, Keith C. "Court Upholds Conviction of Figure in Sturman Case." *Cleveland Plain Dealer,* March 22, 1988, sec. A.

Farmer, Joyce. *Tits & Clits Comix,* no. 3. Laguna Beach, CA: Nanny Goat Productions, 1976.

Fee, Elizabeth, and Nancy Krieger. "Understanding AIDS: Historical Interpretations and the Limits of Biomedical Individualism." *American Journal of Public Health* 83, no. 10 (October 1, 1993): 1477–88.

Frederick, Max. *Book of Amorous Stimulants and Prosthetic Devices,* catalog, 1972. (Kinsey–Sex Aids U.S., 1960).

Fullerton, Patricia. "Dilemma of the Modern Lesbian." *Lavender Woman* 1, no. 3 (May 1972).

Gevins, Adi. "She's Bringing You Good Vibrations." *Berkeley Barb,* June 17, 1977.

Goldman, Andrew. "Panic in Bedrooms as Magic Wand, Cadillac of Vibrators, Disappears." *New York Observer,* June 12, 2000.

Good Vibes Gazette. San Francisco: Good Vibrations, no. 1 (1985). (CSC–Good Vibes)

Good Vibes Gazette. San Francisco: Good Vibrations (June1986). (CSC-Good Vibes)

Good Vibes Gazette. San Francisco: Good Vibrations, no. 3 (March 1987). (CSC–Good Vibes)

Good Vibes Gazette. San Francisco: Good Vibrations, no. 5 (Fall 1988). (CSC–Good Vibes)

Good Vibes Gazette. San Francisco: Good Vibrations, no. 6 (Spring 1989). (CSC–Good Vibes)

Good Vibes Gazette. San Francisco: Good Vibrations, no. 9 (Summer 1990). (CSC–Good Vibes)

Good Vibes Gazette. San Francisco: Good Vibrations, no. 10 (Fall 1990). (CSC–Good Vibes)

Good Vibes Gazette. San Francisco: Good Vibrations, no. 17 (Spring 1995). (CSC–Good Vibes)

Good Vibes Gazette. San Francisco: Good Vibrations, no. 19 (Spring 1996). (CSC–Good Vibes)

Good Vibes Gazette. San Francisco: Good Vibrations, no. 25 (Spring 1999). (CSC–Good Vibes)

Good Vibes Gazette. San Francisco: Good Vibrations (Holiday 1999). (CSC–Good Vibes)

Good Vibes Gazette. San Francisco: Good Vibrations. (Holiday 2002.) (CSC–Good Vibes)

Gosier, Diane, L. N. Gardel, and Alice Aldrich. "NOW or Never." *Off Our Backs*, December 31, 1974.

"Grand Fancy Bijou Catalog of the Sporting Men's Emporium." Philadelphia, Pennsylvania. 1870. (AAS–Trade)

Granville, Joseph Mortimer. "Therapeutics of the Nervous System: Nerve Vibration in the Treatment of Nervous Diseases." *The Journal of Nervous and Mental Disease* (March 1883).

"The Great Playboy Sex Aids Road Test." *Playboy*, March 1978.

Greer, Germaine. *The Female Eunuch.* New York: Paladin, 1970.

Gregory, Martha Ferguson. *Sexual Adjustment: A Guide for the Spinal Cord Injured.* Bloomington, IL: Accent on Living, 1974.

Griffith, John. "Ex-City Man Arrested for Lying in Tax Probe." *Plain Dealer,* March 20, 1984, sec. A.

——— "Sturman Has Dead Man's Passport; Bond Stands." *Plain Dealer,* July 2, 1985.

Griffith, John, and Rosemary Armao. "Sturman Jests as War Tears at Porn Empire." *Plain Dealer,* May 24, 1987, sec. A.

Gross, Jane. "Homosexuals Stepping Up AIDS Education." *New York Times,* September 22, 1985.

Hamilton, Allan McLane. "Vibratory Therapeutics," *Medical News* (February 1898).

Hanisch, Carol. "The Personal Is Political." *Notes from the Second Year: Major Writings of Radical Feminists* 1, no. 1 (1970): 76–78.

Hart, Kelvin. "Adam & Eve Open but Quiet About the Raid." *Burlington Times-News,* June 11, 1986, sec. D.

Harvey Milk Gay Democratic Club, "AIDS Prevention Flyers: Can We Talk?," Pacific University Archives Exhibits, accessed August 6, 2017, http://exhibits.lib.pacificu.edu/items/show/940.

"Health & Beauty." White Cross Vibrator Catalog. Chicago: Linstrom Smith Company, 1911. (AMA–Health Fraud)

Heiman, Julia R., Leslie Lopiccolo, and Joseph Lopiccolo. *Becoming Orgasmic: A Sexual Growth Program for Women.* 1st edition. Englewood Cliffs, NJ: Prentice-Hall, Inc., 1976.

Hernandez, Greg. "Porn Kingpin Who Escaped Prison Arrested: Fugitive: 68-Year-Old Captured in Anaheim Was Serving Time for Federal Racketeering, Obscenity, Income Tax Violations." *Los Angeles Times,* February 10, 1993.

BIBLIOGRAPHY

*

Houston, Paul. "Man Called Largest Porno Seller Indicted." *Los Angeles Times*, October 9, 1987, sec. 1.

Hruby, Kathy. "Sexual Self-Help." *Amazon Quarterly* 3, no. 2 (March 1975).

"Investigate—Before You Invest!!!!" *Roanoke Better Business Bureau Newsletter*, January 15, 1959.

Japenga, Ann. "Sadomasochist Fashions Attracting Suburban Teens." *Los Angeles Times*, March 25, 1983.

Jay, Karla. "The SpiritIs Feminist but the Flesh Is?" *The Lesbian Tide* 4. no. 3, (October 1974).

"John Oster Manufacturing Co. Demonstrators' Manual." December 18, 1949. (NMAH–Mamer)

Johnson, John. "Top Pornographer Reuben Sturman Vanishes from Prison." *Los Angeles Times*, December 14, 1992, sec. VCB.

Johnston, Laurie. "Women's Sexuality Conference Ends in School Here: Older Women Attend." *New York Times*, June 11, 1973.

Katz, Sue. "Smash Phallic Imperialism." *Lavender Vision* 1, no. 1 (1970).

Klemesrud, Judy. "Sex Boutique: 'Middle Ground Between Drugstore Approach and Smut Shop.'" *New York Times*, January 13, 1972.

Koedt, Anne. "The Myth of the Vaginal Orgasm." In *Radical Feminism*, edited by Anne Koedt, Ellen Levine, and Anita Rapone. New York: Quadrangle Books, 1973, 198–207.

Knight, Jerry. "Retailers Racing to Washington." *The Washington Post*, May 12, 1980.

Langelan, Martha. "The Political Economy of Pornography." *Aegis* (Autumn 1981).

Latimer, Dean. "The Chastening of the Blade." *The East Village Other*, March 30, 1971. "Liberating Masturbation." In" Worth Noting," *The Spokeswoman* 5, no. 9 (March 15, 1975).

Lowry, Edith Belle, and Richard Jay Lambert. *Himself: Talks with Men Concerning Himself*. Chicago: Forbes and Company, 1912.

Luther, Marylou. "Shock Chic: The Punk Persuasion." *Los Angeles Times*, July 31, 1977.

Lyvely, Chin, and Joyce Farmer, "The Fuller Bush Person," in *Tits & Clits Comix*, no. 2. Laguna Beach, CA: Nanny Goat Productions, 1976.

Mann, Steve. "Master's Project Turns into Mail-Order Boom." *Burlington Daily Times*, November 27, 1980, sec. F.

Mano, D. Keith. "Tom Swift Is Alive and Well and Making Dildos." *Playboy* (March 1978).

Math, Mara. "Andrea Dworkin Talks About Feminism." *Gay Community News*, December 1985.

Miller, Lindsay. "Women Confer on Sex." *New York Post*, June 11, 1973.

Money, John, and Tom Mazur. "Microphallus: The Successful Use of a Prosthetic Phallus in a 9-Year-Old Boy." *Journal of Sex & Marital Therapy* 3, no. 3 (Fall 1977): 187–96.

"Ms. Magazine Wins Victory For All Women's Press in Library Case." *Media Report to Women*, vol. 7 (July 1, 1979).

"The New Way." *Medical Review* 27, no. 19 (May 1893).

Nussbaum, Paul. "Peddling Sex Accouterments in the Living Room." *Los Angeles Times*, April 22, 1981, sec. G.

"N.Y. World notified by Anthony Comstock to discontinue lottery advertisements; also to be notified to exclude massage, electrical and personal advertisements; also French remedies." *NY Commercial Advertiser*, circa 1900.

Palacios-Jimenez, Louis, and Michael Shernoff. "Facilitator's Guide to Eroticizing Safer Sex." Gay Men's Health Crisis, 1986. (NMAH–HIV)

Passion Parties Business Owners' Product Guide. Passion Parties, Inc., 2003.

Passion Parties' Fact Sheet (2005), https://web.archive.org/web/20050907150624/http://www.passionparties.com/pdf/factsheet.pdf.

Passion Parties' Media Kit (2005), *Pat Davis Biography*.

Peterson, Frederick. "Vibratory Therapeutics." *Medical News* 29 (January 1898).

Queen, Carol. "Sisters Doin' It for Themselves." *On Our Backs*, December 1992.

Rabin, Barry J. *Sensuous Wheeler: Sexual Adjustment for the Spinal Cord Injured*. San Francisco: Barry Rabin, 1980.

Rovner, Ruth. "Women's Sexuality Conference: A Vibrator Connoisseur." *Los Angeles Free Press*, July 20, 1973.

Rubin, Gayle. "Samois." *Leather Times*, Spring 2004.

———— "Thinking Sex." In *Pleasure and Danger: Exploring Female Sexuality*, edited by Carole S. Vance. Boston: Routledge, 1984, 267–319.

Rusk, Howard A. "Roundtable: Sex Problems in Paraplegia." *Medical Aspects of Human Sexuality* (December 1967).

Safran, Clare. "Plain Talk About the New Approach to Sexual Pleasure." *Redbook*, March 1976.

Satchell, Michael. "The Big Business of Selling Smut." *Parade Magazine*, August 19, 1979.

Seajay, Carol. "Vibrators for Sale." *Feminist Bookstore News*, September 1984.

Serrin, William. "Sex Is a Growing Multibillion Business." *New York Times*, February 9, 1981, sec. N.Y. / Region.

Shapiro, Martin. "Obscenity Law: A Public Policy Analysis," *Journal of Public Law* 20:503 (1971).

Shenon, Philip. "Sturm Und Drang Und Pornography." *New York Times*, April 15, 1986, sec. B.

Shulman, Alix Kates, "Organs and Orgasms." In *Women in a Sexist Society*, edited by V. Gornick and B. Moran. New York: Signet, 1971.

Sears Roebuck and Company. *Sears Christmas Book*. Chicago, IL: 1956. (NMAH–Trade Lit)

Sears Roebuck and Company. *Sears, Roebuck & Co. Catalogue No. 111*. Chicago, IL: 1902.

Sears Roebuck and Company. *Sears Special Catalogue of Surgical Instruments and Physicians' Supplies*. Chicago, IL, 1902. (NMAH–Trade Lit)

Seda, Dori, Robert Crumb, and Terri Zwigoff. "Girls Turned into Vibrator Zombies." *Weirdo #8*, 1983. Reprinted in Seda, Dori. *Dori Stories*. San Francisco: Last Gasp, 1999.

Sims, J. Marion. "Cases of Vaginismus, with the Method of Treatment." *Chicago Medical Examiner* 3 no, 6, June 1862.

Snake, R. "Loving Women." *Big Mama Rag* 3, no. 5 (June 1975).

Starrett, Barbara. "I Dream in Female: The Metaphors of Evolution." *Amazon Quarterly* 3, no. 1 (November 1974).

Tarabulcy, E. "Sexual Function in the Normal and in Paraplegia." *Paraplegia* 10, no. 3 (November 1972): 201–8. doi:10.1038/sc.1972.34.

"To Be Destroyed When Read. Private and Confidential." Report from the Y.M.C.A. New York: Jan. 28, 1874. (WISC–Ginzburg)

"Toward Intimacy: Family Planning and Sexuality Concerns of Physically Disabled Women." Planned Parenthood of Snohomish County, Inc., 1977.

Tyco Shop By Mail Catalog. Tyco Inc.: Dobbs Ferry, New York, 1953. (NMAH–Trade Lit)

Vance, Carole S. *Pleasure and Danger: Exploring Female Sexuality*. Boston: Routledge & Kegan Paul, 1984.

Weller, Sheila. "Inside Betty Dodson." *Forum*, February 1976.

Williams, Timothy. "Grand Jury Indicts Pornographer's Ex-Wife." *Los Angeles Times*, November 27, 1993, sec. B.

Winchell, Walter. "It Takes All Kinds to Make World." *Humboldt Standard*, June 24, 1964, C-2.

"Women Protest Sexism on Bar Exam." *The Spokeswoman*, June 15, 1974.

Women's Sexuality Conference Proceedings. New York: National Organization of Women New York Chapter, 1974.

ADVERTISEMENTS

MAGAZINES & MEDICAL JOURNALS

The Advocate, 1978

The Berkeley Barb, 1973

Big Mama Rag: A Feminist News Journal, 1976, 1977

Christian Observer, 1909

Chrysalis, 1977

Echo of Sappho, 1972

Health, 1907

Home Journal, 1855

The Independent, 1914

Lesbian Tide, 1977

Los Angles Free Press, 1973, 1975

McClure's, 1899, 1918

Mother Jones, 1985

Ms., 1974, 1976

The New Way: A Monthly Journal Devoted to the Rational Treatment of Chronic Diseases, 1893

New Woman's Times, 1976–1977

Off Our Backs, 1977

On Our Backs, 1989, 1992

Playgirl, 1975

Suggestion, 1903

Youth's Companion, 1918

NEWSPAPERS

The Chicago (Daily) Tribune, Chicago, Illinoi, 1900–1930

The Des Moines News, Des Moines, Iowa, 1912

The Los Angeles Times, Los Angeles, California. 1900-1930

The New York Times, New York, New York, 1900–1930, 1972

The National Police Gazette, New York, New York, 1888, 1889

The Plain Dealer, 1981, 1982

GOVERNMENT DOCUMENTS

Attorney General's Commission on Pornography: Final Report. U.S. Department of
Justice, 1986.

Commission on Obscenity and Pornography, Final Report. Washington, D.C.: U.S.
Government Printing Office, 1970.

Complaint from viewer in Maple Valley, WA, about "Trojan Triphoria" ad that
aired December 31, 2010, on a *Saturday Night Live* episode that was shown
on VH1. FCC/Enforcement Bureau, IHD–Investigation and Hearings.
Informal complaints received by the Federal Communications Commission
(FCC) regarding the television show "Saturday Night Live," 2008–2012.

Complaint from viewer in Old Tappan, NJ, about *2 Broke Girls* that aired
November 12, 2012 on CBS. Complaint from viewer in Jacksonville,
FL, about *2 Broke Girls* that aired November 11, 2012, on CBS. Informal
complaints received by the Federal Communications Commission (FCC)
regarding the television show "2 Broke Girls," 2011–2013.

U.S. Mail Special Report: Post Office Department. Fiscal Year, 1963.

SECONDARY SOURCES

Angulo, Javier C., Marcos García-Díez, and Marc Martínez. "Phallic Decoration
in Paleolithic Art: Genital Scarification, Piercing and Tattoos." *The
Journal of Urology* 186, no. 6 (December 2011): 2498–503. doi:10.1016/j.
juro.2011.07.077.

Arnott, Stephen. *Sex: A User's Guide.* New York: Bantam Dell, 2002.

Babcock, Glenn D. *History of the United States Rubber Company: A Case Study in
Corporate Management.* Bloomington, IN: The Foundation for the School of
Business: Indiana University, 1966.

Bailey, Beth, *Sex in the Heartland.* Cambridge, MA: Harvard University Press, 1999.

Bailey, Sue. "From Dildo to Dead Man's Pond: The Stories behind Newfoundland
Place Names." *The Canadian Press,* February 23, 2015.

Beato, Greg. "Sexually Transmitted Altruism (SSIR)." *Stanford Social Innovation Review*, Fall 2012.

Borstelmann, Thomas. *The 1970s: A New Global History from Civil Rights to Economic Inequality*. Princeton: Princeton University Press, 2011.

Boyer, Paul. *Purity in Print: Book Censorship in America from the Gilded Age to the Computer Age*, Second edition Madison, WI: University of Wisconsin Press, 2002.

Bright, Susie. *Susie Bright's Sexual Reality: A Virtual Sex World Reader*. Pittsburgh: Cleis Press, 1992.

Broder, Samuel. "The Development of Antiretroviral Therapy and Its Impact on the HIV-1/AIDS Pandemic." *Antiviral Research* 85, no. 1 (January 2010). doi:10.1016/j.antiviral.2009.10.002.

Bronstein, Carolyn. *Battling Pornography: The American Feminist Anti-Pornography Movement, 1976–1986*. Cambridge, UK: Cambridge University Press, 2011.

Bronstein, Phil. "How Feminist Sex Shop Good Vibrations Lost Its Loving Feeling." *San Francisco Chronicle*, August 17, 2009.

Broun, Heywood, and Margaret Leech. *Anthony Comstock: Roundsman of the Lord*. New York, A. & C. Boni, 1927.

Buchanan, Kim Shayo. "Lawrence V. Geduldig: Regulating Women's Sexuality." *Emory Law Review Journal* 56 (2007): 1235–1303.

Cheshes, Jay. "Hard-Core Philanthropist." *Mother Jones*, December 2002.

Chrystal, Paul. *In Bed with the Ancient Greeks*. Stroud, England: Amberley Publishing Limited, 2016.

Clark, Timothy, and C. Andrew Gerstle. *Shunga: Sex and Pleasure in Japanese Art*. Leiden, Netherlands: Brill/Hotei Publishing, 2013.

Cornog, Martha. *The Big Book of Masturbation: From Angst to Zeal*. San Francisco: Down There Press, 2003.

Curtis, Nathan. "Unraveling Lawrence's Concerns About Legislated Morality:

The Constitutionality of Laws Criminalizing the Sale of Obscene Devices."
BYU Law Review, no. 4 (November 1, 2010): 1369–98.

D'Emilio, John, and Estelle B. Freedman. *Intimate Matters: A History of Sexuality in America*. New York: Harper, & Row, 1988.

Dennis, Donna. *Licentious Gotham: Erotic Publishing and its Prosecution in 19th-century New York*. Cambridge: Harvard University Press, 2009.

Dodson, Betty. "Having Sex with Machines: The Return of the Electric Vibrator/," Dodson and Ross, June 8, 2010, http://dodsonandross.com/blogs/betty-dodson/2010/06/having-sex-machines-return-electric-vibrator.

———— *My Romantic Love Wars*. New York: Betty Dodson, 2010.

Doniger, Wendy. "God's Body, Or, The Lingam Made Flesh: Conflicts over the Representation of the Sexual Body of the Hindu God Shiva." *Social Research;* 78, no. 2 (Summer 2011): 485–508, 687.

Downs, Donald. *The New Politics of Pornography*. Chicago: University of Chicago Press, 1989.

Echols, Alice. *Daring to Be Bad: Radical Feminism in America, 1967-1975*. Minneapolis: University of Minnesota Press, 1989.

Ellis, Albert. *Sex Without Guilt*. New York: Lyle-Stewart, 1966.

Ellis, Havelock. *Studies in the Psychology of Sex*. Philadelphia: F. A. Davis Company, 1910.

Findlay, Heather. "Freud's 'Fetishism' and the Lesbian Dildo Debates." *Feminist Studies* 18, no. 3 (Autumn 1992), 563–579.

Fleischer, Doris, and Frieda Zames. *The Disability Rights Movement: From Charity to Confrontation*. Philadelphia: Temple University Press, 2012.

Fox, Stephen. *The Mirror Makers*. Chicago: University of Illinois Press, 1997.

Frank, Thomas. *The Conquest of Cool*. Chicago: University of Chicago Press, 1997.

Freeman, Susan K. *Sex Goes to School: Girls and Sex Education before the 1960s*. Chicago: University of Illinois Press, 2008.

Freitag, Michael. "Neighborhoods in New York Seeing Red Over Blue Videos:

'No Times Square in Greenwich Village,' Protesters Say." *New York Times*, December 28, 1989, sec. Metropolitan News.

Friedan, Betty. *The Feminine Mystique*. New York: W. W. Norton, 1963.

———. *"It Changed My Life": Writings on the Women's Movement*. New York: Laurel, 1991.

Gamson, Joshua. "Rubber Wars: Struggles Over the Condom in the United States." *Journal of the History of Sexuality* 1, no. 2 (October 1990), 262–282.

Gardetta, Dave. "Doctor's Orders." *Los Angeles Magazine*, July 1, 2012. http://www.lamag.com/longform/doctors-orders/.

Geltzer, Jeremy. *Dirty Words and Filthy Pictures: Film and the First Amendment*. Austin, TX: University of Texas Press, 2015.

Gerhard, Jane. *Desiring Revolution: Second-Wave Feminism and the Rewriting of American Sexual Thought, 1920-1982*. New York: Columbia University Press, 2001.

Glasscock, Jessica. *Striptease: From Gaslight to Spotlight*. New York: Harry N. Abrams, 2003.

Godfrey, Phoebe. "The Device That Dare Not Speak Its Name: The State, Sexuality and Dildos in Texas, 1973–2008." *Journal of American Studies* 26 (2011): 101–17.

Griffith, John. "U.S. Accuses Sturman of Massive Tax Dodge." *Plain Dealer*. March 5, 1985, sec. A.

Harvey, Philip D. *The Government vs. Erotica: The Siege of Adam & Eve*. Amherst, NY: Prometheus Books, 2001.

Hatton, Katherine L. "Porn King Tells His Side of the Story." *Cleveland Plain Dealer*, July 20, 1978, sec. Spotlight Section 1, Part 2.

Heidenry, John. *What Wild Ecstasy: The Rise and Fall of the Sexual Revolution*. New York: Simon & Schuster, 1997.

Heinemann, Elizabeth. *Before Porn Was Legal: The Erotica Empire of Beate Uhse*. Chicago: University of Chicago Press, 2011.

Holland, Jack. *A Brief History of Misogyny: The World's Oldest Prejudice.* London: Little, Brown Book Group (Castle and Robinson), 2012.

Hollandsworth, Skip. "Good Vibrations." *Texas Monthly*, September 30, 2004. http://www.texasmonthly.com/articles/good-vibrations/.

Horowitz, Helen Lefkowitz. *Rereading Sex: Battles over Sexual Knowledge and Suppression in Nineteenth-Century America.* New York: Knopf, 2002.

Hughes, Thomas. *American Genesis: A Century of Invention and Technological Enthusiasm.* New York: Viking, 1989.

James, Peter J., Nick Thorpe, and I. J. Thorpe. *Ancient Inventions.* New York: Ballantine Books, 1995.

Jeffreys, Sheila. *The Lesbian Heresy: A Feminist Perspective on the Lesbian Sexual Revolution.* Melbourne, Australia: Spinifex Press, 1993.

Jin, Jessica. "I'm Getting Death Threats for Protesting Guns with Sex Toys." Time.com, October 16, 2015.

Johnson, James William. *A Profane Wit: The Life of John Wilmot, Earl of Rochester.* Rochester, NY: University Rochester Press, 2004.

Jones, James. *Alfred C. Kinsey: A Life.* New York: W. W. Norton, 1997.

Judson, Olivia. *Dr. Tatiana's Sex Advice to All Creation: The Definitive Guide to the Evolutionary Biology of Sex.* New York: Metropolitan Books, 2003.

Kelly, Edward. "A New Image for the Naughty Dildo?" *The Journal of Popular Culture* 7, no. 4 (Spring 1974): 804–809.

Kendrick, Walter. *The Secret Museum: Pornography in Modern Culture.* Berkeley: University of California Press, 1996.

Keuls, Eva C. *The Reign of the Phallus: Sexual Politics in Ancient Athens.* Berkeley: University of California Press, 1993.

Kimmel, Michael, Christine Milrod, and Amanda Kennedy. *Cultural Encyclopedia of the Penis.* London: Rowman & Littlefield, 2014.

Kraig, Gene. *The Sentence, A Family's Prison Memoir.* New York: Greenpoint Press, 2006.

LaMay, Craig. "America's Censor: Anthony Comstock and Free Speech," *Communications and the Law* 19, no. 3 (September 1997).

Laqueur, Thomas. *Solitary Sex: A Cultural History of Masturbation.* New York: Zone Books, 2003.

LaFeber, Walter, Richard Polenberg, and Nancy Woloch. *The American Century: A History of the United States Since 1941: Volume 2.* 5th edition. Boston, MA: McGraw-Hill, 1988.

León, Vicki. *The Joy of Sexus: Lust, Love, and Longing in the Ancient World.* New York: Bloomsbury Publishing, 2013.

Lever, Janet, David A. Frederick, and Letitia Anne Peplau. "Does Size Matter?: Men's and Women's Views on Penis Size across the Lifespan." *Psychology of Men & Masculinity* 7, no. 3 (2006): 129–43. doi:10.1037/1524-9220.7.3.129.

Levy, David. *Love and Sex with Robots: The Evolution of Human-Robot Relationships.* New York: Harper Perennial, 2008.

Lieberman, Hallie. "If You Mold It They Will Come: How Gosnell Duncan's Devices Changed the Sex-Toy Game Forever." *Bitch.* 67. Summer 2015.

——— "Intimate Transactions: Sex Toys and the Sexual Discourse of Second-Wave Feminism." *Sexuality & Culture* 21 (2016). doi:10.1007/s12119-016-9383-9.

——— "Selling Sex Toys: Marketing and the Meaning of Vibrators in Early Twentieth-Century America." *Enterprise & Society* 17, no. 2 (June 2016): 393–433. doi:10.1017/eso.2015.97.

Long, Kat. *The Forbidden Apple: A Century of Sex & Sin in New York City.* Brooklyn: Ig Publishing, 2009.

Maier, Thomas. *Masters of Sex: The Life and Times of William Masters and Virginia Johnson, the Couple Who Taught America How to Love.* New York: Basic Books, 2009.

Mailer, Norman. *The Prisoner of Sex.* New York: Plume, 1985.

Maines, Rachel P. *The Technology of Orgasm: "Hysteria," the Vibrator, and Women's Sexual Satisfaction.* Baltimore: Johns Hopkins University Press, 1999.

Mallants, Charita, and Kristina Casteels. "Practical Approach to Childhood Masturbation Review." *European Journal of Pediatrics* 167, no. 10 (October 2008): 1111–17. doi:10.1007/s00431-008-0766-2.

Margolis, Jonathan. *O: The Intimate History of the Orgasm.* New York: Grove Press, 2005.

Marshall, Barbara L. "'Hard Science': Gendered Constructions of Sexual Dysfunction in the 'Viagra Age.'" *Sexualities* 5, no. 2 (May 2002): 131–58. doi :10.1177/1363460702005002001.

McAuley, Robert J. "Did Woman Juror Turn the Tide in Sturman Verdict?" *Plain Dealer,* July 26, 1978.

McLaren, Angus. *Twentieth-Century Sexuality: A History.* Oxford, UK: Blackwell Publishers, 1999.

Meikle, Jeffrey. *American Plastic: A Cultural History.* New Brunswick, NJ: Rutgers University Press, 1997.

Moya, Cynthia Ann. "Artificial Vaginas and Sex Dolls: An Erotological Investigation." PhD. diss., Institute for Advanced Study of Human Sexuality, 2006.

Murphy, Michelle. "Immodest Witnessing: The Epistemology of Vaginal Self-Examination in the U.S. Feminist Self-Help Movement. *Feminist Studies* 30, no. 1 (Spring 2004).

Nelson, Max. "A Note on the Ὄλισβος." *Glotta* 76, no. 1/2 (2000): 75–82.

Numbers, Ronald L. "Sex, Science, and Salvation: The Sexual Advice of Ellen G. White and John Harvey Kellogg." In *Right Living: An Anglo-American Tradition of Self-Help Medicine and Hygiene,* edited by Charles E. Rosenberg, Baltimore: Johns Hopkins University Press, 2003.

Olivas, Tammy Fonce. "Judge Says State Can't Prohibit Sex Toy Sale." *El Paso Times,* October 11, 2004, 1B.

Parke, Joseph Richardson. *Human Sexuality.* Philadelphia: Professional Publishing Company, 1912.

Phillips, Michael. "What Small Business Experience Teaches Us About Economic Theory." In Paul Elkins, *The Living Economy: A New Economics in the Making*. New York: Routledge, 1986.

Rosen, Ruth. *The World Split Open: How the Modern Women's Movement Changed America*. New York: Penguin Books, 2000.

Rosewarne, Lauren. *American Taboo: The Forbidden Words, Unspoken Rules, and Secret Morality of Popular Culture*. Santa Barbara, CA: Praeger, 2011.

Sandroni, Paola. "Aphrodisiacs Past and Present: A Historical Review." *Clinical Autonomic Research* 11, no. 5 (2001): 303–7. doi:10.1007/BF02332975.

Schlosser, Eric. *Reefer Madness: Sex, Drugs, and Cheap Labor in the American Black Market*. New York: Houghton Mifflin, 2003.

Screech, Timon. *Sex and the Floating World: Erotic Images in Japan, 1700-1820*. Honolulu, HI: University of Hawaii Press, 1999.

Skinner, Marilyn, *Sexuality in Greek and Roman Culture*. Second edition. New York: John Wiley and Sons, 2014.

Snitow, Ann, Christine Stansell, and Sharon Thompson. *Powers of Desire*. New York: Monthly Review Press, 1983.

Stark, Emily L. "Get a Room: Sexual Device Statutes and the Legal Closeting of Sexual Identity." *George Mason University Civil Rights Law Journal* 20, no. 3 (2010): 315–49.

Stone, Lawrence. *The Family, Sex and Marriage in England 1500–1800*. New York: Harper & Row, 1977.

Stricharchuk, Gregory. "Selling Skin: 'Porn King' Expands His Empire with Aid of Businessman's Skills." *Wall Street Journal*, May 8, 1985.

Surnow, Rose. "Babeland Turns 20." *Cosmopolitan*, February 22, 2013.

Tabori, Paul. *The Humor and Technology of Sex*.New York: Julian Press, Inc., 1969.

Taylor, Timothy L. *The Prehistory of Sex: Four Million Years of Human Sexual Culture*. New York: Bantam, 1996.

Tilmouth, Christopher. *Passion's Triumph over Reason: A History of the Moral

Imagination from Spenser to Rochester. Oxford, UK: Oxford University Press, 2010.

Tone, Andrea. *Devices and Desires: A History of Contraceptives in America*. New York: Hill and Wang, 2001.

Uhelszki, Jaan. "Interview: Joan Jett, Queen Of Noise." *The Morton Report*, September 13, 2011.

Van Driel, Mels. *With the Hand: A Cultural History of Masturbation*. Translated by Paul Vincent. London: Reaktion Books, 2013.

Varone, Antonio. *Eroticism in Pompeii*. Los Angeles: J. Paul Getty Museum, 2001.

Warnke, Georgia. *After Identity: Rethinking Race, Sex, and Gender*. Cambridge: Cambridge University Press, 2008.

Whelan, Edward P. "The Prince of Porn." *Cleveland Magazine*, August 1985.

——— "Reuben Sturman and His Amazing Porno Empire!" *Cleveland Magazine*, May 1976.

Whitley, Glenna. "Sex Toy Story." *Dallas Observer*, April 8, 2004. http://www.dallasobserver.com/news/sex-toy-story-6419371.

Williams, Dell, and Lynn Vannucci. *Revolution in the Garden: Memoirs of the Gardenkeeper*. San Francisco: Silver Back Books, 2010.

Williams, Dell. "The Roots of the Garden." *Journal of Sex Research* 27, no. 3 (August 1990): 461–66.

Wolf, Howard, and Ralph Wolf. *Rubber: A Story of Glory and Greed*. New York: Covici Friede Publishers, 1936.

COURT CASES AND LAWS

42nd Congress Session III Chp. 258 1873

Dawn E. Webber, Appellant, v. The State of Texas, No. 03-99-00225-CR (June 15, 2000), Court of Appeals of Texas, Austin

Lawrence v. Texas, 539 U.S. 558 (2003)

PHE ZJ LLC v. State, 2003-CA-00456-SCT (Miss. 2003)

PHE, Inc. v. United States Department of Justice, filed March 26, 1990 in U.S.
  District Federal Court

Reliable Consultants, Inc. v. Earle, 517 F.3d 73

Rhonda Salvail, et. al. v. Nashua Board of Education, 469 F. Supp. 1269 (D. New.
  Hamp., 1979)

Sewell v. Georgia, United States Supreme Court, 435 U.S. 982, 983 (April 24,
  1978) No. 76-1738

Texas. Penal Code Ann. §43.23(a), (f)

Williams v. Attorney Gen. of Ala. (Williams IV), 378 F.3d 1232, 1237 n.8 (11th
  Cir. 2004)

Endnotes

CHAPTER ONE

1. *Lawrence v. Texas*, 539 U.S. 558 (2003).

2. Stark, Emily L. "Get a Room: Sexual Device Statutes and the Legal Closeting of Sexual Identity." *George Mason University Civil Rights Law Journal* 20, no. 3 (2010): 315–49.

3. The Texas statute said that it is illegal if a person "wholesale promotes or possesses with intent to wholesale promote any obscene material or obscene device." Texas Penal Code Ann. § 43.23(a).

4. Godfrey, Phoebe. "The Device That Dare Not Speak Its Name: The State, Sexuality and Dildos in Texas, 1973–2008." *Journal of American Studies*, in Special Edition on Gender Studies, 26 (2011): 101–17.

5. Ibid.

6. *Passion Parties Business Owners' Product Guide*. Passion Parties, Inc., 2003, 4.

7. "Fact Sheet." Passion Parties. 2005. Accessed August 6, 2017 via Web Archive. https://web.archive .org/web/20050424004526/http://www.passionparties.com:80/pdf/factsheet.pdf

8. Texas Penal Code § 43.23(f).

9. Whitley, Glenna. "Sex Toy Story." *Dallas Observer*, April 8, 2004. August 6, 2017. http://www .dallasobserver.com/news/sex-toy-story-6419371.

10. "Texas Woman to Fight Obscenity Law." *UPI NewsTrack*, July 19, 2004. August 6, 2017. http:// www.upi.com/Odd_News/2004/07/19/Texas-woman-to-fight-obscenity-law/34521090250790/.

11. Hollandsworth, Skip. "Good Vibrations." *Texas Monthly*, October 2004. August 8, 2017. http:// www.texasmonthly.com/articles/good-vibrations.

12. Ibid.

13. "Texas Mom Faces Trial for Selling Sex Toys." *CNN*, February 11, 2004. August 6, 2017. http:// edition.cnn.com/2004/LAW/02/11/obscenity.trial.reut.

14. Godfrey, "The Device That Dare Not Speak Its Name," 101–17.

15. *Webber v. The State of Texas*, No. 03-99-00225-CR (Texas Court of Appeals, 2000).

16. *State v. Brenan*, 739 So. 2d 368 (Louisiana Court of Appeals, 1999) and *State v. Brenan*, 772 So. 2d 64 (Supreme Court of Louisiana, 2000).

17. Acosta sued the state because he claimed the anti-sex-toy law was unconstitutional. The Supreme Court refused to hear the case in 2006, so Texas's law continued to be in force. Olivas, Tammy Fonce. "Judge Says State Can't Prohibit Sex Toy Sale." October 2004.

18. Curtis, Nathan. "Unraveling Lawrence's Concerns About Legislated Morality: The Constitutionality of Laws Criminalizing the Sale of Obscene Devices." *Brigham Young University Law Review* no. 4 (November 1, 2010): 1369–98. *Also see Reliable Consultants, Inc. v. Earle*, 517 F.3d 738 (U.S. Court of Appeals, 5th Circuit, 2008).

19. *PHE ZJ LLC v. State*, No. 2003-CA-00456-SCT (Supreme Court of Mississippi, 2003). *Also see* Stark, Emily L. "Get a Room: Sexual Device Statues and the Legal Closeting." George Mason University *Civil Rights Law Journal*, 20 (Summer 2010): 315–49 fn. 109.

20. *Williams v. Attorney General of Alabama*, 378 F.3d 1232, 1237 n.8 (U.S. Court of Appeals, 11th Circuit, 2004).

21. Stark, "Get a Room," 339.

22. *Reliable Consultants, Inc. v. Earle.*

23. Marshall, Barbara L. "'Hard Science': Gendered Constructions of Sexual Dysfunction in the 'Viagra Age.'" *Sexualities* 5, no. 2 (May 1, 2002): 131–58, doi:10.1177/1363460702005002001.

24. *Passion Parties Business Owners' Product Guide.* Passion Parties, Inc., 2003, 8.

25. Bright, Susie. *Susie Bright's Sexual Reality: A Virtual Sex World Reader.* Pittsburgh: Cleis Press, 1992, 34.

26. *Business Owner's Product Guide*, 2003, 61.

CHAPTER TWO

27. "Museum of Prehistory Blaubeuren: Ice Age Europe." Accessed September 15, 2016. http://www.ice-age-europe.eu/visit-us/network-members/museum-of-prehistory-blaubeuren.html.

28. Parke, Joseph Richardson. *Human Sexuality.* Philadelphia: Professional Publishing Company, 1912, 383.

29. Angulo, Javier C., Marcos García-Díez, and Marc Martínez. "Phallic Decoration in Paleolithic Art: Genital Scarification, Piercing and Tattoos." *The Journal of Urology* 186, no. 6 (December 2011): 2498–503, doi:10.1016/j.juro.2011.07.077.

30. "Museum of Prehistory Blaubeuren."

31. Taylor, Timothy L. *The Prehistory of Sex: Four Million Years of Human Sexual Culture.* New York: Bantam, 1997, 128.

32. Parke, *Human Sexuality,* 62.

33. Taylor, *Prehistory of Sex,* 127–29.

34. Ibid.

35. León, Vicki. *The Joy of Sexus: Lust, Love, and Longing in the Ancient World.* New York: Bloomsbury, 2013, 167. *Also see* van Driel, Mels. *With the Hand: A Cultural History of Masturbation.* London: Reaktion Books, 2012, 62.

36. Keuls, Eva C. *The Reign of the Phallus: Sexual Politics in Ancient Athens.* Berkeley: University of California Press, 1993, 82.

37. Nelson, Max. "A Note on the ὄλισβος." *Glotta* 76, no. 1/2 (2000): 75–82. August 6, 2017. http://www.jstor.org/stable/40267098.

38. "Dildo, n.1." The OED Online. March 2014. Accessed May 26, 2014.

39. Arnott, Stephen. *Sex: A User's Guide.* New York: Bantam Dell, 2002, 213.

40. Kimmel, Michael, Christine Milrod, and Amanda Kennedy, eds. *Cultural Encyclopedia of the Penis.* Lanham, Maryland: Rowman & Littlefield, 2014, 52.

41. Bailey, Sue. "From Dildo to Dead Man's Pond: The Stories behind Newfoundland Place Names." *The Canadian Press*, February 23, 2015.

42. Chrystal, Paul. *In Bed with the Ancient Greeks.* Stroud, UK: Amberley Publishing Limited, 2016. *Also see*, Margolis, Jonathan. *O: The Intimate History of the Orgasm.* New York: Grove Press, 2005, 170.

43. Varone, Antonio. *Eroticism in Pompeii.* Los Angeles: J. Paul Getty Museum, 2001, 97.

44. Keuls, *Reign of the Phallus*, 84.

45. Terra Cotta Vessel (amphora, red-figure), attributed by Beazley to the Flying-Angel Painter 500–480 BCE, Paris: Mus. du Petit Palais; The Archive for Research on Archetypal Symbolism, No. 307, 3Ja.032b. Accessed through Artstor, 2017.

46. Keuls, *Reign of the Phallus*, 116–17.

47. *Tanakh: The Holy Scriptures: The New JPS Translation According to the Traditional Hebrew Text.* Philadelphia: Jewish Publication Society, 1985.

48. Other Greek dramas featured dildos too. The Greek poet Herodas wrote a plot where a woman lends her leather dildo out to a friend and it ends up in the hands of her enemy. *see* Skinner, Marilyn. *Sexuality in Greek and Roman Culture, 2nd Ed.* New York: John Wiley and Sons, 2014, 244–45. See also James, Peter J., Nick Thorpe. *Ancient Inventions.* New York: Ballantine Books, 1995, 182. *See also* Henderson, Jeffrey, trans. *Aristophanes: Birds; Lysistrata; Women at the Thesmophoria.* Cambridge, Mass.: Harvard University Press, 2000, 289.

49. Liddell, Henry George, and Robert Scott. "A Greek–English Lexicon, Ὄλισβος." Accessed June 7, 2017. http://www.perseus.tufts.edu/hopper/text?doc=Perseus%3Atext%3A1999.04.0057%3Aentry%3Do)%2Flisbos.

50. In Ancient Rome, a ritual involved a soon-to-be-married woman penetrating herself with "the divine phallus" to ceremonially lose her virginity before marriage in honor of the phallic god Mutunus Tutunus. *See* Tabori, Paul. *The Humor and Technology of Sex.* New York: Julian Press, Inc., 1969, 278.

51. James and Thorpe, *Ancient Inventions*, 184–85.

52. Doniger, Wendy. "God's Body, Or, The Lingam Made Flesh: Conflicts over the Representation of the Sexual Body of the Hindu God Shiva." *Social Research;* 78, no. 2 (Summer 2011): 485–508; 687.

53. Van Driel, *With the Hand*, 63.

54. Nashe wasn't the only one writing about dildos. Around the same time, English poet and playwright John Marston wrote about a woman preferring "'a glassy instrument' to 'her husband's lukewarm bed.'" *See* Ellis, Havelock. *Studies in the Psychology of Sex*. Philadelphia: F.A. Davis Company, 1910, 169–170.

55. It's worth noting that the dildo she uses in the poem was sophisticated for its time. It is a hollow-glass dildo meant to be filled with hot water, milk or urine, with the liquid being used to warm up the dildo or simulate ejaculation. The dildo was then usually covered in a soft material like white velvet or silk. Although these types of dildos were imported from Italy into England in the 17th century—after the poem was written—they may have been available earlier. In fact, Italian dildos were an upper-class item, bought by wealthy, aristocratic women and allegedly so popular that "scarce a lady comes from abroad [to England] without being in possession of one or two." *See* Stone, Lawrence. *The Family, Sex and Marriage in England 1500–1800*. ACLS Humanities E-Book, 2013.

56. Johnson, James William. *A Profane Wit: The Life of John Wilmot, Earl of Rochester*. Rochester, NY: University of Rochester Press, 2004, 106.

57. Tilmouth, Christopher. *Passion's Triumph over Reason: A History of the Moral Imagination from Spenser to Rochester*. Oxford, UK: Oxford University Press, 2010, 260.

58. Holland, Jack. *A Brief History of Misogyny: The World's Oldest Prejudice*. London: Castle and Robinson, 2006, 154.

59. Of course there are some amazing companies run by women today, but the big companies are male-run.

60. Ellis, *Studies in the Psychology of Sex*, 169–70.

61. Tabori, *Humor and Technology of Sex*, 325.

62. Clark, Timothy, and C. Andrew Gerstle. *Shunga: Sex and Pleasure in Japanese Art*. London: British Museum Press, 2013, 28.

63. Ibid., 308–9.

64. Screech, Timon. *Sex and the Floating World: Erotic Images in Japan, 1700-1820*. Honolulu: University of Hawaii Press, 1999, 43.

65. Clark and Gerstle, *Shunga*, 312.

66. Parke, *Human Sexuality*, 382.

67. Ellis, *Studies in the Psychology of Sex*, 168.

68. Kelly, Edward. "A New Image for the Naughty Dildo?" *The Journal of Popular Culture* VII, no. 4 (1974): 804–9, doi:10.1111/j.0022-3840.1974.0704.

69. Tone, Andrea. *Devices & Desires: A History of Contraceptives in America*. New York: Hill and Wang, 2002, 14.

70. "Electro-Thermo Dilators: The Guaranteed Drugless Cure." Electro-Surgical Appliance Co. brochure. Los Angeles, circa 1895. Warshaw Collection of Business Americana, Archives Center, National Museum of American History, Smithsonian Institution, Washington, D.C. (NMAH–Warshaw).

71. Ellis, *Studies in the Psychology of Sex,* 168.

72. "The New Way," *Medical Review* 27, no. 19 (May 1893): 396.

73. "Young's Hard Rubber Rectal Dilators." Advertisement in *The New Way: A Monthly Journal Devoted to the Rational Treatment of Chronic Diseases* 1, no. 5 (April 1893): 6.

74. Babcock, Glenn D. *History of the United States Rubber Company: A Case Study in Corporate Management.* Bloomington, Ind.: Bureau of Business Research, Indiana University, 1966, 12–13.

75. Wolf, Howard, and Ralph Wolf. *Rubber.* New York: Covici Friede, 313.

76. Sims, J. Marion. "Cases of Vaginismus, With the Method of Treatment." *Chicago Medical Examiner* 3 no. 6 (June 1862): 355.

77. Sears Roebuck and Company, *Sears Special Catalogue of Surgical Instruments and Physicians' Supplies,* Chicago, Illinois, 1902. (NMAH-Trade Lit).

78. Dennis, Donna. *Licentious Gotham: Erotic Publishing and Its Prosecution in Nineteenth-Century New York.* Cambridge, Mass: Harvard University Press, 2009.

79. *Grand Fancy Bijou Catalog of the Sporting Man's Emporium.* Philadelphia, 1870, 6. American Antiquarian Society, Worcester, Mass. (AAS–Trade).

80. Ibid., 7.

81. Tabori, *Humor and Technology of Sex,* 295.

82. "TO BE DESTROYED WHEN READ. PRIVATE AND CONFIDENTIAL." Report from the YMCA (New York: January 28, 1874), 2. Ralph Ginzburg Papers, 1848–1964. Wisconsin Historical Society, Madison, Wisc. (WISC–Ginzburg).

83. Ibid., 369.

84. Broun, Heywood, and Margaret Leech. *Anthony Comstock: Roundsman of the Lord.* New York: A. & C. Boni, 1927, 265–266.

85. Kendrick, Walter. *The Secret Museum: Pornography in Modern Culture.* Berkeley: University of California Press, 1987, 140.

86. LaMay, Craig L. "America's Censor: Anthony Comstock and Free Speech." *Communications and the Law* 19 (1997): 1–59, 14.

87. "An Act for the Suppression of Trade in, and Circulation of, obscene Literature and Articles of immoral Use." 42nd Congress: Session III, Chapter 258 (1873).

88. Bennett, D. M. *Anthony Comstock: His Career of Cruelty and Crime; a Chapter from the Champions of the Church.* New York: Liberal and Scientific Publishing House, 1878, 1016.

89. He was also the face of the organization and the national anti-obscenity effort. Horowitz, Helen Lefkowitz. *Rereading Sex: Battles Over Sexual Knowledge and Suppression in Nineteenth-Century America.* New York: Vintage, 2003, 381–84.

90. "TO BE DESTROYED," 4 (WISC–Ginzburg).

91. For examples, see "Rubber Goods" advertisement in *The National Police Gazette*, August 26, 1888, 15; "Rubber Goods" advertisement in *The National Police Gazette*, February 23, 1889, 14.

92. New Life Vibrator featured as "Winner's Gift Number 10-23" in *Youth's Companion*, October 17, 1918, 538. *See also* "Midget Vibrator" advertisement in *Christian Observer*, January 27, 1909, 24. Vibrator ads also ran in *Chicago Tribune, New York Times*, and *Los Angeles Times*.

93. "N.Y. World notified by Anthony Comstock to discontinue lottery advertisements; also to be notified to exclude massage, electrical and personal advertisements; also French remedies." *NY Commercial Advertiser*, circa 1900 (WISC–Ginzburg).

94. I soon realized that I wasn't the only one who'd discovered this. The prominent British historian of technology Iwan Rhys Morus told *The Nation*, "I can safely say that I have come across nothing in my researches on late nineteenth-century electricity and the body that lends any support at all to [this] argument." Another British scholar, Fern Riddell, questions the scholar's sources in her popular book on Victorian sexuality: "I have also not yet found a single reference to a specific 'pelvic massage' in any of the books or pamphlets I have read on the treatment of hysteria in Britain, . . . let alone the later use of vibration in this area." Riddell insists that Victorians were well-informed about orgasms and masturbation, so physicians could not have practiced genital massage "without the knowledge that it was a sexual act." *see* Wypijewski, JoAnn. "Playing Doctor," *The Nation*, June 18, 2012. *aslo see* Riddell, Fern. *The Victorian Guide to Sex: Desire and Deviance in the 19th Century*. South Yorkshire: Pen and Sword Books, 2014.

95. Items housed at Science Museum, Blythe House, London: Hand-cranked vibrator, Chinese or Japanese, late 19th century, no. A116573; Vibrator, air-operated, 19th century, no. A182737; Veedee Vibrator, hand-cranked early 20th century, Germany, no. 1982-1238; Electric Vibrator, France, late 19th early 20th century, no. A602312; Mechanical Eureka Massager, New York, no. A602769, circa 1900–1930.

96. Maines, Rachel P. *The Technology of Orgasm: "Hysteria," the Vibrator, and Women's Sexual Satisfaction*, revised edition. Baltimore: Johns Hopkins University Press, 2001, 11; 15; 93–94; 98–99.

97. Granville, Joseph Mortimer. "Therapeutics of the Nervous System: Nerve Vibration in the Treatment of Nervous Diseases." *The Journal of Nervous and Mental Disease* (March 1883): 172.

98. Peterson, Frederick. "Vibratory Therapeutics." *Medical News.* (January 1898): 141.

99. Hamilton, Allan McLane. "Vibratory Therapeutics," *Medical News* (February 1898): 248.

100. *Journal of the American Medical Association* to Samuel Hopkins Adams, February 11, 1915. Historical Health Fraud Collection, Box 243, Lindstrom Smith (File), Folder 3, American Medical Association Archives, Chicago (AMA–Health Fraud). The AMA wrote multiple letters to consumers and doctors, warning them of the inefficacy of White Cross and New Life vibrators. Another letter from the same file (September 14, 1916) is to the consumer Mr. F. R. Lawrence, saying the White Cross vibrator book *Health and Beauty* is "false and misleading." A letter from the Hamilton Beach file contains similar criticisms. *See JAMA* to Dr. J. M. Donelan, December 16, 1912. File Hamilton Beach, Box 231, Folder 3 (AMA–Health Fraud).

101. Vibratile Advertisement. *McClure's.* April 1899, 158.

102. Arnold Vibrator ads began running in the *New York Times* on May 26, 1908; Eureka Vibrator ads on October 4, 1909; and Swedish Massage Vibrator ads on March 17, 1909. Hygeia Vibratory Co.

began running ads in the *Chicago Tribune* on November 16, 1902, and Lindstrom Smith's White Cross Vibrator ads began running in *Health* magazine on December 1907 and in the *Chicago Tribune* on November 4, 1908.

103. Star Vibrator advertisement. *McClure's*. December 1918, 29.

104. Laqueur, Thomas W. *Solitary Sex: A Cultural History of Masturbation*, revised edition. New York: Zone Books, 2004, 66–74.

105. Hygeia Vibrator Ad. *Suggestion* 10, no 6. (June 1, 1903): 284.

106. Lowry, E. B., and R. J. Lambert. *Himself: Talks With Men Concerning Themselves*. Chicago: Forbes Company, 1912, 67–68.

107. Dickinson, Robert Latou, and Lura Beam. *A Thousand Marriages: A Medical Study of Sex Adjustment*. Baltimore: Williams & Wilkins, 1931, 421.

108. [Masturbation Female Photographs] 1920-1934. Photo no. 50466; 1920–1934 50466, 50467, 50468, 50469, 50470,-50471, 50472. Kinsey Institute Special Collections, Bloomington, Ind. (Kinsey).

109. "Snow White Makes Bashful Grow Bold!! And He Loves It." Circa 1930s–1940s. Eight-pager no. 6808 (Kinsey).

110. *Hank O'Hare Presents Tillie VI*. Circa 1930s–1940s. Eightpager no. 7456 c.1 (Kinsey).

111. *Novelties*. Detroit: Johnson Smith & Co., 1941, 519. Smithsonian National Museum of American History Trade Literature Collection, Washington, D.C. (NMAH–Trade Lit).

112. "Oster Vibrator." *Tyco Shop By Mail Catalog*. Dobbs Ferry, NY, 1953, 50 (NMAH–Trade Lit).

113. "Kenmore Vibrator." *Sears Christmas Book*. 1956, 372 (NMAH–Trade Lit).

114. Jones, James H. *Alfred C. Kinsey: A Life*. New York: W. W. Norton & Company, 2004, 689.

115. Rosen, Ruth. *The World Split Open: How the Modern Women's Movement Changed America*. New York: Penguin Books, 2000, 4–36.

116. "Investigate—Before You Invest!!!!" *Roanoke Better Business Bureau Newsletter*. January 15, 1959. "Mechanical Devices Special Data 1958–1962" (AMA–Health Fraud).

117. Yet you could send vibrators if they weren't sold as sex toys.

CHAPTER THREE

118. "Democratic Convention Opens with Carnival Atmosphere." *Redlands Daily Facts*. July 11, 1960, 9.

119. LaFeber, Walter, Richard Polenberg, and Nancy Woloch. *The American Century: A History of the United States Since 1941: Volume 2*. Boston: McGraw-Hill, 1988, 402–3.

120. Author interview with Marche's son (October 4, 2016).

121. Ibid.

122. "Ending Southwest Tour: Stars Spend Night in Flag." *Arizona Daily Sun.* June 4, 1958, 1.

123. Winchell, Walter. "It Takes All Kinds to Make World." *Humboldt Standard.* June 24, 1964, C-2.

124. "Our Get Acquainted Christmas Party." The Davis Plan Advertisement, *The Press-Courier* (Oxnard, Ca.). Dec. 3, 1959. *See also* "See Ted Marche and His Talking Pig at Market Basket in San Bernardino." *The San Bernardino County Sun.* July 9, 1959, C-9. *See also* "Ventriloquist Set." *Valley News* (Van Nuys, Ca.). March 6, 1965, 19.

125. Beltair, Mark. "The Town Crier: Remember the Yanks." *Detroit Free Press.* May 29, 1965, B14.

126. Letter to Charles S. Nelson from Oliver Field. August 27, 1963. Box 242, Folder 7 (AMA–Health Fraud).

127. As in the 1940s and 1950s, during the 1960s and 1970s, companies could send vibrators if they were disguised as massage devices.

128. *Griswold v. Connecticut,* 381 U.S. 479 (1965).

129. Boyer, Paul. *Purity in Print.* Madison, WI: University of Wisconsin Press, 2002, 40–42.

130. As quoted in Ibid., 276.

131. Ginzburg received over more than thirty-five thousand complaints. See *Special Report: U.S. Mail.* Fiscal Year 1963. Post Office Department, 24. Ralph Ginzburg Papers, Unprocessed Collection, 1961–1988, Eros Box 1 (WISC–Ginzburg).

132. Ibid.

133. Author interview with Marche's son (October 4, 2016). *See also* Heidenry, John. *What Wild Ecstasy.* New York: Simon & Schuster, 2002, 75–76. (Note: Marche's son said that some of the information about his father's company in this book is incorrect.)

134. Ibid. *See also* Mano, D. Keith. "Tom Swift Is Alive and Well and Making Dildos." *Playboy,* March 1978, 122.

135. LaFeber, Polenberg, and Woloch, *The American Century,* 412–13.

136. *Sewell v. Georgia,* 435 U.S. 982, 983 (1978).

137. Author interview with Marche's son (October 4, 2016).

138. Commission on Obscenity and Pornography. *The Report of the Commission on Obscenity and Pornography.* Washington: U.S. Government Printing Office, 1970, 101; 129.

139. Author interview with Marche's son (October 4, 2016).

140. Ibid.

141. Friedan, Betty. *The Feminine Mystique.* New York: W. W. Norton, 1963.

142. Rosen, *The World Split Open,* 4–6.

143. Dodson, Betty. *Sex for One: The Joy of Selfloving.* New York: Harmony, 1996, 14.

144. Mallants, Charita, and Kristina Casteels. "Practical Approach to Childhood Masturbation: A Review." *European Journal of Pediatrics* 167, no. 10 (October 2008): 1111–17, doi:10.1007/s00431-008-0766-2. About 44 percent of girls ages two to five masturbate.

145. Dodson, Betty. *Liberating Masturbation: A Meditation on Self Love*. New York. Bodysex Designs, 1974, 1.

146. Dodson letter to Jacqui. Box 3, Folder 66, Dell Williams Papers, 1922–2008, Cornell Human Sexuality Collection, Ithaca, NY (Cornell–Williams).

147. Ibid.

148. Dodson, Betty. *My Romantic Love Wars*. New York: Betty Dodson, 2010, 28–38.

149. Side note: Kinsey did observe people having sex, but he denied it and didn't use the data for his research.

150. Maier, Thomas. *Masters of Sex: The Life and Times of William Masters and Virginia Johnson, the Couple Who Taught America How to Love*. New York: Basic Books, 2009, 98–101; 162; 242.

151. "Best Seller List." *New York Times*, July 31, 1966, 203; "Best Seller List." *New York Times*, December 11, 1966, 372.

152. Mailer, Norman, and Pete Hamill. *Prisoner of Sex*. New York: Plume, 1985, 73; 80.

153. Ibid., 88.

154. Author interview with Marche's son (October 4, 2016).

155. Ibid. *See also* Mano, "Tom Swift"; Heidenry, *What Wild Ecstasy*, 75–77.

156. *Guide to the American Medical Association Historical Health Fraud and Alternative Medicine Collection*. American Medical Association, 1992, vii.

157. Letter from Frank E. Wilson to Oliver Field, Director of Research at AMA, September 11, 1967 (AMA–Health Fraud).

158. Letter from Frank E. Wilson to Oliver Field, Director of Research at AMA, August 18, 1967 (AMA–Health Fraud).

159. As quoted in Downs, Donald. *The New Politics of Pornography*. Chicago: University of Chicago Press, 1989, 15–16.

160. Ibid., 16.

161. Geltzer, Jeremy. *Dirty Words and Filthy Pictures: Film and the First Amendment*. Austin: University of Texas Press, 2015, 247.

162. Weller, Sheila. "Inside Betty Dodson." *Forum*, February 1976.

163. Dodson, *Liberating Masturbation*, 24.

164. Dodson, *My Romantic Love Wars*, 42.

165. Dodson, *Liberating Masturbation*, 8.

166. Ibid.

167. Ibid.

168. Weller, "Inside Betty Dodson."

169. Dodson, Betty. "Having Sex with Machines: The Return of the Electric Vibrator." Dodson and Ross, June 8, 2010. Accessed May 5, 2014. http://dodsonandross.com/blogs/betty-dodson/2010/06/having-sex-machines-return-electric-vibrator

170. Judson, Olivia. *Dr. Tatiana's Sex Advice to All Creation*. New York: Metropolitan Books, 2002, 88. *See also* Cornog, Martha. *The Big Book of Masturbation from Angst to Zeal*. San Francisco: Down There Press, 2003, 101.

171. Hughes, Thomas. *American Genesis: A Century of Invention and Technological Enthusiasm*. New York: Viking, 1989, 447.

172. Ibid.

173. Dodson, "Having Sex with Machines."

174. Ibid.

175. Dodson, *Sex for One*, 30.

176. Ibid., 85.

177. Dodson, *My Romantic Love Wars*, 84.

178. Dodson, *Sex for One*, 32.

179. Ibid., 32.

180. Ibid., 187.

181. Ibid., 32.

182. Author interview with Farley Malorrus (October 4, 2016).

183. Gamson, Joshua. "Rubber Wars: Struggles over the Condom in the United States." *Journal of the History of Sexuality* 1, no. 2 (1990): 262–82.

184. Farley Malorrus said this to me in an interview, but I haven't been able to confirm it elsewhere.

185. Author interview with Farley Malorrus (October 4, 2016).

CHAPTER FOUR

186. Mano, "Tom Swift."

187. Moya, Cynthia Ann. "Artificial Vaginas and Sex Dolls: An Erotological Investigation." Ph.D. diss., Institute for Advanced Study of Human Sexuality, 2006, 80–81.

188. Mano, "Tom Swift."

189. Brochure for Premier Vaginal Prosthesis, 2. Box 786, Folder 4 (AMA–Health Fraud).

190. Author interview with Farley Malorrus (October 4, 2016).

191. Letter from Dr. Kenneth D. Campbell to Mr. Oliver Field, February 14, 1967. Box 786, Folder 4 (AMA–Health Fraud).

192. Author interview with Marche's son (October 4, 2016).

193. In my research, I've found no evidence of other companies producing such things.

194. Ellis, Albert. *Sex without Guilt.* New York: Lyle-Stewart, 1966, 29–30. This chapter was a revised edition of a 1956 article he wrote for *The Independent.*

195. Frederick, Max. *Book of Amorous Stimulants and Prosthetic Devices.* Catalog, 1972 (Kinsey).

196. "The Great Playboy Sex Aids Road Test." *Playboy.* March 1978,137; 208.

197. Mano, "Tom Swift." *Also,* author interview with Marche's son (October 4, 2016).

198. Sandroni, Paola. "Aphrodisiacs Past and Present: A Historical Review." *Clinical Autonomic Research* 11, no. 5 (2001): 303–7, doi:10.1007/BF02332975.

199. Author interview with Dr. Michael D. Lieberman, practicing physician in Alexandria, Virginia (1970s–2014) and President of Medical Staff of Mount Vernon Hospital (1993–95) (October 10, 2016).

200. Geltzer, *Dirty Words and Filthy Pictures.*

201. Sandroni, "Aphrodisiacs Past and Present," 306.

202. Ben Wa Novelty Catalog. Circa 1970s, 18. Gosnell Duncan Papers, Author's Personal Collection (Duncan).

203. Mano, "Tom Swift."

204. Whelan, Edward P. "Reuben Sturman and His Amazing Porno Empire!" *Plain Dealer,* May 1976. *See also* Hatton, Katherine L. "Porn King Tells His Side of the Story." *Plain Dealer,* July 30, 1978, 1.

205. Kraig, Gene. *The Sentence: A Family's Prison Memoir.* New York: Greenpoint Press, 2006.

206. Hatton, "Porn King," 1.

207. Author interview with David Sturman (December 7, 2016).

208. Stricharchuk, Gregory. "Selling Skin: 'Porn King' Expands His Empire with Aid of Businessman's Skills." *Wall Street Journal,* May 8, 1985, 2.

209. Schlosser, Eric. *Reefer Madness: Sex, Drugs, and Cheap Labor in the American Black Market.* Boston: Mariner Books, 2004, 118.

210. Hatton, "Porn King," 1.

211. Schlosser, *Reefer Madness*, 118.

212. *Attorney General's Commission on Pornography: Final Report.* U.S. Department of Justice, 1986, vol. 2, 1066; 1180.

213. Whelan, "Reuben Sturman," 49.

214. Schlosser, *Reefer Madness*, 124–25; 130.

215. Heidenry, *What Wild Ecstasy*, 73.

216. Whelan, "Reuben Sturman," 52.

217. Stricharchuk, "Selling Skin," 1.

218. Heidenry, *What Wild Ecstasy*, 47.

219. Ibid., 55.

220. *New York*, November 4, 1968, 15.

221. Dodson, *Liberating Masturbation*, 13.

222. Dodson, *My Romantic Love Wars*, 105.

223. Koedt, Anne. "The Myth of the Vaginal Orgasm." *Radical Feminism*, eds. Anne Koedt, Ellen Levine, and Anita Rapone. New York: Quadrangle Books, 1973, 198–207.

224. Shulman, Alix Kates. "Organs and Orgasms." *Women in a Sexist Society*, eds. V. Gornick and B. Moran. New York: Signet, 1971.

225. *Women and Their Bodies: A Course.* Boston Women's Health Collective, 1970, 22–23; 26.

226. Dodson, *My Romantic Love Wars*, 110–12; 166–67.

227. Mary Phillips, "The Fine Art of Lovemaking: An Interview with Betty Dodson," *Evergreen Review* 87 (February 1971). *See also* Dodson, *My Romantic Love Wars*, 110–12; 166–67.

CHAPTER FIVE

228. Dodson, *My Romantic Love Wars*, 84.

229. Author interview with Dell Williams (January 9, 2015); Williams, Dell, and Lynn Vannucci, *Revolution in the Garden*. San Francisco: Silverback Books, 2005, 131.

230. Author interview with Dell Williams (January 9, 2015).

231. Williams and Vannucci, *Revolution in the Garden*, 132.

232. Ibid., 20.

233. Ibid.

234. Author interview with Dell Williams (January 9, 2015).

235. Freeman, Susan K. *Sex Goes to School: Girls and Sex Education before the 1960s.* Champaign, IL: University of Illinois Press, 2008, 45.

236. Calculation made using www.measuringworth.com.

237. Williams and Vannucci, *Revolution in the Garden,* 49–54; 60–62; 66–74.

238. Ibid., 80–86.

239. Author interview with Dell Williams (January 9, 2015).

240. Williams and Vannucci, *Revolution in the Garden,* 103–6.

241. "The 35th Academy Awards." Academy of Motion Picture Arts and Sciences, 1963. Accessed June 6, 2017. https://www.oscars.org/oscars/ceremonies/1963.

242. Fox, Stephen. *The Mirror Makers: A History of American Advertising and Its Creators.* Champaign, IL: University of Illinois Press, 1997, 293–94.

243. Williams and Vannucci, *Revolution in the Garden,* 108–13; 129–33.

244. Author interview with Dell Williams (January 9, 2015).

245. Bronstein, Carolyn. *Battling Pornography: The American Feminist Anti-Pornography Movement, 1976–1986.* Cambridge, UK: Cambridge University Press, 2011, 40–41.

246. Ibid., 43.

247. Hanisch, Carol. "The Personal Is Political." *Notes from the Second Year: Major Writings of Radical Feminists* 1, no. 1 (1970): 76–78.

248. Murphy, Michelle. "Immodest Witnessing: The Epistemology of Vaginal Self-Examination in the U.S. Feminist Self-Help Movement." *Feminist Studies* 30, no. 1 (2004) 115–147.

249. Dodson, *Sex for One,* 45.

250. Ibid., 49.

251. Friedan, Betty. *It Changed My Life.* New York: Laurel, 1991, 86.

252. Echols, Alice. *Daring to Be Bad: Radical Feminism in America 1967-1975.* Minneapolis: University of Minnesota Press, 1989, 82; 145–46.

253. Ibid., 149, 163.

254. Gerhard, Jane. *Desiring Revolution: Second-Wave Feminism and the Rewriting of American Sexual Thought, 1920 to 1982.* New York: Columbia University Press, 2001, 111–12.

255. Dodson, *Sex for One,* 49.

256. Snitow, Ann, Christine Stansell, and Sharon Thompson. *Powers of Desire*. New York: Monthly Review Press, 1983, 27.

257. Echols, *Daring to Be Bad*, 149.

258. Dodson, *My Romantic Love Wars*, 98.

259. Dodson, *Sex for One*, 50.

CHAPTER SIX

260. Author interview with Gosnell Duncan (August 2, 2013).

261. Author interview with Lurline Martineau, Gosnell Duncan's niece (January 10, 2015).

262. Ibid.

263. Jokobsen, May Kristin, trans. "A Cellarfull of Dildoes: Olav Andre Manum Visits Dildo Makers Scorpio Novelty Products." *Hverdag Products* (August 6, 1990): 2.

264. Rabin, Barry J. *Sensuous Wheeler: Sexual Adjustment for the Spinal Cord Injured*. San Francisco: Barry Rabin, 1980, v.

265. Author interview with Lurline Martineau (January 10, 2015).

266. Fleischer, Doris, and Frieda Zames. *The Disability Rights Movement: From Charity to Confrontation*. Philadelphia: Temple University Press, 2012, 36–43.

267. Gregory, Martha Ferguson. *Sexual Adjustment: A Guide for the Spinal Cord Injured*. Bloomington, IL: Accent on Living, 1974, 1–2.

268. Author interview with Gosnell Duncan (August 2, 2013).

269. Ibid.

270. It is possible that a company may have sold silicone dildos earlier than Duncan because a catalog in Gosnell Duncan's papers from the Pen-Vibe company (Malorrus's spin-off company) shows two silicone rubber dildos. The catalog has no date on it, although Duncan has written "1970" in pencil on the front page. See *Pen-Vibe Catalog*, circa 1970, 2 (Duncan).

271. Author interview with Lurline Martineau (January 10, 2015).

272. Meikle, Jeffrey. *American Plastic: A Cultural History*. New Brunswick, NJ: Rutgers University Press, 1997, 83–85.

273. Author interview with Gosnell Duncan (August 2, 2013).

274. Meikle, *American Plastic*, 83–85.

275. Author interview with Gosnell Duncan (August 2, 2013).

276. Jokobsen, "A Cellarfull of Dildoes," 4.

277. Author interview with Gosnell Duncan (August 2, 2013).

278. Letter to *The Squeaky Wheel* June 1973, reprinted in *Proceeding of the Workshop Continuing Education in the Treatment of Spinal Cord Injuries.* Chicago: National Paraplegia Foundation, 1973, 3.

279. Tarabulcy, Edward, M.D. "Sexual Function in the Normal and in Paraplegia." *Paraplegia* (1972) vol. 10, no. 3, 10; 201–208.

280. Task Force on Concerns of Physically Disabled Women. "Toward Intimacy: Family Planning and Sexuality Concerns of Physically Disabled Women." Planned Parenthood of Snohomish County, Inc., 1977, 48–49.

281. Therapeutic Sex Aids Brochure. Paramount Therapeutic Products early 1970s (Duncan).

282. Letter from W. H. Verduyn, M. D., to Gosnell Duncan, April 19, 1983; Letter from Gosnell Duncan to W. H. Verduyn, M.D., April 26, 1983 (Duncan).

283. Letter from Gosnell Duncan to Ms. Joynce Leffler, May 11, 1979 (Duncan); Letter from Gosnell Duncan to Dr. Matthew Lee, Jan 4, 1978 (Duncan). *See also* Fleischer and Zames. *The Disability Rights Movement: From Charity to Confrontation*, 22.

284. Letter from Mary Romano to Gosnell Duncan, March 18, 1975 (Duncan).

285. Letter from A. S. Crouse at General Electric, Silicone Products Department, to Gosnell Duncan, October 24, 1975 (Duncan).

286. Rusk, Howard A., M.D, moderator. "Roundtable: Sex Problems in Paraplegia." *Medical Aspects of Human Sexuality.* December 1967, 48.

287. Therapeutic Sex Aids Brochure. Paramount Therapeutic Products, early 1970s (Duncan).

288. *The Report of the Commission on Obscenity and Pornography* (1970), 105 (Duncan).

289. Letter from customer to Gosnell Duncan, May 14, 1976 (Duncan).

290. Shapiro, Martin. "Obscenity Law: A Public Policy Analysis." 20.2 *Journal of Public Law.* 503, 522 (1971), 516–17.

291. Post Office Department Prohibitory Order No. 14762 to Gosnell Duncan, January 23, 1970 (Duncan).

292. *The Report of the Commission on Obscenity and Pornography* (1970), 18.

293. These studies were limited, but they are some of the only market research available.

294. *The Report of the Commission on Obscenity and Pornography* (1970), 51.

295. Ibid., 53.

296. Geltzer, *Dirty Words and Filthy Pictures*, 255.

297. Schlosser, *Reefer Madness*, 135.

298. Letter from a female customer to Gosnell Duncan, February 4, 1983; Letter from a male customer to Gosnell Duncan, June 19, 1984 (Duncan).

299. Letter from a male customer to Gosnell Duncan, June 8, 1984 (Duncan).

300. Letter from a female customer to Gosnell Duncan, February 17, 1980 (Duncan).

301. Letter from a female customer to Gosnell Duncan, February 20, 1980 (Duncan).

302. Gosnell Duncan interview with customer n.d. (Duncan).

303. Letter from a customer to Gosnell Duncan, February 17, 1980 (Duncan).

304. Letter from a customer to Gosnell Duncan, May 27, 1975 (Duncan).

305. Letter from a customer to Gosnell Duncan, late 1970s or early 1980s (Duncan).

306. Letter from a customer to Gosnell Duncan, November 14, 1978 (Duncan).

307. Letter from Chuck to Gosnell Duncan, February 24, 1980 (Duncan).

308. Bright, *Susie Bright's Sexual Reality*, 31.

CHAPTER SEVEN

309. Picture of Colglazier, late 1970s. Pleasure Chest Store Corporate Archives, Los Angeles (Pleasure Chest).

310. Author interview with Brian Robinson (March 23, 2016).

311. Mano, "Tom Swift," 228.

312. *Pleasure Chest Catalog*. Pleasure Chest, circa 1978 (Pleasure Chest).

313. Mano, "Tom Swift," 228.

314. Numbers, Ronald. "Sex, Science and Salvation: The Sexual Advice of Ellen G. White and John Harvey Kellogg." *Right Living: An Anglo-American Tradition of Self-Help Medicine and Hygiene*. Charles E. Rosenberg, ed. 206–25. Baltimore: Johns Hopkins University Press, 2003.

315. Author interview with Brian Robinson (March 23, 2016).

316. Ibid. *See also* "Duane Lee Colglazier (1944–1988). Find a Grave. Accessed June 8, 2017. https://www.findagrave.com/cgi-bin/fg.cgi?page=gr&GRid=128609617.

317. Long, Kat. *The Forbidden Apple: A Century of Sex & Sin in New York City*. Brooklyn: Ig Publishing, 2009, 147.

318. D'Emilio, John, and Estelle B. Freedman. *Intimate Matters: A History of Sexuality in America*. New York: Harper and Row, 1988, 321.

319. Klemesrud, Judy. "Sex Boutique: 'Middle Ground Between Drugstore Approach and Smut Shop.'" *New York Times*, January 13, 1972. August 6, 2017. https://www.nytimes.com/1972/01/13/archives/sex-boutique-middle-ground-between-drugstore-approach-and-smut-shop.html.

320. *Pleasure Chest Catalog.* Pleasure Chest, circa 1971 (Pleasure Chest).

321. *Pornography in New York.* Documentary film. USA, 1972. (The section described begins at 37:05 in the movie).

322. Klemesrud, "Sex Boutique," 36.

323. Author interview with Chad Braverman (July 6, 2016).

324. Gardetta, Dave. "Doctor's Orders." *Los Angeles Magazine,* July 1, 2012. August 6, 2017. http://www.lamag.com/longform/doctors-orders/.

325. Author interview with Chad Braverman (July 6, 2016).

326. Author interview with Ron Braverman (December 27, 2016).

327. Mahoney, E. R. *Human Sexuality.* New York: McGraw-Hill, 1983, 475.

328. Author interview with Farley Malorrus (October 4, 2016).

329. Levy, David. *Love and Sex with Robots: The Evolution of Human-Robot Relationships.* New York: Harper Perennial, 2008, 236–37.

330. Ibid., 237.

331. Ibid., 247.

332. It's unclear if this was the same doll as the one Orient Industries made.

333. "Auto-Girl" Advertisement (Page C). *Los Angeles Free Press,* April 20, 1973.

334. "Love and the Living Doll." *Love, American Style: Season 1.* ABC. October 6, 1969. Accessed June 8, 2017. http://www.tv.com/shows/love-american-style/love-and-the-living-doll-166362/.

335. I was unable to find statistics on sex-doll ownership.

336. Author interview with Farley Malorrus (October 4, 2016).

337. "Bosko, the Auto-Girl Company" Advertisement (Page C). *Los Angeles Free Press,* August 24, 1973. Other dolls with artificial vaginas were available two years earlier, however.

338. "Auto-Girl" Advertisement. *Berkeley Barb,* May 4–10, 1973, 38; and "Auto-Sex" Advertisement. *Los Angeles Free Press,* April 6–16, 1973, C. Malorrus ran more than sixty ads in these publications between 1972 and 1973.

339. Author interview with Farley Malorrus (October 4, 2016).

340. The earliest Pleasure Chest catalog I've found with his blow-up dolls is from 1978, but some of the other old catalogs between 1971 and 1978 have been impossible to obtain, so it could be earlier.

341. "No Place to Go but Up." *Time,* April 19, 1971.

342. Latimer, Dean. "The Chastening of the Blade." *The East Village Other,* March 30, 1971, 11.

343. Klemesrud, "Sex Boutique."

344. Long, *The Forbidden Apple*, 168.

345. D'Emilio and Freedman, *Intimate Matters*, 300.

346. Independent Voices search of underground publications (1968–72): sixty-four mentions of "marital aids" versus twenty-four of "sex toys."

347. Mano, "Tom Swift," 228.

348. Author interview with Ted Marche's son (September 30, 2016).

349. Mano, "Tom Swift," 228.

350. Mahoney, *Human Sexuality*, 475.

351. Author interview with Farley Malorrus (October 4, 2016).

352. Ibid.

353. *The Pleasure Chest Compendium of Amorous & Prurient Erotica, Paraphernalia, et. al. or Do Unto Others As You Would Have Others Do Unto You.* New York City: Pleasure Chest Ltd., early 1970s, 45 (Pleasure Chest).

354. *The Pleasure Chest Compendium*, 45 (Pleasure Chest).

355. Klemesrud, "Sex Boutique," 36.

356. "Pleasure Chest" Advertisement. *Echo of Sappho*, August/September 1972, 12.

357. *Big Mama Rag*, November/December 1977, 1.

358. "Listen." *Los Angeles Times*, January 18, 1980, H1.

359. Rubin, Gayle. "Samois." *Leather Times*, Spring 2004, 4.

360. *Pornography in New York*. Documentary film. USA, 1972.

361. *The Pleasure Chest Compendium*, 7 (Pleasure Chest).

CHAPTER EIGHT

362. Author interview with Betty Dodson (January 15, 2014).

363. Author interview with Dell Williams (January 9, 2015). *See also* Williams and Vannucci, *Revolution in the Garden*, 140.

364. Author interview with Dell Williams (January 9, 2015).

365. Ibid.

366. Williams, Dell. Writings about 1973 workshops with Betty Dodson, for "Sexually Speaking" article series. *Sappho's Isle*, Box 3, Folder 64, 1 (Cornell–Williams).

367. Author interview with Dell Williams (January 9, 2015).

368. Williams and Vannucci, *Revolution in the Garden,*" 141.

369. Dodson, *My Romantic Love Wars*, 174.

370. Williams and Vannucci, *Revolution in the Garden*, 142.

371. Dell Williams Papers, Box 3, Folder 64, 2 (Cornell–Williams).

372. Williams and Vannucci, *Revolution in the Garden*, 143.

373. Ibid., 143.

374 Dell Williams Papers, Box 3, Folder 64, 4 (Cornell–Williams).

375. Williams and Vannucci, *Revolution in the Garden*, 144.

376. Dell Williams Papers, Box 3, Folder 64, 4 (Cornell–Williams).

377. Williams and Vannucci, *Revolution in the Garden*, 144–45.

378. *The Report of the Commission on Obscenity and Pornography* (1970), 101; 129.

379. "January Sale of Drugs, Toilet, and Manicure Goods" Advertisement. Macy's Department Store. *New York Times*, January 26, 1910, 7.

380. Williams and Vannucci, *Revolution in the Garden*, 146–8.

381. Dodson, *Liberating Masturbation*, 10. *See also* Williams, Writings about 1973 workshops with Betty Dodson, *Sappho's Isle*, Box 3, Folder 64, 1 (Cornell–Williams).

382. Dodson, *My Romantic Love Wars*, 177.

383. *Women's Sexuality Conference Proceedings*. New York: National Organization of Women New York Chapter, 1974, 8–10.

384. Miller, Lindsay. "Women Confer on Sex." *New York Post*, June 11, 1973. *See also* Johnston, Laurie. "Women's Sexuality Conference Ends in School Here: Older Women Attend." *New York Times*, June 11, 1973.

385. Johnston, "Women's Sexuality Conference."

386. Williams, Dell. "To Explore, Define, and Celebrate Our Sexuality." *Women's Sexuality Conference Proceedings*. New York: National Organization of Women New York Chapter, 1974, 6.

387. Author interview with Dell Williams (January 9, 2015).

388. Dodson, *My Romantic Love Wars*, 181.

389. Dodson, Betty. *Women's Sexuality Conference Proceedings*. New York: National Organization of Women New York Chapter, 1974, 10.

390. "Betty's Talk—NOW's Sexuality Conference in 1973." Posted January 18, 2012. YouTube video. https://www.youtube.com/watch?v=w6oAGPA8MSs.

391. Rovner, Ruth. "Women's Sexuality Conference: A Vibrator Connoisseur." *Los Angeles Free Press*, July 20, 1973, 13–14. Reprinted in *Women's Sexuality Conference Proceedings*. New York: National Organization of Women New York Chapter, 1974, 55–56.

392. "Panasonic" Advertisement. *New York Times*, May 4, 1972.

393. "Panabrator" Advertisement (Embedded in Abercrombie and Fitch Advertisement). *New York Times*, November 25, 1972.

394. "Speakout to the NOW Sexuality Conference." June 1973. Box 7, tr. 8025a. (Cornell–Williams).

395. Rovner, "Women's Sexuality Conference," 13.

396. Comfort, Alex, ed. *The Joy of Sex: A Gourmet Guide to Love Making*. New York: Simon & Schuster, 1972, 176; 220; 239.

397. "Speakout to the NOW Sexuality Conference." Box 8, tr. 8025a.

398. Dodson, *My Romantic Love Wars*, 180–82.

399. Greer, Germaine. *The Female Eunuch*. New York: Paladin, 1970.

400. Bronstein, *Battling Pornography*, 2.

401. Dodson, *My Romantic Love Wars*, 182.

402. Author interview with Dell Williams (January 9, 2015).

403. Dodson, *My Romantic Love Wars*, 217.

404. Ibid.

405. Dodson, Betty. "Getting to Know Me." *Ms.* (August 1974). Reprinted in Escoffier, Jeffrey, ed. *Sexual Revolution*. New York: Thunder's Mouth Press, 2003.

406. Dodson, *My Romantic Love Wars*, 219.

407. Ibid., 221.

408. Mahoney, *Human Sexuality*, 166.

409. As far as I know.

410. Dodson, *Liberating Masturbation*, 2.

411. Ibid., 12.

412. Rosen, *The World Split Open*, 149.

413. A positive review in *Big Mama Rag* (vol. 4, no. 2, February 1976, 11) supports Dodson's project to

make masturbation the center of sexual knowledge but warns that "without a political analysis of the pleasure of orgasm, it may be used to placate women in their relationships with men, discouraging their consciousness of the political reality of these relationships."

414. Gerhard, *Desiring Revolution*, 7.

415. "Liberating Masturbation," in "Worth Noting." *The Spokeswoman* 5 (March 15, 1975): 9.

416. Hruby, Kathy. "Sexual Self-Help." *Amazon Quarterly* 3, no. 2 (March 1975): 61. Other lesbian journals recommended the book. In an article about masturbation in *Lesbian Connection* (vol. 2, no. 3, July 1976, 2), Dodson's theories are espoused and her book is recommended.

417. Dodson, *Liberating Masturbation*, 48.

418. Ibid,, 28.

419. Ibid., 1.

420. Ibid., 51.

421. Williams, Dell. "The Roots of the Garden." *Journal of Sex Research* 27, no. 3 (August 1990): 461–66.

422. Author interview with Betty Dodson (January 15, 2014).

423. Williams and Vannucci, *Revolution in the Garden*, 160–61.

CHAPTER NINE

424. Author interview with Dell Williams (January 10, 2015). Quote is Williams's summation of Reich's argument.

425. Williams, Dell. Writings about Betty Dodson. Box 3, Folder 64 (Cornell–Williams).

426. Eve's Garden Media Kit. Box 6, Folder 69 (Cornell–Williams).

427. Author interview with Dell Williams (January 10, 2015). Quote is Williams's summation of Reich's argument.

428. Author interview with Dell Williams (January 10, 2015).

429. Williams and Vannucci, *Revolution in the Garden*, 16.

430. Ibid.,18.

431. Ibid.

432. Ibid., 180.

433. Bronstein, *Battling Pornography*, 148.

434. Borstelmann, Thomas. *The 1970s: A New Global History from Civil Rights to Economic Inequality.* Princeton, NJ: Princeton University Press, 2011, 164.

435. Author interview with Dell Williams (January 10, 2015).

436. Williams and Vannucci, *Revolution in the Garden*, 179.

437. Customer letter, August 5, 1983. Customer Correspondence. Box 5, Folder 1 (Cornell–Williams).

438. Author interview with Dell Williams (January 9, 2015); Customer letter to Dell Williams, January 7, 1977; "The Eve's Garden Guide to More Fun and Pleasure," Box 3, Folder 144; "Saying Hello to Your Vibrator," Box 3, Folder 4. (Cornell–Williams).

439. Glasscock, Jessica. *Striptease: From Gaslight to Spotlight*. New York: Harry Abrams, 2003, 161.

440. In fact, strip clubs already had a rich history in New York in the 1970s, as they had made the city their home since the 1920s. *See* Glasscock, *Striptease*, 11–12.

441. Author interview with Dell Williams (January 9, 2015).

442. Jacqui Ceballos interview with Dell Williams. Transcript, Box 1, Folder 14, 33 (Cornell–Williams).

443. Customer correspondence to Eve's Garden, November 6, 1975. Box 5, Folder 2 (Cornell–Williams).

444. Letter from Williams to a customer, November 1, 1975. Box 5, Folder 2 (Cornell–Williams).

445. Customer correspondence to Eve's Garden, March 1984. Box 4, Folder 2 (Cornell–Williams).

446. Gosier, Diane, L. N. Gardel, and Alice Aldrich. "NOW or Never." *Off Our Backs*, December 31, 1974.

447. Califia, Pat. "In Response to Dorchen Leidholdt's 'Lesbian S/M: Radicalism or Reaction.'" *New Women's Times* 8, no. 9 (October 1982): 15. *See also* Letter to editor signed Berkeley, Ca. *Lesbian Connection*, 6 (July 1975): 24.

448. Rubin, Gayle. "Thinking Sex." *Pleasure and Danger: Exploring Female Sexuality*. Boston: Routledge, 1984, 267–319.

449. Echols, *Daring to Be Bad*. 52; 68. For example, New York Radical Women promoted a "one-dress" uniform for members of their organization that would demonstrate their members were not consumers beholden to the fashion industry.

450. Rosen, *The World Split Open*, 204.

451. Frank, Thomas. *The Conquest of Cool*. Chicago: University of Chicago Press, 1997, 155–56.

452. Author interview with Dell Williams (January 9, 2015).

453. Customer correspondence to Eve's Garden, February 7, 1985. Box 5, Folder 3 (Cornell–Williams).

454. Williams and Vannucci, *Revolution in the Garden*, 18.

455. Author interview with Betty Dodson (January 15, 2014).

456. "Dell's account of store inception and expansion and struggle" of Eve's Garden, 1982. Box 3, Folder 2 (Cornell–Williams).

457. Letter from Dell Williams to Ms. Eddie Greenberg, January 13, 1976. Business correspondence, 1970s. Box 3, Folder 142 (Cornell–Williams).

458. "Eve's Garden" Advertisement. *Big Mama Rag: A Feminist News Journal,* vol. 4, no. 3 (March 1976): 10; *Big Mama Rag,* 4, no. 12 (December 1976): 9; *Big Mama Rag* 5, no. 1 (January–February 1977): 7; *Chrysalis* 2 (1977): 142; *Lesbian Tide* 6, no. 5 (March–April 1977): 22.

459. "Eve's Garden" Advertisement. *New Women's Times,* vol. 2, no. 11 (December 1976–January 1977): 15.

460. Customer correspondence to Eve's Garden, April 1975. Box 5, Folder 1 (Cornell–Williams).

461. Customer correspondence to Eve's Garden, October 4, 1975. Box 5, Folder 6 (Cornell–Williams).

462. Barbach, Lonnie Garfield. *For Yourself: The Fulfillment of Female Sexuality.* Revised and updated edition. New York: Anchor, 1976, 119.

463. Safran, Claire. "Plain Talk About the New Approach to Sexual Pleasure." *Redbook,* March 1976.

464. Heiman, Julia R., Leslie Lopiccolo, and Joseph Lopiccolo. *Becoming Orgasmic: A Sexual Growth Program for Women.* First edition. Englewood Cliffs, NJ: Prentice-Hall, Inc., 1976, 105; 431–32.

465. Author interview with Phil Harvey (February 3, 2017).

466. Cheshes, Jay. "Hard-Core Philanthropist." *Mother Jones.* Accessed January 23, 2017. http://www.motherjones.com/politics/2002/09/hard-core-philanthropist-phil-harvey.

467. Harvey, Philip D. *The Government vs. Erotica: The Siege of Adam & Eve.* Amherst, NY: Prometheus Books, 2001, 41–42.

468. Ibid., 42.

469. Author interview with Phil Harvey (February 3, 2017).

470. Harvey, *The Government vs. Erotica,* 43.

471. "Our History." Marie Stopes International. Accessed February 5, 2017. https://mariestopes.org/about-us/our-history/.

472. Harvey, *The Government vs. Erotica,* 4; 43–44.

473. Author interview with Phil Harvey (February 3, 2017).

474. Harvey, *The Government vs. Erotica,* 107.

475. Author interview with Phil Harvey (February 3, 2017).

476. Harvey, *The Government vs. Erotica,* 45.

477. "Adam and Eve. Deluxe Vibrator Massager" Advertisement. *Playgirl,* August 1975.

478. Author interview with Phil Harvey (February 3, 2017).

479. Harvey, *The Government vs. Erotica,* 44.

480. McLaren, Angus. *Twentieth-Century Sexuality: A History.* Oxford, UK: Blackwell Publishers, 1999, 18.

481. "Our History." Marie Stopes International.

482. Whelan, "Reuben Sturman," 48.

483. Gardette, Dave. "Doctor's Orders." *Los Angeles Magazine,* July 1, 2012. http://www.lamag.com/longform/doctors-orders/.

484. Whelan, "Reuben Sturman," 48.

485. Author interview with David Sturman (December 7, 2016).

486. Whelan, Edward P. "The Prince of Porn." *Cleveland Magazine,* August 1985.

487. Heidenry, *What Wild Ecstasy,* 200.

488. Whelan, "Reuben Sturman," 51.

489. *Attorney General's Commission on Pornography: Final Report* (1986), vol. 2, 1108–10.

490. Whelan, "Reuben Sturman," 75.

491. Schlosser, *Reefer Madness,* 145.

492. Whelan, "Reuben Sturman," 46.

493. Ibid., 50.

494. *The Report of the Commission on Obscenity and Pornography* (1970), 347.

495. Money, John, and Tom Mazur. "Microphallus: The Successful Use of a Prosthetic Phallus in a 9-Year-Old Boy." *Journal of Sex and Marital Therapy,* 3, no. 3 (Fall 1977): 187–96.

496. Ibid., 191.

497. Warnke, Georgia. *After Identity: Rethinking Race, Sex, and Gender.* Oxford, UK: Cambridge University Press, 2008, 15–29. For the complete story, *see also* Colapinto, John. *As Nature Made Him: The Boy Who Was Raised as a Girl.* New York: HarperCollins, 2013.

498. Money and Mazur, "Microphallus," 191.

499. Ibid., 193.

500. Ibid., 193–95.

501. Author interview with Marche's son (September 30, 2016).

502. The FDA does regulate "genital vibrators for therapeutic use in the treatment of sexual dysfunction or as an adjunct to Kegel's exercise (tightening of the muscles of the pelvic floor to increase muscle tone)." The FDA also regulates clitoral vacuum devices and vibrators "for climax control of premature ejaculation." See §884.5960, §884.5970, §876.5020 of the Electronic Code of Federal Regulations.

503. "The Porno Plague." *Time*, April 5, 1976.

CHAPTER TEN

504. Satchell, Michael. "The Big Business of Selling Smut." *Parade Magazine*, August 19, 1979, 4–5.

505. Ibid.

506. Author interview with Chad Braverman (July 6, 2016).

507. Author interview with Marche's son (September 30, 2016).

508. Author interview with Ron Braverman (December 27, 2016).

509. Author interview with Chad Braverman (July 6, 2016).

510. Lever, Janet, David A. Frederick, and Letitia Anne Peplau. "Does Size Matter? Men's and Women's Views on Penis Size Across the Lifespan." *Psychology of Men & Masculinity* 7, no. 3 (2006): 129–43.

511. Author interview with Ron Braverman (December 27, 2016).

512. Ibid.

513. Ibid.

514. Author interview with Chad Braverman (July 6, 2016).

515. Cook, James. "The X-Rated Economy." *Forbes*, September 18, 1978, 84.

516. Author interview with Ron Braverman (December 27, 2016).

517. Cook, "The X-Rated Economy," 84.

518. *"Doc" Johnson Marital Aids Catalog.* Cleveland, Ohio: "Doc" Johnson, 1976, front cover. Doc Johnson Corporate Collection.

519. Ibid., 34.

520. "Anal Intruder Kit" Advertisement. *The Advocate*, January 11, 1978, 24. Lesbian, Gay, Bisexual, and Transgender (LGBT) Collection, Archives Center. National Museum of American History, Smithsonian Institution. (NMAH–LGBT).

521. Blystone, Richard. "Residents Deploy Porno Atmosphere." *Carroll Daily Times Herald*, June 9, 1976.

522. Whelan, "Reuben Sturman," 51.

523. Stricharchuk, "Selling Skin," 26.

524. Author interview with Farley Malorrus (October 4, 2016).

525. Ibid.

526. Customer correspondence to Eve's Garden, circa 1975–1985. Box 5, Folder 1 (Cornell–Williams).

527. Customer correspondence to Eve's Garden, 1976. Box 5, Folder 4 (Cornell–Williams).

528. Customer correspondence to Eve's Garden, March 14, 1983. Box 5, Folder 2 (Cornell–Williams).

529. Ibid.

530. Customer correspondence to Eve's Garden, circa 1975–1985. Box 5, Folder 1 (Cornell–Williams).

531. For example, see *off our backs*, 7 no. 1 (February 1977): 23.

532. Author interview with Dell Williams (November 22, 2013).

533. Customer correspondence to Eve's Garden, December 12, 1977. Box 5, Folder 1 (Cornell–Williams).

534. Customer correspondence to Eve's Garden, n.d. Box 5, Folder 15 (Cornell–Williams).

535. Author interview with Dell Williams (January 9, 2015).

536. Brannon, Lynette: Austin Center for Human Resources. 1976-1977. "Goodbye to All That: Good Vibrations at Eve's Garden." Box 1, Folder 49. (Cornell–Williams).

537. Letter from Lynette Brannon to Dell Williams, February 1, 1977. Box 1, Folder 49 (Cornell–Williams).

538. Ibid.

539. Brannon, Lynette: Austin Center for Human Resources. 1976-1977. "Female Sexuality: An Awareness Workshop." Box 1, Folder 49. (Cornell–Williams).

540. Author interview with Joani Blank (March 23, 2015).

541. Author interview with Joani Blank (April 1, 2014).

542. Sullivan, Elizabeth. "Godmother of Sex Ed: Maggi Rubenstein." FoundSF. Accessed June 10, 2014. http://foundsf.org/index.php?title=Godmother_of_SexEd:_Maggi_Rubenstein.

543. Author interview with Joani Blank (March 23, 2015).

544. Barbach, *For Yourself*, 107. *See also* "About Dr. Barbach." Accessed April 5, 2014. http://www.lonniebarbach.com/.

545. Author interview with Joani Blank (April 1, 2014).

546. Ibid.

547. Barbach, *For Yourself*, 107.

548. Author interview with Joani Blank (April 1, 2014).

549. Ibid.

550. Blank, Joani. *A Playbook for Women About Sex*. San Francisco: Down There Press, 1975, 8.

551. Ibid.

552. Sullivan, Elizabeth. "Carol Seajay, Old Wives Tales and the Feminist Bookstore Network." FoundSF. Accessed January 21, 2017. http://www.foundsf.org/index.php?title=Carol_Seajay,_Old_Wives_Tales_and_the_Feminist_Bookstore_Network.

553. Seajay, Carol. "Vibrators for Sale." *Feminist Bookstore News*, September 1984, 16. Note: After Good Vibes opened up, Old Wives Tales stopped carrying vibrators.

554. Author interviews with Joani Blank (April 1, 2014) and Dell Williams (November 22, 2013, and January 9, 2015).

555. Ibid.

556. Author interview with Joani Blank (April 1, 2014).

557. Ibid.

558. Author interview with Dell Williams (November 22, 2013).

559. Author interview with Joani Blank (April 1, 2014).

560. Gevins, Adi. "She's Bringing You Good Vibrations." *Berkeley Barb*, June 17, 1977, 5.

561. Author interview with Joani Blank (April 1, 2014).

562. Bronstein, *Battling Pornography*, 141.

563. Ibid.

564. Author interview with Joani Blank (March 23, 2015).

565. Phillips, Michael. "What Small Business Experience Teaches Us About Economic Theory." In Elkins, Paul. *The Living Economy*. London: Routledge, 1986, 274–75.

566. Ibid., 2.

567. Author interview with Joani Blank (March 23, 2015).

568. Ibid.

569. "The Story." Beate Ushe. Accessed February 27, 2017. http://www.beate-uhse.ag/index.php/the-story.html.

570. Heineman, Elizabeth. *Before Porn Was Legal: The Erotic Empire of Beate Uhse*. Chicago: University of Chicago Press, 2011.

571. "Sex Supermarket." *East Village Other*, March 1, 1967, 12.

572. "D.W. Writings on Masturbation and Vibrators. "Eve's Garden's Guide to Masturbation and Vibrator Use. Do You Love Yourself?" p. 7. Box 3 Folder 4 (Cornell-Williams) .

573. Doc Johnson customer sales tax forms. Box 3, Folder 5 (Cornell–Williams).

CHAPTER ELEVEN

574. Author interview with Ron Braverman (December 27, 2016).

575. Ibid.

576. Author interview with Gosnell Duncan (August 2, 2013).

577. This probably occurred around 1977 because that's when the earliest invoice is from.

578. Author interview with Gosnell Duncan (August 2, 2013).

579. Dworkin, Andrea. *Pornography: Men Possessing Women.* New York: Perigee Books, 1981.

580. Koedt, Anne. "The Myth of the Vaginal Orgasm." In Anne Koedt, Ellen Levine, and Anita Rapone, eds. *Radical Feminism.* New York: Quadrangle Books, 1973, 198–207.

581. The phallic object in *The Exorcist* was a crucifix. *See* Starrett, Barbara. "I Dream in Female: The Metaphors of Evolution." *Amazon Quarterly,* 3. 1 (November 1974): 15. *See also* Lieberman, Hallie. "If You Mold It, They Will Come: How Gosnell Duncan's Devices Changed the Feminist Sex-Toy Game Forever." *Bitch Media.* Accessed June 9, 2017. https://www.bitchmedia.org/article/if-you-mold-it-they-will-come-dildo-history-feminist-sex-toy-stores.

582. Katz, Sue. "Smash Phallic Imperialism." *Lavender Vision,* 1, no. 1 (1970): 5.

583. Fullerton, Patricia. "Dilemma of the Modern Lesbian." *Lavender Woman,* 1, no. 3 (1972): 5.

584. Jay, Karla. "The Spirit Is Feminist but the Flesh Is?" *The Lesbian Tide,* vol. 4. no. 3 (October 1974): 15.

585. Findlay, Heather. "Freud's 'Fetishism' and the Lesbian Dildo Debates." *Feminist Studies,* 18, no. 3 (Fall 1992): 564–65. Findlay was writing in the 1990s, but the terms of the debate were similar in the 1970s.

586. Leigh and M. Duck Brody. "Two Views on Loving Women." *Lavender Woman,* 4. no. 3 (June 1975): 10.

587. Snake, R. "Loving Women" Review. *Big Mama Rag,* 3, no. 5 (June 1975): 13.

588. "Dongs: The Images of Men." "Doc Johnson Marital Aids Catalog," 1977. Sex Aids Dealers, 1970–79 (Kinsey).

589. Author interview with Gosnell Duncan (August 2, 2013).

590. Williams and Vannucci, *Revolution in the Garden,* 192.

591. Author interview with Dell Williams (November 19, 2013).

592. Williams and Vannucci, *Revolution in the Garden,* 192–93.

593. Eve's Garden catalog, 1990, 14 (Cornell–Williams).

594. Williams and Vannucci, *Revolution in the Garden*, 218.

595. Letter from Williams to Wardell B. Pomeroy, April 9, 1975. Business correspondence, 1970s. Box 3, Folder 142 (Cornell–Williams).

596. Ibid.,183.

597. Eve's Garden Media Kit. Box 6, Folder 69 (Cornell–Williams).

598. McAuley, Robert J. "Did Woman Juror Turn the Tide in Sturman Verdict?" *Plain Dealer*, July 26, 1978, 1. *See also* Hatton, "Porn King."

599. Heaton, Michael. "Famed Hotel Owner Jim Swingos Takes a Long Look Back on the Glory Days." Cleveland.com. Accessed December 20, 2016. http://www.cleveland.com/entertainment/index .ssf/2013/11/famed_hotel_owner_jim_swingos.html.

600. Griffith, John. "U.S. Accuses Sturman of Massive Tax Dodge." *Plain Dealer*, March 5, 1985, sec. A, 1;7.

601. Cook, "The X-Rated Economy," 84.

602. Ibid., 87.

603. Uhelszki, Jaan. "Interview: Joan Jett, Queen of Noise." *The Morton Report*, September 13, 2011. http://www.themortonreport.com/entertainment/music/interview-joan-jett-queen-of-noise/.

604. Pleasure Chest catalog, 1978, 6 (Pleasure Chest).

605. Luther, Marylou. "Shock Chic: The Punk Persuasion." *Los Angeles Times*, July 31, 1977, sec. V, 15.

606. Japenga, Ann. "Sadomasochist Fashions Attracting Suburban Teens." *Los Angeles Times*, March 25, 1983, sec. V, 1; 8.

607. Pleasure Chest catalog, circa 1978, 3 (Pleasure Chest).

608. Pleasure Chest job advertisement. *Los Angeles Free Press*, July 11–17, 1975.

609. Freitag, Michael. "Neighborhoods in New York Seeing Red Over Blue Videos: 'No Times Square in Greenwich Village,' Protesters Say." *New York Times*, December 28, 1989.

610. Pleasure Chest catalog, 1978 (Pleasure Chest).

611. Pleasure Chest catalog, 1981 (Pleasure Chest). *See also* "Pleasure Chest Goes Back to School," circa 1981. Sex Aids Dealers. United States. 20th century, 1980–1999. (Kinsey).

612. Serrin, William. "Sex Is a Growing Multibillion Business." *New York Times*, February 9, 1981. http://www.nytimes.com/1981/02/09/nyregion/sex-is-a-growing-multibillion-business-first-of-two-articles.html.

613. Knight, Jerry. "Retailers Racing to Washington." *Washington Post*, May 12, 1980.

614. It was probably no longer operating at this time, although exact details on how long it stayed open are unknown.

615. Williams and Vannucci, *Revolution in the Garden*, 218.

616. "Dell's account of store's inception and expansion and struggle." Account of Eve's Garden, 1982. Box 3, Folder 2, 3 (Cornell–Williams).

617. Letter from William J. Ryan to Marilyn Carten, November 23, 1981. Business correspondence, 1981. Box 3, Folder 5 (Cornell–Williams).

618. "Dell's account of store's inception and expansion and struggle." Account of Eve's Garden, 1982. Box 3, Folder 2, 4 (Cornell–Williams).

619. Williams and Vannucci, *Revolution in the Garden*, 220.

620. Letter to five of Dell Williams's friends, 1981; Letter about financial crisis. Box 3, Folder 4 (Cornell–Williams).

621. Williams and Vannucci, *Revolution in the Garden*, 220.

622. "Dell's account of store's inception and expansion and struggle." Account of Eve's Garden, 1982. Box 3, Folder 2, 6. (Cornell–Williams).

623. Langelan, Martha. "The Political Economy of Pornography." *Aegis*, Autumn 1981, 7.

624. Ann Summers catalog, 1982. Accessed August 7, 2017. http://i1.adis.ws/i/annsummers/1982-new -cat5toys.jpg?%24brandtimeline-lg%24.

625. *United States v. Ronald A. Braverman*, 829 F.2d 1126 (6th Cir. 1987).

626. Whelan, "Reuben Sturman," 78.

627. Heidenry, *What Wild Ecstasy*, 317.

628. "John Oster Manufacturing Co. Demonstrators' Manual." December 18, 1949. Louisan E. Mamer Rural Electrification Administration Papers 1927–2002, Box 4, Folder 4, "Demonstrator Scripts." Archives Center. (NMAH–Archives).

629. Blank, Joani. *Good Vibrations: The Complete Guide to Vibrators*. Burlingame, CA: Down There Press, 1982, 20.

630. Bumiller, Elisabeth. "Our Bodies, Our Salves: The Erotica Party Comes to Silver Spring." *Washington Post*, May 30, 1980, C1.

631. Nussbaum, Paul. "Peddling Sex Accouterments in the Living Room." *Los Angeles Times*, April 22, 1981, sec. G, 8.

632. "Lovelay In-Home Parties" Advertisement. *Plain Dealer*, November 1, 1981, G1; *Plain Dealer*, January 5, 1982, B3.

633. Nussbaum, "Peddling Sex Accouterments in the Living Room," 1; 8.

634. Auerbach, Stuart. "Mail Order Company Called Just a Tease; Complaints Cite Undelivered Goods." *Washington Post*, June 4, 1983.

CHAPTER TWELVE

635. Auerbach, "Mail Order."

636. Pleasure Chest photographs, circa 1980s (Pleasure Chest).

637. Altman, Lawrence K. "Rare Cancer Seen in 41 Homosexuals." *New York Times*, July 3, 1981, http://www.nytimes.com/1981/07/03/us/rare-cancer-seen-in-41-homosexuals.html.

638. Peyton, Jackson. "AIDS Prevention for Gay Men: A Selected History and Analysis: The San Francisco Experience, 1982-1987." John-Manuel Andriote Victory Deferred Collection, Box 10, Folder 6 (NMAH–Archives).

639. Long, *The Forbidden Apple*, 185.

640. Gross, Jane. "Homosexuals Stepping Up AIDS Education." *The New York Times*, September 22, 1985, 56.

641. Peyton, "AIDS Prevention for Gay Men," 9.

642. "Designing an Effective AIDS Prevention Campaign Strategy for San Francisco: Results Form the First Probability Sample of an Urban Gay Male Community." Prepared for the San Francisco AIDS Foundation by Research & Decisions Corporation. December 1984, Appendix F. John-Manuel Andriote Victory Deferred Collection, Box 10, Folder 5 (NMAH–Archives).

643. Palacios-Jimenez, Louis, and Michael Shernoff. "Facilitator's Guide to Eroticizing Safer Sex." Gay Men's Health Crisis, 1986. HIV/AIDS Collection #1134, Box 1, Folder 33, 28 (NMAH–HIV).

644. Fee, Elizabeth, and Nancy Krieger. "Understanding AIDS: Historical Interpretations and the Limits of Biomedical Individualism." *American Journal of Public Health*, 83, no. 10 (October 1, 1993): 1477–88.

645. Harvey Milk Gay Democratic Club, "AIDS Prevention Flyers: Can We Talk?," Pacific University Archives Exhibits, accessed August 6, 2017, http://exhibits.lib.pacificu.edu/items/show/940.

646. "Women, Sex, and AIDS." Pamphlet, 1988. #1134, Box 1, Folder 10 (NMAH–HIV).

647. Vance, Carole S. *Pleasure and Danger: Exploring Female Sexuality*. Boston: Routledge & Kegan Paul, 1984, 3.

648. Ibid., 6.

649. Kubala, Juliana M. "Sex Wars." In Bonnie Zimmerman, ed. *Encyclopedia of Lesbian and Gay Histories and Cultures: An Encyclopedia. Gay Histories and Cultures. Vol. 2.* New York: Taylor & Francis, (2000) 683.

650. Author interview with Susie Bright (July 7, 2016).

651. Ibid.

652. "Seda, Dori, Robert Crumb, and Terri Zwigoff. "Girls Turned into Vibrator Zombies." *Weirdo #8*, 1983. Reprinted in Seda, Dori. *Dori Stories*. San Francisco: Last Gasp, 1999.

653. Farmer, Joyce. *Tits & Clits Comix*, no. 3. Laguna Beach, Ca.: Nanny Goat Productions, 1976, front cover.

654. Ibid.

655. Chevli, Lyn, and Joyce Farmer. "The Fuller Bush Person," in *Tits & Clits Comix*, no. 2. Laguna Beach, Ca.: Nanny Goat Productions, 1976, 9–11.

656. Ibid., 9.

657. Ibid.

658. Ibid.

659. Bailey, Beth. *Sex in the Heartland.* Cambridge, MA: Harvard University Press, 1999, 169–74.

660. "How're We Doin'." *Good Vibes Gazette* 2. Sex Aids Dealers, United States, 1980–1999. (Kinsey).

661. Williams and Vannucci, *Revolution in the Garden*, 179.

662. Author interview with Joani Blank (April 1, 2014).

663. Ibid.

664. Blank, Joani. "Bad Vibes." Letter to the Editor, *WomaNews*, March 1983, 2.

665. Author interview with Joani Blank (April 1, 2014).

666. Allen, Donna, ed. "Ms. Magazine Wins Victory for All Women's Press in Library Case." *Media Report to Women,* vol. 7 (July 1, 1979): 1–2.

667. *Rhonda Salvail, et. al. v. Nashua Board of Education,* 469 F. Supp. 1269 (D. New Hamp., 1979).

668. She recounts this story in *Good Vibes Gazette* (March 1987, 1), so it's possible that it happened in 1987, and not 1983 as she told.

669. Author interview with Joani Blank (April 1, 2014).

670. Friedan, *It Changed My Life*, 86.

671. I asked Gloria Steinem about this story, and her assistant contacted me and said he asked Steinem, but she had no recollection of the situation with Joani Blank.

672. *Good Vibes Gazette.* San Francisco: Good Vibrations, no. 3 (March 1987), 1 (CSC–Good Vibes).

673. "Ms. Magazine." *Feminist Bookstore News*, April 1987, 20.

674. One of the ads Good Vibes ran in *Mother Jones* showed a drawing of the Hitachi Magic Wand and said, "It's fun to use at home or with a partner." *Mother Jones*, May 1985, 47.

675. *Good Vibes Gazette.* San Francisco: Good Vibrations, no. 5 (Fall 1988), 1 (CSC–Good Vibes).

676. *Good Vibes Gazette.* San Francisco: Good Vibrations, no. 10 (Fall 1990), 4 (CSC–Good Vibes).

677. "Censorship." *Feminist Bookstore News*, August 1989, 25.

678. *Good Vibes Gazette*. San Francisco: Good Vibrations, no. 9 (Summer 1990), 1 (CSC–Good Vibes).

679. Author interview with Joani Blank (April 1, 2014).

680. Author interview with Susie Bright (July 7, 2016).

681. Author interview with Ron Braverman (December 27, 2016).

682. *Attorney General's Commission on Pornography: Final Report* (1986), vol. 2, 1447–50. During this time, about half the sex toys sold in the United States were sold through retail.

683. Griffith, John. "U.S. Accuses Sturman of Massive Tax Dodge." *Plain Dealer*. March 5, 1985, A7.

684. Ibid.

685. Ibid.

686. "Sturman Released as Checks Check Out." *Plain Dealer*, July 10, 1985, sec. B.

687. Griffith, John. "Sturman Has Dead Man's Passport; Bond Stands." *Plain Dealer,* July 2, 1985, A, 1.

688. Geltzer, *Dirty Words and Filthy Pictures*, 257.

689. "Sturman Counts Reinstated in New Indictment." *Cleveland Plain Dealer*, July 25, 1987, sec. B, 3.

690. Epstein, Keith C. "Court Upholds Conviction of Figure in Sturman Case." *Cleveland Plain Dealer*, March 22, 1988, sec. A, 8.

691. Author interview with Susie Bright (July 7, 2016).

692. Ibid.

693. Author interview with Joani Blank (April 1, 2014).

694. Author interview with Susie Bright (July 7, 2016).

695. Letter from a customer to Gosnell Duncan, circa late 1970s–early 1980s (Duncan).

696. Author interview with Gosnell Duncan, August 3, 2013 (Duncan).

697. Good Vibrations catalog, circa late 1980s–1990 (Duncan).

698. Letters from a female customer to Gosnell Duncan, December 17, 1975, and Duncan to customer, and January 21, 1976 (Duncan).

699. Letter from an activist to Gosnell Duncan, August 31, 1984 (Duncan).

700. Letter from an activist to Gosnell Duncan, December 17, 1984 (Duncan).

701. *Good Vibes Gazette*. San Francisco: Good Vibrations, no. 1 (1985) (CSC–Good Vibes).

702. Bright, Susie. "Toys for Us." *On Our Backs,* September-October 1984, 13.

703. Math, Mara. "Andrea Dworkin Talks About Feminism." *Gay Community News,* December 1985, 8.

704. Customer correspondence to Eve's Garden, October 19, 1987. Box 5, Folder 2 (Cornell–Williams).

705. Author interview with Susie Bright (July 7, 2016).

706. "Come Again Erotic Emporium Celebrating 10th Anniversary." Press release, November 16, 1991 (Duncan).

707. Advertisement for Gosnell Duncan's dildos showing U.S. stores carrying them. *On Our Backs,* November-December 1989, 9.

708. Bright, "Toys for Us," 8.

709. Bright, Susie. "Bay Area Bulletin: Good Vibrations Offers Home Parties." *Good Vibes Gazette.* San Francisco: Good Vibrations, 1986 (CSC–Good Vibes).

710. Jeffreys, Sheila. *The Lesbian Heresy: A Feminist Perspective on the Lesbian Sexual Revolution.* Melbourne, Australia: Spinifex Press, 1993, 28–29.

711. GMHC sextoy certificate. Susie Bright Papers, Box 20, Folder 2. Human Sexuality Collection. Division of Rare and Manuscript Collections, Cornell University Library (Cornell–Bright).

CHAPTER THIRTEEN

712. Geltzer, *Dirty Words and Filthy Pictures,* 304–06.

713. Shenon, Philip. "Sturm Und Drang Und Pornography." *The New York Times,* April 15, 1986, sec. B6.

714. Scott, Joseph E. "Book Review: Attorney General's Commission on Pornography." *Journal of Criminal Law and Criminology* (Winter 1988). Accessed February 28, 2017, via LexisNexis Academic.

715. Broder, Samuel. "The Development of Antiretroviral Therapy and Its Impact on the HIV-1/AIDS Pandemic." *Antiviral Research* 85, no. 1 (January 2010): 1.

716. Author interview with Brian Robinson (March 23, 2016) [doi:10.1016/j.antiviral.2009.10.002].\\ uc0\\u8221{} {\\i{}Antiviral Research} 85, no. 1 (January 2010).

717. "Duane Colglazier Services Held." *Holyoke Enterprise,* Holyoke, CO, March 1988.

718. Author interview with Brian Robinson (March 23, 2016).

719. Mills, Kim I. "Lesbians Urge 'Safe Sex' as AIDS Precaution." Associated Press, December 30, 1987. Box 13, Folder 88 (Cornell–Bright).

720. *Good Vibes Gazette.* San Francisco: Good Vibrations, no. 5 (Fall 1988): 2 (CSC–Good Vibes).

721. "Women, Sex and AIDS" pamphlet, 1988. #1134 HIV/AIDS. Box 1, Folder 10. (NAMH–HIV).

722. "AIDS: A Woman's Health Issue." Whitman-Walker Clinic Inc., Washington, D.C., Maryland, Virginia, circa 1990s, 5 (NAMH–HIV).

723. "Feeling the Heat: An Evening of Erotic Entertainment for Women Only." Fund-raiser, 1988. Box 13, Folder 84 (Cornell–Bright).

724. *A View from the Garden.* Eve's Garden Newsletter. Fall 1990, 1. Box 3, Folder 24 (Cornell-Williams).

725. Letter from Cynthia Madansky to Dell Williams, June 2, 1993. Charity correspondence, 1992–1994. Box 3, Folder 9 (NMAH–HIV).

726. Author interview with Carol Queen (July 17, 2016).

727. Griffith, John, and Rosemary Armao. "Sturman Jests as War Tears at Porn Empire." *Plain Dealer,* May 24, 1987, sec. A, 1; 17.

728. Houston, Paul. "Man Called Largest Porno Seller Indicted." *Los Angeles Times,* October 9, 1987, sec. 1, 20.

729. Heidenry, *What Wild Ecstasy,* 318–20.

730. Johnson, John. "No Heir Apparent for Toppled Porn King." *Los Angeles Times,* December 4, 1989. *See also* Henderson, Karen E. "Sturman Trial Goes to Jury." *Plain Dealer,* November 7, 1989.

731. "Pornographer Gets $10 Years, $2.46 Million Fine." *Los Angeles Times,* February 13, 1990, sec. B2.

732. Hendersen, Karen E. "Porn Czar Gets Prison Term, Fined $2 Million." *Plain Dealer,* February 13, 1990, A1, A7.

733. Mann, Steve. "Master's Project Turns into Mail-Order Boom." *Burlington Times-News,* November 27, 1980, sec. F6.

734. Hart, Kelvin. "Adam & Eve Open But Quiet About the Raid." *Burlington Times-News,* June 11, 1986, sec. D2.

735. Ibid.

736. Harvey, *The Government vs. Erotica,* 34.

737. Ibid.

738. Author interview with Phil Harvey (February 1, 2017).

739. Harvey, *The Government vs. Erotica,* 34; 66–67; 82; 125.

740. Ibid., 84–87.

741. Harvey, *The Government Vs. Erotica,* 21.

742. Ibid., 82–86.

743. Heidenry, *What Wild Ecstasy,* 319.

744. Ibid., 320.

745. "Pornography Given 4-Year Sentence." *Los Angeles Times,* June 11, 1992, sec. A41.

746. Johnson, John. "Top Pornographer Reuben Sturman Vanishes from Prison." *Los Angeles Times*, December 14, 1992, sec. B5.

747. Williams, Timothy. "Grand Jury Indicts Pornographer's Ex-Wife." *Los Angeles Times*, October 27, 1993, sec. B4.

748. Author interview with David Sturman (December 7, 2016).

749. Hernandez, Greg. "Porn Kingpin Who Escaped Prison Arrested: Fugitive: 68-Year-Old Captured in Anaheim Was Serving Time for Federal Racketeering, Obscenity, Income Tax Violations." *Los Angeles Times*, February 10, 1993. Accessed August 7, 2017. http://articles.latimes.com/1993-02-10/local/me-1306 _1_income-tax-violations.

750. Author interview with Shay Martin (September 6, 2016).

751. Ibid.

752. Ibid.

753. Ibid.

754. Ibid.

755. Ibid.

756. Scorpio Products advertisement. *On Our Backs*, November/December 1989, 9.

757. Author interview with Susie Bright (July 7, 2016).

758. Scorpio Products advertisement. *On Our Backs*, November/December 1989, 9.

759. *Good Vibes Gazette*, San Francisco: Good Vibrations, no. 6 (Spring 1989) (CSC–Good Vibes).

760. Author interview with Gosnell Duncan (August 2–3, 2013).

761. Letter from Gosnell Duncan to Honey Lee Cottrell, March 13, 1993 (Duncan).

762. Solid Penis Device brochure, circa early 1990s (Duncan).

763. Disabled & Able-bodied Adults Erotic Toys" catalog mock-up, early 1990s (Duncan).

764. "A Cellarfull of Dildoes: Olav Andre Manum Visits Dildo Makers Scorpio Novelty Products." *Cupido*, No. 2 (1990): 5. Translated from Danish by May Kristin Jokobsen. Hverdag Products (Duncan).

765. Author interview with Susie Bright (July 7, 2016).

766. Letter from Susie Bright to Gosnell Duncan, circa February 1993 (Duncan).

767. Bright, Susie. "What a Friend We Have in Dildos." *The Advocate*, September 10, 1991, 67.

768. *Good Vibes Gazette*. San Francisco: Good Vibrations. (Holiday 2002). (CSC–Good Vibes).

769. *GV Store's Afterhours News*, 1990s (CSC–Good Vibes).

770. *Good Vibes Gazette*. San Francisco: Good Vibrations, no. 17 (Spring 1995), 2. (CSC–Good Vibes).

771. Queen, Carol. "Sisters Doin' It for Themselves." *On Our Backs*, December 1992, 39.

772. Wall History of Good Vibrations (2004), 1992 panel (CSC-Good Vibes).

773. Surnow, Rose. "Babeland's Co-Founder Talks 20 Years of Vibrators and Lube." *Cosmopolitan*, February 22, 2013. Accessed August 7, 2017. http://www.cosmopolitan.com/sex-love/advice/babeland-turns-20.

774. Wall History of Good Vibrations (2004), 1992 panel (CSC-Good Vibes).

CHAPTER FOURTEEN

775. Gardetta, "Doctor's Orders."

776. Author interview with Phil Harvey (February 3, 2017). *See also* Harvey, *The Government vs. Erotica*, 127; 130–32.

777. *PHE, Inc. v. U.S. Dept. of Justice*, 743 F. Supp. 15 (D.D.C. 1990). *See also* Harvey, *The Government vs. Erotica*, 145–8; 200.

778. Hentoff, Nat. "The Justice Department's Tainted Fruit." *Washington Post*, July 25, 1992, sec. A21

779. "PHE Battle Unifies Two Usual Opponents." *Burlington N.C. Times-News*, June 22, 1993, sec. C2. *See also* Beato, Greg. "Sexually Transmitted Altruism (SSIR)." *Stanford Social Innovation Review*, Fall 2012. 10: 4, 66-71

780. "PHE Battle Unifies Two Usual Opponents."

781. Mail-Order Firm Clears Legal Hurdle to Relocate." *Burlington N.C. Times-News*, March 15, 1994, sec. C2.

782. *Good Vibes Gazette*. San Francisco: Good Vibrations, no. 17 (Spring 1995), 1 (CSC–Good Vibes).

783. Author interview with Joani Blank (April 1, 2014).

784. Wall History of Good Vibrations (2004), 1996 panel (CSC–Good Vibes).

785. Wall History of Good Vibrations (2004), 1995 panel (CSC–Good Vibes).

786. Queen, "Sisters Doin' It for Themselves," 20–22; 38. *See also* Ad for Gosnell Duncan's dildos. *On Our Backs*, November/December 1989, 9.

787. *Good Vibes Gazette*. San Francisco: Good Vibrations (Holiday 2002), 4 (CSC–Good Vibes).

788. *Good Vibes Gazette*. San Francisco: Good Vibrations, no.19 (Spring 1996), 1 (CSC–Good Vibes).

789. *Good Vibes Gazette*. San Francisco: Good Vibrations, no. 25 (Spring 1999), 3 (CSC–Good Vibes); *Good Vibes Gazette*. San Francisco: Good Vibrations (Holiday 1999), 1 (CSC–Good Vibes).

790. Author interview with Brian Robinson (March 23, 2016).

791. Author interview with Sarah Tomchesson (February 15, 2016).

792. Author interview with Shay Martin (September 6, 2016).

793. "The Turtle and the Hare." *Sex and the City: Season 1.* HBO, 1998.

794. *Good Vibes Gazette.* San Francisco: Good Vibrations, no. 25 (Spring 1999), 1 (CSC–Good Vibes).

795. Author interview with Shay Martin (September 6, 2016).

796. "My Motherboard, My Self." *Sex and the City: Season 4.* HBO, 2001.

797. "Critical Condition." *Sex and the City: Season 5.* HBO, 2002. Even dildos cause problems. Samantha throws out her back when using a strap-on dildo to have sex with her girlfriend. *See also* "Ghost Town." *Sex and the City: Season 4.* HBO, 2001.

798. For more on this scene and the vibrator in American popular culture, see Rosewarne, Lauren. *American Taboo: The Forbidden Words, Unspoken Rules, and Secret Morality of Popular Culture.* Santa Barbara, CA: Praeger, 2011, 211–35.

799. *Not Another Teen Movie.* Directed by Joel Gallen. Columbia Pictures, 2001.

800. Goldman, Andrew. "Panic in Bedrooms as Magic Wand, Cadillac of Vibrators, Disappears." *New York Observer*, June 12, 2000.

801. Author interview with Shay Martin. (September 6, 2016).

802. Ibid.

CHAPTER FIFTEEN

803. *Good Vibes Gazette.* San Francisco: Good Vibrations (Holiday 2000) (CSC–Good Vibes).

804. DeBare, Ilana. "Good News for Good Vibrations—It's Being Sold." *SFGate*, September 27, 2007. Accessed June 8, 2017. http://www.sfgate.com/business/article/Good-news-for-Good-Vibrations-it-s -being-sold-2501063.php.

805. Vega, Cecilia M. "Transgender Pioneer Rises to Powerful Spot." *SFGate*, May 12, 2007. Accessed March 1, 2017. http://www.sfgate.com/politics/article/Transgender-pioneer-rises-to-powerful-spot-2595344.php.

806. Bronstein, Phil. "How Feminist Sexshop Lost Its Loving Feeling." *San Francisco Chronicle*, August 17, 2009. Accessed August 7, 2017. http://www.sfgate.com/opinion/article/How-feminist-sexshop-lost -its-loving-feeling-3289154.php.

807. Note: There is debate about whether or not phthalates are harmful.

808. Cassell, Heather. "Good Vibrations Announces Merger." *Bay Area Reporter*, October 4, 2007. Accessed March 1, 2017. http://www.ebar.com/news/article.php?sec=news&article=2281.

809. Author interview with Susie Bright (July 7, 2016).

810. Bronstein, "How Feminist Sexshop Lost Its Loving Feeling."

811. Sara J. "Good Vibrations Yelp Review." Yelp, August 3, 2008. Accessed August 7, 2017. https://www.yelp.ca/biz/good-vibrations-berkeley?hrid=pT_2yxjkWj4VbPncnZGoxA&. The name of the corporation that owns Good Vibrations has changed from GVA-TWN. It is now the corporation Barnaby Ltd. which was founded by Kaminsky.

812. Author interview with Walter Fallon (April 1, 2016).

813. Williams and Vannucci, *Revolution in the Garden,* 248.

814. Reinholz, Mary. "Sex Shop Founder Dell Williams Dies." *NY Press,* March 19, 2015. Accessed March 2, 2017. http://www.nypress.com/local-news/20150319/sex-shop-founder-dell-williams-dies.

815. Author interview with David Keegan, AEFC general manager (February 13, 2017).

816. Author interview with Phil Harvey (February 1, 2017).

817. Bowles, Nellie. "It's Hard Out There for a Sex-Toy Entrepreneur." *Recode,* October 17, 2014. Accessed August 8, 2017. http://www.recode.net/2014/10/17/11631986/its-hard-out-there-for-a-sex-toy-entrepreneur.

818. "Fifty Shades of Grey Charlie Tango Classic Vibrator." Lovehoney.com. Accessed March 6, 2017. https://www.lovehoney.com/product.cfm?p=29338.

819. Research on obscene devices laws was done by my father, Erik R. Lieberman, who is an attorney, and his legal intern.

820. Buchanan, Kim Shayo. "Lawrence v. Geduldig: Regulating Women's Sexuality." *Emory Law Review Journal,* 56 (2007): 1235–1303.

821. "Donald Trump Plug. " Shapeways.com. Accessed March 2, 2017. https://www.shapeways.com/product/SCD3B2NJD/donald-trump-plug.

822. Complaint from viewer in Maple Valley, WA, about "Trojan Triphoria" ad that aired December 31, 2010, on a *Saturday Night Live* episode that was shown on VH1. FCC/Enforcement Bureau, IHD-Investigation and Hearings. Informal complaints received by the Federal Communications Commission (FCC) regarding the television show "Saturday Night Live," 2008–2012. Other consumers have complained about sex toys being discussed on *2 Broke Girls. See:* Complaint from viewer in Old Tappan NJ, about *2 Broke Girls* that aired November 12, 2012, on CBS; Complaint from viewer in Jacksonville, FL, NJ about *2 Broke Girls* that aired November 11, 2012 on CBS. Informal complaints received by the Federal Communications Commission (FCC) regarding the television show "2 Broke Girls," 2011–2013, Released Date December 5, 2013. Obtained from Government Attic, accessed August 20, 2014. http://www.governmentattic.org/10docs/FCC_Complaints2BrokeGirls_2011-2013.pdf

823. Jin, Jessica. "I'm Getting Death Threats for Protesting Guns With Sex Toys." Time.com. October 16, 2015. Accessed August 7, 2017. http://time.com/4074728/campus-carry-sex-toys.

824. Craver, Jack. "Madison Politiscope: Isthmus Cover Photo Too Much for Metcalfe's Market." Madison.com, August 25, 2012. Accessed March 5, 2017. http://host.madison.com/news/local/govt-and-politics/politiscope/madison-politiscope-isthmus-cover-photo-too-much-for-metcalfe-s/article_e6e09852-ee5d-11e1-8c48-0019bb2963f4.html.

825. Harvey's nonprofit DKT helps distribute vibrating cock rings along with condoms, and in Brazil they help distribute regular vibrators, but they don't usually subsidize them.

Acknowledgments

Writing this book was at turns joyous, maddening, hilarious, and inspiring. These are some of the people who helped me on the way.

I couldn't have asked for a better editor than Iris Blasi at Pegasus Books, who shepherded my project from dissertation to book. From the beginning, she not only understood the type of story I was trying to tell, but perhaps even more important, why the story needed to be told. Her skill was invaluable in shaping my book.

Thanks also to Torrey Sharp for creating an amazing book cover design that perfectly conveys the message of the book. Designer Sabrina Plomitallo-González carried the theme throughout the pages of the book in a clever, beautiful way. Copyeditor Mary Hern's and proofreader Andrea Monagle's work was much appreciated.

My agent, Lydia Shamah, took a chance on me and provided much guidance throughout the process of writing a proposal and finding a publisher. The Carol Mann Agency also provided me with a lot of support.

Without the kindness generosity of the sexual pioneers who spent endless hours with me, telling their stories, I would not have been able to write this book. They opened up their archives for me and were willing to answer any questions I had. I hope this book does their stories justice. Thanks to Chad, Erica, and Ron Braverman of Doc Johnson; Brian Robinson, owner of the Pleasure Chest; Sarah Tomchesson, Walter Fallon, and Chris Cherrie, also of the Pleasure Chest; Joani Blank and Carol Queen of Good Vibrations;

Susie Bright, sexpert extraordinaire, founder of *On Our Backs*, former manager of Good Vibrations; Betty Dodson, masturbation & vibrator advocate, artist, iconoclast; Gosnell Duncan, inventor of the silicone dildo and disability advocate; David Sturman, erotic store owner and son of Reuben; Farley Malorrus of United Sales; Dell Williams, founder of Eve's Garden; Shay Martin, founder of Vibratex, and Eddie Romero, also of Vibratex; Phil Harvey, founder of Adam & Eve and DKT; and David Keegan of Adam &Eve.

Metis Black, founder of Tantus Silicone, introduced me to Gosnell Duncan's incredible story and encouraged me to contact him. Duncan's niece Lurline Martineau was incredibly kind. She opened his home to me, explained his sex-toy making process, and gifted his archives to me.

Kjerstin Johnson, then editor-in-chief of *Bitch*, published my story on Duncan and gave me my first "yes" after an endless string of "no"s. This gave me the hope I needed to continue.

Thanks to my advisor Dr. Stephen Vaughn at the University of Wisconsin–Madison for letting me study sex toys for my dissertation, and for introducing me to Ralph Ginzburg's Papers at the Wisconsin Historical Society. Dr. William Reese, also at the University of Wisconsin, has always encouraged my research.

Thanks to all the archivists and librarians who gave me invaluable help and turned me on to so many different collections. Alison L. Oswald, Kay Peterson, Franklin Robinson, and Mallory Warner at Smithsonian's National Museum of American History tracked down all manner of amazing artifacts and documents hidden in the collections and made my experience at the Smithsonian not only incredibly fruitful for my research but also incredibly fun during the summer I spent as a Lemelson Fellow. Brenda J. Marston at Cornell University helped me discover all the gems within Dell Williams's and Susie Bright's Papers while I was Phil Zwickler grant recipient. Micaela Sullivan-Fowler at University of Wisconsin–Madison found all the weird vibrator brochures for me in their collections. Elizabeth Ihrig at the Bakken Museum and Library shared her knowledge of the rich vibrator collections during my time there as a Bakken Travel Grant Recipient. Shawn Wilson at Kinsey Institute was unbelievably patient and even tracked down an eight-pager in the stacks to check punctuation. Dr. Debby Herbenick at Indiana University shared her endless knowledge on sexual health with me, supported this project from the beginning, and helped me navigate the Kinsey Institute's collection. Amber Dushman at the American Medical Association and Selina Hurley at the Science Museum also took the time to help me with my research. Lindsay Morse shared her expertise with Ancient Greek and Latin sources, which was invaluable.

The University of Wisconsin–Madison supported me with multiple grants that allowed me to focus on my research while I was writing my dissertation.

Allison Murray shared her encyclopedic knowledge of popular culture, was willing to answer my questions at all hours of the day, and always encouraged me and alleviated my anxieties. Rachel Lenerz has always been there for me, supported me when I was at my lowest, and boosted my confidence.

Thanks to my uncle Dr. Michael D. Lieberman, who inspired me with his ability to talk without embarrassment about the human body in all its weirdness.

Special thanks to Eric Schatzberg for being my boyfriend, one of the most difficult tasks in the world. He believed in me even when the rest of the world didn't.

Thanks to my parents, Ann and Erik Lieberman, for being incredibly supportive, both emotionally and financially. They gave me the greatest gift in the world: the confidence that I could be anything I wanted to be.

Lulu and Miss Yvonne gave all the love.

Finally, thanks to everybody in the sex-toy industry who was willing to withstand personal criticism in order to follow their dreams of making the world a better place.

About the Author

Hallie Lieberman obtained her PhD from the University of Wisconsin–Madison in 2014, with a dissertation on Sex Toy History. Her writing has been published in *Bitch*, *Bust*, *Eater*, *The Forward*, and *Inside Higher Ed*, among others. She has given talks at many university events and conferences. She lives in Atlanta, Georgia.